PENIN∫ULA

TALES & TRAILS

*Commemorating the Thirtieth Anniversary of the
Midpeninsula Regional Open Space District*

DAVID WEINTRAUB

GRAPHIC ARTS BOOKS

Library of Congress Cataloging-in-Publication Data
Weintraub, David, 1949-
  Peninsula tales and trails : commemorating the thirtieth anniversary of
the Midpeninsula Regional Open Space District / by David Weintraub.
    p. cm.
Includes bibliographical references and index.
  ISBN 1-55868-850-1 (softbound)
  1. Hiking—California—San Francisco Peninsula—Guidebooks. 2. Hiking
California—Santa Cruz Mountains Region—Guidebooks. 3. Trails—
California—San Francisco Peninsula—Guidebooks. 4. Trails—California—
Santa Cruz Mountains Region—Guidebooks. 5. San Francisco Peninsula
(Calif.)—Guidebooks. 6. Santa Cruz Mountains Region (Calif.)—
Guidebooks. I. Midpeninsula Regional Open Space District (Santa Clara
County, Calif.) II. Title.
  GV199.42.C22S269959 2004
  917.94'9—dc22   2004010009

Graphic Arts Books
An imprint of Graphic Arts Center Publishing Company
P.O. Box 10306, Portland, Oregon 97296-0306
503/226-2402; www.gacpc.com

President: Charles M. Hopkins
Associate Publisher: Douglas A. Pfeiffer
Editorial Staff: Timothy W. Frew, Tricia Brown, Kathy Howard,
  Jean Bond-Slaughter
Production Staff: Richard L. Owsiany, Heather Doornink
Design: Jean Andrews
Printed by Haagen Printing, www.haagen.com
Bound by Lincoln & Allen, www.lincolnandallen.com

Printed and bound in the United States of America

*This book is dedicated to those
extraordinary individuals who, in 1972,
had the foresight and vision to create the
Midpeninsula Regional Open Space District.
It is equally dedicated to the constituents who
thereafter supported this vision, enabling the
District to provide the public with a legacy of
permanently protected open space lands
on the San Francisco peninsula.*

—Carleen Bruins

TABLE OF CONTENTS

ACKNOWLEDGMENTS

~

Many people helped to make this book. Of course, the District itself would still be only a dream without the support of the wise taxpayers who deemed open space a precious community value. More immediately, however, District staff took time out from their busy schedules to give me valuable information about the preserves and trails; District board members spoke with me about the creation of the Midpeninsula Regional Open Space District, and setting priorities for wise land management. District volunteers described some of the participatory activities that bring the community into closer touch with the land. A variety of other people involved with open space shared stories and historical information pertaining to particular areas and issues.

Thanks, then, to the following folks for putting up with my tape recorder and my endless questions: Lorraine Alleman, Rodger Alleman, Marc Auerbach, Craig Britton, Kerry Carlson, Patrick Congdon, Elizabeth Dana, Dennis Danielson, Mary Davey, John Escobar, Ken Fisher, Herb Grench, Nonette Hanko, Larry Hassett, Jane Huber, Dave Knapp, Tom Lausten, Mort Levine, Allan Lindh, Deane Little, Ken Miller, Joyce Nicholas, Ward Paine, Elizabeth Salveter, Stephen Salveter, David Sanguinetti, Janet Schwind, Pete Siemens, Carrie Sparks-Hart, Steve Tedesco, Jay Thorwaldson, David Topley, and Lisa Zadek.

I was lucky to have the help of the following generous people, who provided essential background information, and answers to questions when I was stumped: Chet Bardo, Matt Freeman, Jed Manwaring, Paul McKowan, Ann Powell, Jeff Powell, Cindy Roessler, and John Woodbury. The District's archives are full of treasures, and I helped myself to some of them, including memos and reports on local history by Lois Adams, Karin Bivens, Alice Cummings, Joyce Nicholas, Craig Weicker, and Joan Young.

Thanks to members of the District book committee—Kristi Altieri, Craig Britton, John Escobar, Stephanie Jensen, John Kowaleski, Michael Newburn, and David Sanguinetti—for their fine work. Kristi Altieri and Anne Koletzke beautifully captured the District's history and vision for the future in the writing of the preface and the epilogue. Ruthie Harari-Kremer, Matt Sagues, and Sumudu Welaratna produced the maps for the route descriptions featured in this book. Chris MacIntosh and Andrew Martin performed flawless fact-checking, consulting multiple authoritative sources and logging editors' comments. Chris Braley and Andrew Martin researched and obtained historic photographs and maps. The task of catching errors and omissions fell to Kristi Altieri, Craig Britton, Jo Combs, John Escobar, Stephanie Jensen, Michael Newburn, Del Woods, and David Sanguinetti, and they performed admirably.

Stephanie Jensen, the District's former public affairs manager, outlined the book project, then gave it to me and let me run with it—for that I am very grateful. I relied heavily on the help of Kristi Altieri, the District's public affairs specialist, who managed the project through to publication, who was always there when I needed her, and whose enthusiasm for the project and love of open space were inspirational. Finally, I would like to thank my wife, Maggi, for her love and support during this odyssey.

—David Weintraub

FOREWORD:
THE MANY FACES OF OPEN SPACES

~

I first looked up at a portion of the Skyline Ridge, looming above Los Gatos like a great shoulder of wilderness, when I was three years old. Within a year, I was riding a horse behind my older sister Cynthia up into the 2,000 acres of trails of the Charles Moore estate—now the El Sereno Open Space Preserve.

It was the beginning of a lifelong adventure of exploration, and love for the green ridges, the deep and rugged canyons, the occasional grassy hilltop and ridgeline that make up the Santa Cruz Mountains and the heart of the Midpeninsula Regional Open Space District.

By age five, I was riding my own horse into the hills—big, gentle Sam, a retired cowhorse; and at eight was given Baby, the meanest pinto pony in the West. But I survived, and together, feuding all the way, we explored Mt. Umunhum to the south of town; we spent many hours in an open meadow on a ridge looking down on Los Gatos; we rode miles over brush-covered El Sereno to the west and ultimately down to the old town of Alma, now flooded by Lexington Dam. We found back trails to Saratoga, old ranches long vacant, deep-shade bay-tree dells, and a huge oak reaching the ground at one end of a football-field-sized meadow we dubbed "Horse's Paradise."

And from these ridges we saw the valley's endless apricot and prune orchards give way to homes and highways in a sad, but seemingly inevitable, roll of market demand and economic reality. Before silicon became the heart of computers, this was called the "Valley of Heart's Delight."

At thirteen and fourteen, I was called upon by a former U.S. Senator, Sanborn Young, to track his beloved beagle dogs when they escaped (almost every other month) with my pet bloodhound, Annie Oakley, who pulled me

View of Rogue Valley in Rancho San Antonio Open Space Preserve

through endless brush and poison oak, past rattlesnakes and alligator lizards of Mt. Umunhum. The dogs always returned on their own.

Later, trading Baby for a '49 Dodge coupe, I discovered Skyline Boulevard and its many side roads, followed rumors of survivalist camps, visited the old Holy City religious settlement, and met strange old Father Riker. I discovered Sky Londa with its historic Alice's Restaurant (not the one in the song), La Honda's Applejack's bar, and—one wild, stormy night when I was hopelessly lost on an endless road—Pescadero and its classic Duarte's Restaurant and Bar (locals call it "doo-arts").

Taking a drive on Skyline became a staple of my youth, with friends, girl-friend (later wife), and alone—just to see the sunset, the storm, the occasional snow; to smell the Douglas-fir on a hot day; to feel a cool breeze; to explore hidden nooks, find old logging camps, wonder on a drizzly day at Castle Rock and its scooped-out overhang where a woman schoolteacher, the story goes, camped for several years a century or so ago.

When it wasn't possible to "go to Skyline"—during the hectic years of college, getting a job, starting a family—the great bulk of dark ridge and the grassy ridges and oak valleys of the lower hills were always there, a backdrop for the scenes of life. And they were almost always there in my mind, a mental respite from the pace and responsibilities of life.

Years later, reporting for the erstwhile *Palo Alto Times,* an assignment sent an editor and me up to explore Devil's Canyon, to check on reports of an illegal hippie encampment. We found it above a waterfall, complete with a young man glowing golden in the afternoon sun, meditating nude on the utmost edge of a rock cliff.

Living off Swett Road, I learned from historian Ken Fisher more history of the northern Skyline region than I knew existed, of the "suicide" death of shingle king Purdy Pharis and the moving in of the graft kingpins of nineteenth-century San Francisco, the burning of the old lumber camp/village of Grabtown on Tunitas Creek Road.

I learned that every ridge and valley of the hills has a history, some of it noble, some dark deeds and illegal doings, from the clear-cutting of the old redwoods for shingles in the 1800s to bootlegging on Kings Mountain in the 1920s—a lookout could spot the feds chugging up Highway 92. I learned that members of the Younger clan, part of Jesse James's bunch, hid out in La Honda before they went east to scope out a bank in Northfield, Minnesota.

I was shown the site of the tragic 1953 crash of a passenger plane flying 200 feet too low in the fog to clear a ridge—in which eighteen persons died, including world-famous pianist William Kapell. It was San Mateo County's worst air crash, remarkably.

And as a journalist in Palo Alto in the 1960s, I began to learn that I was not alone in my special relationship with the ridges and valleys of the Peninsula's great backbone. I talked with and interviewed dozens, scores of persons who shared stories, and feelings, about the hills. Some had spent their lives there and recalled earlier generations and characters (lots of characters); some had recently discovered it and were out to buy land or desired to build homes along the ridges.

"Isn't that a beautiful ridge?" one developer asked me rhetorically, waving his hand toward an oak-lined, descending slope as we bounced in a rented Chevy across the main field of what is now Palo Alto's Arastradero Preserve. He meant for 1,776 houses. I agreed it was a beautiful ridge—as did the City Council at the time, in rejecting the plan.

In the late 1960s, development proposals began circulating more frequently. Cities and the two counties that shared the foothills and ridge lands began experimenting with zoning and slope restrictions. In 1969, a young Palo Alto couple personally conducted a survey and found that residents of northern Santa Clara County said they valued the open lands enough that they would pay a modest amount of taxes to preserve them.

In 1970, *Palo Alto Times* Editor Alexander Bodi called me into his office one afternoon and complained about Palo Alto trying to "confiscate private property" by enacting a slope-density formula to control how many houses could be built on steeper lands, and a slope-grading standard for the foothills—how steep the gradient below housing pads could be. There was an endless debate underway on whether the graded slope should be 12 versus 14 degrees—the significance of which was that the average slope of the lower foothills was 13 degrees, and at 12 degrees half the housing pads would stretch to infinity and couldn't be built.

As Al fulminated about the issue, he seemed surprised when I agreed with him, and told him of a running discussion I was having with a Palo Alto woman who would complain emotionally about my coverage of the foothills issues before the Planning Commission. "I told her if they want to preserve the hills they should do what they did in the East Bay in 1934: create a district and buy the land at fair-market value."

Al thought, smiled, and said, "Yeah. Draft me an editorial." It was printed on Feb. 16, 1970—the year *Time Magazine* discovered the environmental movement with its Earth Day cover, also a Palo Alto/Stanford–based phenomenon.

The housewife who cared so deeply, Nonette Hanko, convened a brain-storming meeting in her home. From that eventually (and not without struggle, doubts, opposition, and hard work by thousands of supporters) emerged the Midpeninsula Regional Open Space District, better known by its unpronounceable acronym, MROSD.

This introduction should have been written by the late Wallace Stegner, who could look from his home toward the hills as he composed his literature of the West, his writings that helped so many of us Westerners *see* ourselves. He also helped us *see the hills* when he wrote of early efforts "to try to save for every-one, for the hostile and indifferent as well as the committed, some of the health that flows down across the green ridges from the Skyline, and some of the beauty and refreshment of spirit that are still available to any resident of the valley who has a moment, and the wit, to lift up his eyes unto the hills."

As this is written just past thirty years since voters formed the District, MROSD is approaching 50,000 acres of permanently protected lands, threaded with trails for hikers, equestrians, mountain bikers, and Buddhist meditators—rather than lined with barbed-wire fences and "No Trespassing" signs as in earlier decades.

These incredibly rugged, vulnerable open spaces are filled with faces—of the deer, fox, coyote, owl, creatures large and small, and now of humans of all ages: grandparents with grandchildren flying kites off Windy Hill, faces behind protective biking gear, awed faces of flatlanders exploring new terrain, of veteran hikers who have explored every trail and canyon, of volunteers doing trail work or leading walks for the wilderness challenged.

Faces of us.

—JAY THORWALDSON

PREFACE

❧

Peninsula Tales and Trails: Commemorating the Thirtieth Anniversary of the Midpeninsula Regional Open Space District is a celebration of the public land that is forever protected, its raw beauty perched on the Skyline Ridge and along the San Francisco Bay edge, all on the urban fringe of Silicon Valley—a celebration of the people willing to spend their time and money to preserve open space for future generations—a celebration of a small group of people who made a difference.

The late 1960s in the "Valley of Heart's Delight" was a scene of rapid growth—lush acres of blossoming orchards and grassy meadows being replaced by tract housing and commercial development. The spectacular scenic backdrop to the cities of the San Francisco midpeninsula that also served as a "greenbelt" and the potential for readily accessible recreation in a natural, unspoiled setting for future generations to enjoy was in jeopardy. In less than a generation, peninsula residents saw the open fields, which once separated their cities, give way to unrelieved suburbanization. The population explosion resulted in pressure to develop the foothills and baylands, especially in the cities that had relatively little undeveloped "flatlands" remaining. A reversal of this trend had to be achieved to ensure the preservation of the irreplaceable foothill and bayland natural resources.

A key figure advocating for the preservation of the foothills and baylands was Nonette Hanko, a Palo Alto resident and District founding member. Hanko's interest in politics began in 1967 when the "residentialists" (City of Palo Alto councilmembers who were pre-environmentalists—"environmentalist" wasn't yet a common term), who were concerned about increased development in the City and preserving the quality of life, were recalled from the City Council. One of the people proposed to be recalled was Byron Sher, who went on to become a distinguished California State Legislator from 1980 to 2004. The recall had been brought about by a group of people known as the "establishment," who were more development oriented and generally supportive of urban expansion.

Hanko began attending all of the Palo Alto Council and Planning Commission meetings, and with some prompting by then *Palo Alto Times* (now the *Palo Alto Weekly* editor) reporter Jay Thorwaldson, she encouraged one of the new council members, John Berwald, to go forward with the idea of developing a plan for all of Palo Alto's nine square miles of undeveloped foothill land, but done in an environmentally sound way. The Council approved the hiring of a consultant to conduct a study of land use, and, in 1969, the Livingston & Blaney Foothills Environmental Design Study was released. Amidst growing development pressures, the Study's cost benefit analysis found the property tax revenue generated by development of the foothills would not even pay for the area's required municipal services. The Study also recommended the formation of a special park district to preserve, not only the foothills above Palo Alto, but also all of the remaining open space lands south of the San Francisco Crystal Springs Watershed.

During this time, another conservationist who was instrumental in raising awareness, funds, and spirits on behalf of open space preservation was District founding member (and Board member since 1994) Mary Davey. She also served on the Board of the Trust for Hidden Villa and was active in the Committee for Green Foothills and Sempervirens Fund. Davey recalls Wallace Stegner as "an early ringleader in the philosophical sense." Stegner was a nationally acclaimed writer of both fiction and non-fiction, a Stanford University professor, and an environmentalist who resided in Los Altos Hills. In his "Wilderness Letter" of 1960, written to the University of California Wildland Research Center, he provided environmental proponents with a vision and grand design that proclaimed if you wanted open space, you had to own it so you could keep it "open" forever.

On February 16, 1970, Editor Alexander Bodie of the *Palo Alto Times* ran an editorial that was primarily an attack on the environmentalists' strategy of fighting rear guard battles against foothills development and suggested that to be permanently effective environmentalists should acquire open space at market value like was done by the park district in the East Bay. Hanko felt the editorial was meant for her, as she and Thorwaldson had been debating for several months over who should be responsible for preserving the foothills, if not the City of Palo Alto.

Deciding to accept Thorwaldson's challenge, Hanko called Stanford law professor Bob Girard, and together they created a list of people to invite to her home who would be knowledgeable and politically astute about permanently preserving the foothills. The twelve-member group met on April 9, 1970. Attendees included Stan Norton, a former Palo Alto assistant city attorney, and, at that time, a member of the Palo Alto Planning Commission. Norton served on a regional hillside planning committee encompassing San Mateo and Santa Clara counties and was later elected to the Palo Alto City Council, and Mayor. Another individual was new-lawyer-in-town Larry Klein, who in time became a Planning Commissioner, Councilmember, and Mayor.

By the next meeting, lawyers Klein and Fadlo Mousalam recommended to the group that the existing state law (Public Resources Code 5500) used to create the East Bay Regional Park District in the 1930s would serve the purpose without having to develop new legislation. Another attendee was Bill Spangle, a consulting planner for Portola Valley and Woodside, who went on to draft the plan for the new District boundaries. The group was on its way. It drew in Los Altos residents Tom and Joan Brown, who had founded Friends of the Foothills. It also attracted Saratoga Mayor Jerry Smith, who went on to be appointed to the California Court of Appeals, Cupertino resident Nancy Hertert, and Matt Allen, who went on to become Mayor of Mountain View.

In October 1970, supporters of a park and open space district conducted a random sample public opinion poll of 4,600 registered voters to determine the level of support for formation of a new regional park district. This new regional park district would be distinct and different from county parks in that it would be a single-purpose agency, focusing solely on open space acquisition and preservation, with separate funding and its own elected officials. The poll yielded results greater than what was hoped for with 72 percent favoring a regional park plan as a way to prevent the "Los Angelization" of the midpeninsula.

Nonette Hanko, District founding member, submits signatures to the Local Agency Formation Commission for creation of a regional park district to be put before voters in the November 1972 election.

Tom Brown, Mary Davey, Nonette Hanko, Larry Klein, and Stan Norton, in coordination with other regional park district proponents, began outreach to various peninsula communities, providing presentations to local city councils to gain support for the creation of a park district. Hanko said Mary Davey knows everyone in Santa Clara County and Stan Norton knows all the public officials in San Mateo County. Brown, another District founder, recalls a presentation to the Graders and Pavers Association of Santa Clara County: "I'm standing in front of all of these people who are looking pretty somber. They have just gotten off of their backhoes and graders, and they're looking at this guy (me), and I look at my notes and I look back at them, and I said, 'There must be some mistake. I was told this was the Audubon Society.' That softened the group up a little. And, if not their acceptance, we got their neutrality."

In March 1971, Hanko, Klein, and Norton, the legal proponents of the Local Agency Formation Commission (LAFCo) petition, won permission from Santa Clara County's LAFCo to circulate petitions favoring a regional park district. Hundreds of people volunteered to help. Groups actively supporting the proposed district included the League of Women Voters, the American Association of University Women, the Sierra Club, the Committee for Green Foothills, Friends of the Foothills, and the Junior League of Palo Alto. More than 10,000 signatures were collected and submitted to the Board of Supervisors in both counties.

The regional park district proposal was dealt a disappointing blow in August 1971 when the then "metropolitan-minded" San Mateo County Board of Supervisors rejected the opportunity for the district to extend into that county by a 3-to-2 vote. In October 1971, however, the proposal came before the Santa Clara County Board of Supervisors and, to the relief and elation of everyone involved in the effort, received approval and the opportunity to go before Santa Clara County voters in November of the following year.

The Measure R campaign materials chosen by Carole Norton rang with prose:

A "yes" vote on Measure R will preserve open space by creating the Midpeninsula Regional Park District. Open space is our green backdrop of hills. It is rolling grasslands—cool forests in the Coast Range—orchards and vineyards in the sun. It is the patch of grass between communities where children can run. It is uncluttered baylands where water birds wheel and soar, where blowing cordgrass yields its blessings of oxygen, where the din of urban life gives way to the soft sounds of nature. It is the serene, unbuilt, unspoiled earth that awakens all our senses and makes us whole again . . . it is room to breathe.

The Midpeninsula Regional "Park" District was "swept into being" on November 7, 1972, as Measure R passed by more than a two-thirds vote: 67.71 percent for and 32.29 percent against. The first five directors were also elected on the same ballot—Daniel Condron, Katherine Duffy, Nonette Hanko, William Peters, and Daniel Wendin. The boundaries encompassed Cupertino, Los Altos, Los Altos Hills, Los Gatos, Monte Sereno, Mountain View, Palo Alto, Saratoga, and Sunnyvale. During this same election year, the voters of Marin and Monterey counties also approved regional park district measures in their respective counties, thus creating a total of four such districts in the state.

At first, the Midpeninsula Regional Park District focused on establishing a new public agency. The small, competent staff included the first general manager, Herb Grench, a former Lockheed manager, Palo Alto Planning Commission member, and a leader in the local Audubon Society and the Committee for Green Foothills. The District set up headquarters, developed a Basic Policy and Master Plan, collected a modest property tax and began buying land for open space.

Although the regional park district advocates were disheartened by the San Mateo County Board of Supervisors' denial of the District's proposal to include portions of San Mateo County within its boundaries, the group knew they could go back later and fulfill that part of their dream. With concern mounting among California taxpayers in the mid-1970s, *Times* reporter Jay Thorwaldson nudged the District to get busy if they wanted to include part of San Mateo County. The District still did not have the approval of San Mateo County Supervisors to get on the ballot; yet, the visible open space enjoyed by both counties transcended the political boundary between Santa Clara County and San Mateo County.

In November 1974, a new plan to annex the southern San Mateo County cities of Atherton, East Palo Alto, Menlo Park, Portola Valley, Redwood City, San Carlos, and Woodside was activated by the District and its supporters. The plan emphasized the need for annexation, as County park funds were limited and could only provide for minor land purchases, not for preservation of substantial foothill and bayland areas threatened by development. A Citizens Committee for Annexation to the Midpeninsula Regional Park District, formed in July 1975 and led by Lennie Roberts and Harry Turner, conducted a survey that showed 65 percent of southeastern San Mateo County residents favored annexation. The Committee gathered the required petition signatures and in early 1976, LAFCo and the District board approved a ballot measure to go before voters in June.

A 'yes' vote on Proposition D will preserve open space in its natural state as 'room to breathe' in our hills and baylands. The foothills and baylands are two prime natural resources of the midpeninsula. Both provide nearby recreation, greenbelts around urban areas, and aesthetic relief from the strains of urban life. These resources are threatened by the same development pressures that eliminated open fields between our cities and created sprawling suburbanization in one generation. —From the Yes on Proposition D Campaign Materials

It was a difficult, hard-fought campaign, but despite opposition of the San Mateo County Grand Jury and the *Redwood City Tribune* (the *Times'* sister newspaper), Proposition D passed—51.52 percent for and 48.48 percent against.

To reflect its mission more accurately—preserving a continuous greenbelt of open space land and featuring a low-impact, "light footprint" approach to public recreational use—the District sponsored state legislation to expand the definition of "District" to include "open space." Once signed into law in 1977, the District changed its name to Midpeninsula Regional Open Space District, becoming the familiar MROSD that is now approaching 50,000 acres of preserved open space land, with hundreds of miles of trails and scenic vistas for present and future generations to explore and enjoy. See the epilogue, "The Other Side of the Mountain," for the next chapter in the District's journey to preserve the San Francisco midpeninsula's irreplaceable open space lands.

Special commendations: Thank you to early organizers Tom Brown, Mary Davey, Bob Girard, Barbara Green, Nonette Hanko, Larry Klein, Carole and Stan Norton, Lennie Roberts, Harry Turner, and many other friends—Pat Barrentine, Victor Calvo, Kirke Comstock, Barbara Eastman, Herb Grench, Lois Hogle, Barbara and Fadlo Mousalam, Jay Thorwaldson, Ward Winslow, and Alexander Bodi of the *Palo Alto Times*—for having the vision to set in motion the preserving of the Midpeninsula's open space heritage and ensuring "room to breathe" for generations to come.

Special mention of all former District board members for their contributions toward furthering the District's mission: Gerry Andeen, Ginny Babbitt, Richard Bishop, Daniel Condron, Betsy Crowder, Wim de Wit, Katherine Duffy, Barbara Green, Teena Henshaw, Robert McKibbin, William Peters, George Seager, Edward Shelley, David Smernoff, Harry Turner, Daniel Wendin.

Never doubt that a small group of thoughtful, committed citizens can change the world. Indeed, it is the only thing that ever has. —Margaret Mead

—Kristi Altieri

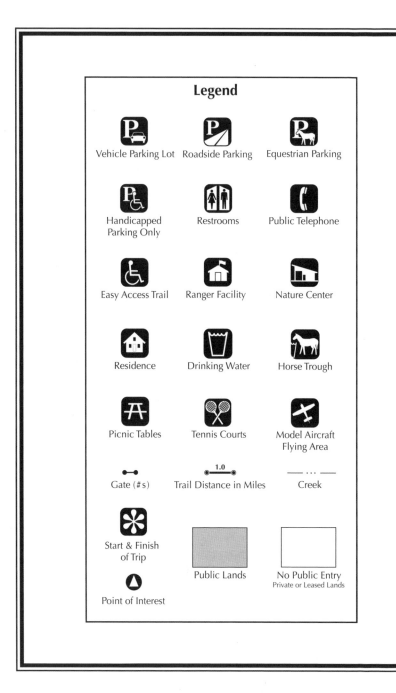

Legend

Vehicle Parking Lot

Roadside Parking

Equestrian Parking

Handicapped Parking Only

Restrooms

Public Telephone

Easy Access Trail

Ranger Facility

Nature Center

Residence

Drinking Water

Horse Trough

Picnic Tables

Tennis Courts

Model Aircraft Flying Area

Gate (# s)

1.0
Trail Distance in Miles

Creek

Start & Finish of Trip

Public Lands

No Public Entry
Private or Leased Lands

Point of Interest

Regional Open Space Preserves

	Preserves	Acres	🚶	🐎	🚲	🐕	♿	P	🏕
1.	Bear Creek Redwoods	1,345	●¹	●¹				□¹	
2.	Coal Creek	502	●	●	●	●		▮	
3.	El Corte de Madera Creek	2,821	●	●	●			▮	
4.	El Sereno	1,412	●	●	●			□	
5.	Foothills	212	●	●		●		□	
6.	Fremont Older	739	●	●	●	●		▮	●
7.	La Honda Creek	2,078	●¹	●¹				□¹	
8.	Long Ridge	1,971	●	●	●	●¹		▮	
9.	Los Trancos	274	●	●				■	
10.	Monte Bello	2,954	●	●	●		●	■	●
11.	Picchetti Ranch	308	●	●			●	■	●
12.	Pulgas Ridge	366	●			●	●	□	
13.	Purisima Creek Redwoods	3,120	●	●	●		●	■	●
14.	Rancho San Antonio	3,800	●	●	●		●	■	●
15.	Ravenswood	373	●		●		●	■	
16.	Russian Ridge	1,827	●	●	●			■	●
17.	Saratoga Gap	1,291	●	●	●			■	
18.	Sierra Azul (Kennedy-Limekiln and Cathedral Oaks Areas)	5,319	●	●	●	●²		□	
	Sierra Azul (Mt. Umunhum Area)	11,761	●	●	●			▮	
19.	Skyline Ridge	2,143	●	●	●		●	■	●
20.	St. Joseph's Hill	268	●	●	●	●		▮	●
21.	Stevens Creek Shoreline Nature Study Area	55	●			●	●	■	
22.	Teague Hill	626	●	●					
23.	Thornewood	164	●	●		●		▮	
24.	Windy Hill	1,308	●	●	●	●	●	■	●

■ Ample Parking   ▮ Limited Parking   □ Very Limited Parking

1 In designated area by permit only

2 Kennedy-Limekiln area only

Symbols and other information on these 2 pages refer to the master map on page 22, as well as to other maps throughout the book.

INTRODUCTION

~

BAY AREA OPEN SPACE

The Bay Area consists of the nine counties that encircle San Francisco Bay—Alameda, Contra Costa, Marin, Napa, San Francisco, San Mateo, Santa Clara, Solano, and Sonoma. These counties are generally arranged to form four regions: the East Bay, the North Bay, the South Bay, and the Peninsula. The definitions of the Peninsula and the South Bay sometimes overlap, but for the purposes of this book, the Peninsula covers San Francisco, San Mateo, and the northwestern part of Santa Clara County, and the South Bay takes in the balance of Santa Clara County. This is an incredibly diverse area, containing some of California's most heavily developed urban areas and also some of its most beautiful open spaces. Blessed by a Mediterranean climate and a large number of parks and preserves close to urban centers, the Bay Area is overflowing with opportunities for outdoor recreation. The landscape is wonderfully varied, containing wave-washed coastlines, forested canyons, rushing rivers, flower-carpeted grasslands, chaparral-clad hillsides, and windswept summits. Whatever your favorite outdoor activity, you are almost sure to find a place to pursue it in the Bay Area.

What makes the Bay Area's climate so ideal? The moderating effect of the Pacific Ocean tempers both summer's heat and winter's cold. A cooling blanket of fog often shrouds the coast and the coastal hills in summer, spilling picturesquely over ridgelines in billowing, wavelike patterns. In winter, the ocean provides a moderating influence, keeping temperatures mostly above freezing. The farther inland you go, the less pronounced is this moderating influence.

The Bay Area lies within a geological province called the Coast Ranges, which stretches from Arcata to near Santa Barbara, and inland to the edge of

Tree silhouetted against sky at Monte Bello Open Space Preserve

the Central Valley. Several important subranges run through the Bay Area, including the Diablo Range in the East Bay and South Bay; the Sonoma, Mayacmas, and Vaca Mountains in the North Bay; and the Santa Cruz Mountains on the Peninsula and in the South Bay. Numerous year-round creeks and seasonal streams flow to the Pacific coast or empty into San Francisco or San Pablo bays. As everyone knows, the Bay Area is prone to earthquakes, with the last major one occurring in 1989. Many earthquake faults run through the Bay Area; the most famous, the San Andreas, runs through the Santa Cruz Mountains.

The public parklands and open spaces of the Bay Area, about 1 million acres total, are administered by an alphabet soup of local, state, and federal agencies. Among those with the largest land holdings open to the public are: California State Parks, about 225,000 acres in the nine-county area; East Bay Regional Park District (EBRPD), about 94,500 acres in Alameda and Contra Costa counties;

Craig Britton, the District's general manager, says the District today owns about 50,000 acres of land that cost roughly $200 million to acquire, for an average of $4,000 per acre. At today's prices, in most cases at least double the average historic cost, some of the District's best-loved urban preserves would have been unaffordable. "I think we [the District] made some excellent decisions," Britton says. "It's an incredible asset to the people of the Midpeninsula. I think it improves our quality of life. If you look up to hills in southern California, you see—when you can see—housing. Here, when you look up, you see natural areas, and that was the whole idea."

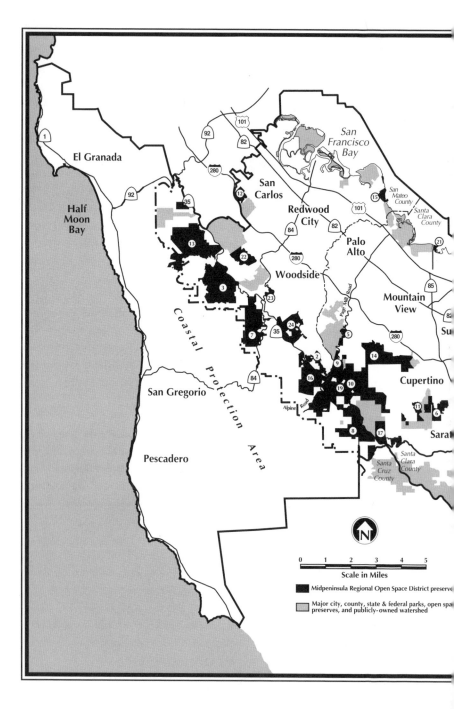

Scale in Miles

■ Midpeninsula Regional Open Space District preserve

▨ Major city, county, state & federal parks, open spa
preserves, and publicly-owned watershed

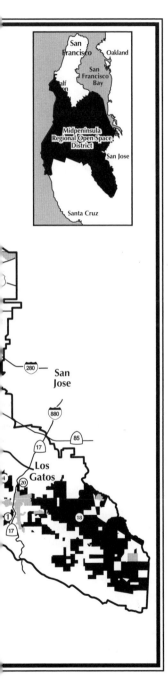

the Golden Gate National Recreation Area (GGNRA), about 75,000 acres in Marin, San Francisco, and San Mateo counties; Sonoma County Agricultural Preservation and Open Space District, about 59,000 acres; Midpeninsula Regional Open Space District (MROSD), about 50,000 acres in San Mateo, Santa Clara, and Santa Cruz counties; Santa Clara County Parks and Recreation, about 45,000 acres; East Bay Municipal Water District (EBMUD), about 27,000 acres in Alameda and Contra Costa counties; U.S. Fish and Wildlife Service, about 22,000 acres in San Francisco and San Pablo bays; Marin Municipal Water District, about 19,000 acres; Marin County Open Space District (MCOSD), about 14,000 acres; San Mateo County Parks and Recreation, about 14,000 acres; and Sonoma County Regional Parks, about 5,000 acres.

The Midpeninsula Regional Open Space District (hereafter referred to simply as the District) currently has twenty-five preserves (twenty-four of which are open to the public), with about 220 miles of trails. Two of these preserves, Bear Creek and La Honda Creek, require a special entry permit. Along with Sierra Azul, these preserves are undergoing major planning processes and will be opened to the public in the future. District preserves are free and open to the public year-round from sunrise to one-half hour after sunset.

Voters created the District in northwestern Santa Clara County in 1972, using the same enabling legislation that was passed in 1933 by the California legislature to create the East Bay Regional Park District. A vote in 1976 expanded the District's boundaries to include southeastern San Mateo County. In 1992, the District annexed a small part of Santa Cruz County, making it the first park or open space district in California to extend into three counties. Nonette Hanko is one of the District founders and a current board member. She remembers tagging along in the late 1960s on a tour for planning commissioners conducted by the late Frances Brenner, a member of the Palo Alto City Council, who was active in the conservation movement, especially with regard to protecting watersheds: "She took us all up and showed us the foothills of Palo Alto. Because of the beauty and vistas, I wasn't paying attention, nor was anybody else. [She] showed us the Stevens Creek watershed and where it began, right there on Monte Bello Ridge. Standing on this one place that overlooked Los Trancos on one side and Monte Bello on the other, you could see Mt. Umunhum, the highest mountain in the distance. And to the north, you could see San Francisco. The San Andreas Fault came through there, about a quarter of a mile wide. You could see the sag ponds, where the 1906 earthquake happened. The fact is that these lands were both in San Mateo and Santa Clara counties, which made it clear that any agency trying to protect those lands would have to cover both counties. And so when we started talking about putting together a special district, it seemed pretty obvious that it had to cross county boundaries."

Most of the District's land is along the crest of the Santa Cruz Mountains, which stretch from Pacifica to near Watsonville. However, other important properties lie on the doorstep of Silicon Valley. Deciding which land to purchase was, and still is, a challenge. Craig Britton, District general manager, says his philosophy of open space acquisition is a simple one: "They're printing money every day, but they aren't making more land. We should borrow, like every property owner, and buy every piece of strategic open space land we can get hold of. I really have to appreciate the fact that Fremont Older, Rancho [San Antonio], Picchetti [Ranch], and others

Redwoods at Purisima Creek Redwoods Open Space Preserve

View of Stevens Canyon from the Water Wheel Creek Trail in Monte Bello Open Space Preserve

were acquired early. Because the one thing I found in acquisition is that the most difficult properties to acquire are the ones that are right up against the urban boundary. We've always had difficulty because they're adjacent to existing public services, making the land easy to develop. And the owners have grander ideas of developing the land, rather than seeing it become open space."

Jay Thorwaldson is the editor of the *Palo Alto Weekly* and a longtime area resident. He remembers the pressures on land development that spurred the creation of the District. He says a study in the late 1950s projected 50,000 residents in the hills above Palo Alto. "They actually ran utilities up Page Mill Road. Water was run up under the pavement of Page Mill Road, telephone and electrical poles too."

Santa Clara Valley was also feeling the effects of development, Thorwaldson says. "I literally saw the valley fill up year after year. In Los Gatos one year, a subdivision showed up about five miles out of town called Blossom Hill Manor. It was the first curvilinear-street subdivision, and I didn't notice at the time, but then it sort of blossomed out. It's all developed now, but it was this little, bright clustering of houses among green trees. Later on I discovered it was the property tax laws that did it." Thorwaldson says the appraised value of the subdivisions boosted the value of the surrounding agricultural land and raised property taxes. This, in turn, forced out the orchards and other agricultural enterprises from the "Valley of Heart's Delight," as the Santa Clara Valley was then known. "Some of the richest, most fertile land in the world," he says. "The beauty of that valley! In the spring, cherry and apricot blossoms with the yellow mustard weed under the trees."

"Open space is still a mantra, I think, among the general public," says Ward Paine, a founder of Peninsula Open Space Trust. "Look at the $2.9 billion Proposition 40 election in March 2002. People really are enthusiastic about open space. They like having open space. People understand when they go down to Los Angeles, and they don't want that. They made a lot of mistakes down there and people up here don't want to repeat it. They also have seen what happened in Daly City with the string of houses along the edge of those hills. They don't want that to happen down here."

THE DISTRICT'S ROLE

The mission of the Midpeninsula Regional Open Space District is as follows: "To acquire and preserve a regional greenbelt of open space land in perpetuity; protect and restore the natural environment; and provide opportunities for ecologically sensitive public enjoyment and education." The District defines open space as "land area that is allowed to remain in or return to its natural state." Among the important functions of open space are:

- Protecting and preserving areas of scenic beauty
- Safeguarding natural habitats important to plants and animals, especially rare, threatened, or endangered species
- Providing opportunities for public recreation, education, and escape from the pressures of modern urban life
- Enhancing public safety by preventing development in floodplains, fire zones, and geologically unstable areas
- Establishing limits on urban growth
- Providing "Room to Breathe"

The District's Master Plan identifies the environmental challenges that faced the San Francisco Bay Area in the 1970s, many of which are still present today: "Uncontrolled urban sprawl and leapfrog development have been destructive to agriculture, have made efficient local government difficult and provision of urban services costly, and have aggravated pollution and transportation problems. This destructive and wasteful process of urban development must be controlled by careful planning and proper land use regulation, and by the phased extension of urban services and facilities." The District was formed to create an urban greenbelt in the Santa Cruz Mountains that would help provide a scenic backdrop and help define the rapidly growing communities of the Peninsula.

The scenic corridor of Skyline Boulevard anchors the District firmly atop the Santa Cruz Mountains. District lands extend downhill from the ridgeline, southwest toward the San Mateo coast and northeast along the shore of San Francisco Bay. Many District purchases were important pieces of the jigsaw puzzle that represents open space on the Peninsula. For example, one of the District's earliest gifts established Saratoga Gap Open Space Preserve, which today provides an important link in the Bay Area Ridge Trail and connections to Sanborn Skyline County Park, Castle Rock State Park, Big Basin State Park, Portola Redwoods State Park, Upper Stevens Creek County Park, and other District preserves. The District's largest preserve, Sierra Azul, borders on both Lexington Reservoir and Almaden Quicksilver parks in Santa Clara County.

Many other District preserves are near or adjacent to state and county parks, including Pulgas Ridge (near Edgewood County Park, and the San Francisco Crystal Springs watershed lands); Purisima Creek Redwoods (near Phleger Estate of the Golden Gate National Recreation Area, and Huddart Park); Teague Hill (near Huddart Park); El Corte de Madera Creek (near Wunderlich Park); Foothills (near Palo Alto Foothills Park, and Hidden Villa); Los Trancos (near Foothills Park); Monte Bello (near Hidden Villa, and Upper Stevens Creek County Park);

District Board of Directors in 2004
Back row from left to right: Pete Siemens (Ward 1), Kenneth C. Nitz (Ward 7), Deane Little (Ward 4), Larry Hassett (Ward 6), Jed Cyr (Ward 3); Front row from left to right: Nonette G. Hanko (Ward 5), Mary C. Davey (Ward 2)

Hikers on the Woods Trail at Sierra Azul Open Space Preserve; this trail was dedicated as part of the Bay Area Ridge Trail.

Rancho San Antonio (near Hidden Villa, and Rancho San Antonio County Park); Long Ridge (near Portola Redwoods State Park); Picchetti Ranch (near Stevens Creek County Park); Fremont Older (near Stevens Creek County Park); El Sereno (near Sanborn Skyline County Park); St. Joseph's Hill (near Town of Los Gatos Novitiate Park, and Lexington Reservoir County Park); Ravenswood (near Palo Alto Baylands Nature Preserve, and Don Edwards San Francisco Bay National Wildlife Refuge); and Stevens Creek Shoreline Nature Study Area (near Shoreline-at-Mountain View Park). Britton says the proximity of District preserves to county and state parks greatly benefits the public. "If a person's visiting one of these parks, you have a dual regional component," he says. "You can come and do more active things with your family in the park, or you can go up and have a more passive wilderness-type recreational experience in the open space preserve."

District preserves are free of charge and open to the public year-round from sunrise to one-half hour after sunset. They have few introduced amenities. Most have a gravel parking area and many have a vault toilet. None have trash cans, so you must pack out what you pack in. Some have small roadside parking areas and no facilities. The attraction, of course, is the land itself and the natural beauty, with trails running through that are among the best in the Bay Area. Dennis Danielson, a supervising ranger at the District's Skyline office, said, "We're almost like a mini–wilderness area. We don't even have one garbage can, and proudly so. And very few picnic tables. No ball fields. No barbecues. But there are the city and county parks that accommodate those needs very, very well. So we've been able to focus more on land conservation, and the idea of having low-intensity recreational use. We do allow mountain bikes, which some people would argue is not a low-intensity use, but it is a compatible trail use."

Deane Little is a District board member. "I expect state parks and county parks to be more crowded, and to have people there who are looking for more of an active recreational experience, rather than a contemplative or meditative experience offered on the open space preserves. The Open Space District's sites get to the root of the environment, for me, much more than do parks. And I think it's because there's so little of mankind that's layered on them. The county parks have all those developed facilities. From my perspective, mankind intrudes on those spaces much more than it does on the Open Space District's lands."

The District works with local, state, and federal agencies to preserve the greenbelt and develop a regional trail system. Among these agencies are the sixteen cities and three counties within the District's boundary; the California Department of Parks and Recreation (State Parks); the California Department of Fish and Game; the Wildlife Conservation Board; the Coastal Conservancy; and the Golden Gate National Recreation Area (GGNRA). In addition, the District cooperates with special districts, such as the Santa Clara Valley Water District, and regional agencies, such as the San Francisco Bay Conservation and Development Commission (BCDC) and the Association of Bay Area Governments (ABAG). Finally, the District has several unique relationships with local government agencies. At the northern end of the District, the District made a significant contribution to fund the acquisition of the Phleger Estate, which is owned and managed by GGNRA. Neighbors of Pulgas Ridge formed a special assessment district to raise tax money to help the District create the preserve. Across Edgewood Road from Pulgas Ridge Open Space Preserve is Edgewood Park and Preserve, which represents a partnership between the District, San Mateo County, and the (federal) Land and Water Conservation Fund. Farther south, the District manages Rancho San Antonio County Park—the main gateway to Rancho San Antonio Open Space Preserve—for Santa Clara County. Deer Hollow Farm, one of Rancho San Antonio's best-loved attractions, is a cooperative venture between the District, the County of Santa Clara,

Sticky monkeyflower

and the City of Mountain View. The Town of Los Gatos shared the purchase cost of St. Joseph's Hill with the District, and has contributed more toward buying open space than any of the other towns in the District, says Britton. "The entire backdrop to Los Gatos is our St. Joseph's Hill, Sierra Azul, and El Sereno Open Space Preserves. I think they put in nearly five million dollars toward open space acquisition. So it's very important to them. Los Gatos was very forward thinking."

Many nonprofit land trusts and advocacy groups share the District's philosophy concerning open space. The District has benefited from its relationship with, among others, Peninsula Open Space Trust (POST), Sempervirens Fund, the Nature Conservancy, Save-the-Redwoods League, and the Bay Area Ridge Trail Council. Whole Access, a nonprofit group dedicated to improving outdoor recreation opportunities for people with disabilities, gave the District assistance and advice on the planning and construction of several trails designed for visitors with wheelchairs. Private individuals and organizations also play important roles in the preservation of open space, and the District works with them to protect land from development, using open space easements, life-estate arrangements, and other methods.

In terms of regional trail connections, the District, in concert with Santa Clara County Parks, is trying to acquire the balance of rights to connect Stevens Creek and Upper Stevens Creek county parks with Saratoga Gap Open Space Preserve. The District is looking to the future, when it might be able to secure continuous trail alignments that will connect the Bay Trail to the Bay Area Ridge Trail, and from there to the Coastal Trail, making it possible to walk unhindered from San Francisco Bay to the Pacific Ocean.

Bay Area Ridge Trail

The Bay Area Ridge Trail is a proposed five-hundred-mile route that would circle the Bay Area along the ridges of its nine counties. About half of the trail system has been completed so far, mostly using existing trails in established parks and preserves. The Bay Trail is a similar effort to ring San Francisco and San Pablo bays. The District supports both the Bay Area Ridge Trail and the Bay Trail, and actively seeks to obtain trail alignments to promote the completion of these regional trail systems. Currently, the District is involved with planning segments through La Honda Creek, Windy Hill, and Sierra Azul Open Space Preserves.

Peninsula Open Space Trust

The District and the Peninsula Open Space Trust (POST) have enjoyed a special and productive partnership for more than twenty years, which has resulted in the preservation of thousands of acres of open space. The two organizations have collaborated on many successful projects, including preservation of Windy Hill Preserve and creation of the easy-access Redwood Trail at Purisima Creek Redwoods Preserve. For more information about this key preservation partner organization, please see pages 331-333.

THE LAND

Plant Communities

California is blessed with a rich variety of plant life. The state has more than five thousand native plant species and an estimated one thousand introduced species. About 30 percent of the native plants occur nowhere else—these are called endemics. Common endemic plants include many species of manzanita *(Arctostaphylos)* and monkeyflower *(Mimulus)*. In terms of evolution, the state has some of the oldest species and also some of the youngest. For example, coast redwoods date back to the dinosaurs, whereas certain species of tarweed *(Madia)* have evolved within the past several thousand years. Botanists divide the plant kingdom into several major groups: flowering plants; conifers; ferns and their allies; mosses; and algae. The members of these groups that grow together in a distinct habitat are a plant community. Because District lands stretch from San Francisco Bay to the Santa Cruz Mountains, you can find many different plant communities represented in the District's various preserves.

Redwood Forest

Shady, cool, and often fogbound, redwood forests are dominated by their namesake tree, the coast redwood. Associated with redwoods are a number of plant species, including tanbark oak, California bay, hazelnut, evergreen huckleberry, wood rose, redwood sorrel, and western sword fern. Redwood groves were once extensive in a coastal band that stretched from central California to southern Oregon. Coast redwoods are the world's tallest trees and also among the fastest-growing. Commercially valuable, they were heavily logged in the Santa Cruz Mountains and elsewhere. The remnants of this ancient forest are in isolated pockets on federal, state, and private land.

Some individual old-growth trees remain on District land, and you can visit these giants, along with fine stands of second-growth redwoods, in several preserves, including Bear Creek Redwoods, El Corte de Madera Creek, and Purisima Creek Redwoods.

Douglas-fir Forest

In many areas of the Santa Cruz Mountains, Douglas-fir is the most common conifer, easily told by its distinctive cones, which have protruding, three-pointed bracts. Douglas-fir and coast redwood are California's two most important commercial trees. Douglas-fir often grows mixed with redwoods or adjacent to redwood groves, but also in drier conditions that do not favor redwood growth. Some of the common plants associated with Douglas-fir in the Bay Area are the same as those associated with coast redwood, namely California bay, tanbark oak, and western sword fern. Others include blue blossom, coffeeberry, and poison oak. Enjoy wandering through a Douglas-fir forest at La Honda Creek, Saratoga Gap, and Skyline Ridge Open Space Preserves.

Mixed Evergreen Forest

As its name implies, this forest contains a mixture of evergreen trees, including California bay, canyon oak, coast live oak, and madrone. The understory to this forest often contains shrubs such as toyon, blue elderberry, hazelnut, buckbrush, snowberry, thimbleberry, oceanspray, and poison oak. Carpeting the forest floor may be an assortment of wildflowers, including milkmaids, fairy bells, mission bells, hound's tongue, and western heart's-ease. A mixed evergreen forest is a good place to practice "birding by ear," the technique of identifying birds by their songs, notes, and calls. Take a stroll through a mixed evergreen forest at Long Ridge, Monte Bello, Rancho San Antonio, Saratoga Gap, and Sierra Azul Open Space Preserves.

Oak Woodland

District lands contain a variety of oaks, some of them venerable, photogenic specimens, others stunted shrubs. The oaks on District preserves include coast live oak, canyon oak, interior live oak, valley oak, black oak, blue oak, Oregon oak, scrub oak, leather oak, Shreve oak, and oracle oak (a hybrid). Tanbark oak, although not in the same genus *(Quercus)* as the true oaks, is important in oak woodlands. Especially with oaks, slope aspect and elevation determine where different species occur. A woodland containing oaks or other trees growing in widely spaced stands is sometimes called a savanna. Oaks provide shelter and

Oak woodland at Rancho de Guadalupe Area of Sierra Azul Open Space Preserve

food for wildlife, and acorns were an important food source for Native Americans. Common trees and shrubs associated with oak woodlands are California buckeye, California bay, buckbrush, toyon, coffeeberry, snowberry, and poison oak. Explore the District's oak woodlands at Long Ridge, Los Trancos, Rancho San Antonio, and Russian Ridge Open Space Preserves.

Riparian Forest

Members of this moisture-loving community are usually found in shady canyons beside rivers, creeks, and streams. Among the most common riparian trees are bigleaf maple, white alder, red alder, California bay, and various willows. Other plants that share this unique habitat include California rose, poison oak, California wild grape, elk clover, and giant chain fern. Many animals depend for their survival on the water, shade, food, and cover provided by riparian forests. Riparian forests provide the best locations in the Bay Area to see fall colors. Although the display here is modest compared to New England's, visitors can enjoy the changing seasons at El Corte de Madera Creek, Monte Bello, Purisima Creek Redwoods, and Sierra Azul Open Space Preserves.

Grasslands

Native grasslands are threatened throughout California and the rest of North America, according to scientists. Destructive grazing practices, fire suppression, farming, and the invasion of nonnative plant species have taken their toll on grasslands, and only a few grassland areas in the Santa Cruz Mountains retain their native character. Perennial bunchgrasses, such as purple

Chaparral at Sierra Azul Open Space Preserve

needlegrass, have, in large part, been replaced with nonnative grasses like wild oat and Harding grass. Restoration is underway on some of the District's grasslands to return them to a more natural state. Many grasslands still have showy displays of wildflowers in spring and summer. Among the most common are bluedicks, California poppy, owl's-clover, checker mallow, lupine, coyote brush, and blue-eyed grass. Seek out these enchanting areas at Fremont Older, La Honda Creek, Long Ridge, Rancho San Antonio, Russian Ridge, and Windy Hill Open Space Preserves.

Chaparral and Coastal Scrub

Chaparral is a fascinating plant community that thrives in poor soils under hot, dry conditions. The word itself comes from a Spanish term for dwarf or scrub oak, but in the Santa Cruz Mountains it is chamise, toyon, buckbrush, silk tassel, mountain mahogany, yerba santa, and various species of manzanita that dominate this community. Chaparral is adapted to fire. Certain species of manzanita survive extremely hot fires by sprouting new growth from ground-level burls, whereas other plants reseed themselves. Despite the harsh environment in which it grows, chaparral can be beautiful year-round, with some manzanitas blooming predominantly white flowers as early as December, and other plants continuing into spring and summer. Coastal scrub, sometimes called soft chap-

arral, consists mostly of shrubs and grasses growing in the fog belt near the coast. Among the most common members are California sagebrush, coyote brush, toyon, sticky monkeyflower, and various brooms. You can see examples of both chaparral and coastal scrub when you visit El Corte de Madera Creek, El Sereno, La Honda Creek, Pulgas Ridge, Purisima Creek Redwoods, Sierra Azul, and St. Joseph's Hill Open Space Preserves.

Salt Marsh

Salt marshes are found at the edges of bays and estuaries, and contain plants that can tolerate salt in varying degrees. At the lowest level of the marsh, which is flooded twice daily by the tide, are various cord grasses *(Spartina)*, some of which have come to San Francisco Bay from Humboldt Bay and the East Coast. Growing at higher elevations in the marsh are pickleweed and salt marsh dodder, a parasitic plant that sends out orange threads to encircle its host. Salt grass, alkali heath, and sea lavender, also called marsh rosemary, grow at a level reached only by the highest tides. The yellow flowers of gumplant and brass buttons bloom in salt marshes nearly year-round. Salt marshes are highly productive ecosystems, providing food, shelter, nesting areas, and spawning grounds for birds, fish, and small mammals. Approximately 80 percent of San Francisco Bay's wetland habitats have been lost to development. The District has two preserves that contain salt marshes, Ravenswood Open Space Preserve and Stevens Creek Shoreline Nature Study Area.

For a comprehensive, searchable listing of the flora and fauna found on District preserves, visit the Natural Resources DataBase at *www.nrdb.org*.

Geology

The Santa Cruz Mountains are part of the southern Coast Ranges. The earth's continents and oceans are not fixed in place but rather travel on ever-shifting plates, whose motions are controlled by forces deep within the earth. Geologists say that California's Coast Ranges were formed when the heavier Pacific plate was dragged beneath the North American plate, scraping off material and building it up on the continent's western edge. Forces then cracked and folded this material, forming the ridges and valleys we see today. These ridges and valleys trend northwest to southeast, paralleling the San Andreas and other faults.

The San Andreas fault is the most important player on the geological stage in the Bay Area, bisecting the Santa Cruz Mountains. West of the San Andreas fault is a formation called the Salinian block, which is actually a chunk of southern Sierra Nevada granite that has been slowly creeping northwest with the Pacific plate at the rate of about two to three inches per year. To the east of the fault is the Franciscan complex, which extends from the Bay Area to the Central Valley. The Franciscan complex consists generally of sandstone, or graywacke, accompanied by other rocks such as chert and serpentine

Serpentine outcrop at Jacques Ridge Area of Sierra Azul Open Space Preserve

(California's state rock). Serpentine forms a soil that is toxic to many plant species, but some have adapted to it, including various chaparral shrubs and grassland wildflowers. The Santa Cruz Mountains are just an accidental assemblage of rocks, geologists say. Their eastern and western slopes are sliding by each other like two trains moving in opposite directions.

You can learn a lot about the geological forces at work in the Santa Cruz Mountains by visiting selected District preserves on routes described in this book. A walk along the San Andreas Fault Trail in Los Trancos Open Space Preserve vividly illustrates various aspects of earthquake geology. On this trail, you straddle the San Andreas fault and walk on both the Pacific and the North American plates. Tim Hall, a former professor of geology at Foothill College, designed the trail. Stevens Creek Canyon in nearby Monte Bello Open Space Preserve follows the course of the San Andreas fault, and the Stevens Creek Nature Trail explores terrain shaped by the fault. Along the way, you pass several sag ponds, formed when earth movement caused the ground to subside in various places. The low points fill seasonally with rainwater or are fed year-round by underground springs.

Topography

Most District lands are draped across the spine of the Santa Cruz Mountains in an area stretching from Los Gatos in the south to San Carlos in the north, and reaching to the baylands. Other preserves are located near urban areas at the edge of Silicon Valley and along the shore of San Francisco Bay. Skyline Boulevard, or Highway 35, is the major ridge-top route through the Santa Cruz Mountains. The major roads running across the Santa Cruz Mountains from San Francisco Bay to the Pacific coast are, from north to south, Highway 92, Highway 84, Highway 9, and Highway 17. Several other roadways provide access to Skyline Boulevard from the east, including Kings Mountain Road and Page Mill/Alpine Road. Many of the roads traversing the Santa Cruz Mountains follow alignments of old logging and ranching roads, which in turn may have traced paths used by Native Americans, Spanish missionaries, and Mexican settlers. Many of the trails on District preserves are also old logging and ranching roads, although many single-track trails have been constructed more recently. Thus, the trail systems follow the topography, with rolling routes along ridge tops, and steep, switchbacking paths up and down hillsides.

District preserves can be sorted into five distinct topographical categories: West-facing from Skyline Boulevard, East-facing from Skyline Boulevard, Valley Edge, Lexington Basin, and San Francisco Bay Shoreline.

Riparian habitat at Bear Creek Redwoods Open Space Preserve

West-facing from Skyline Boulevard

Purisima Creek Redwoods, El Corte de Madera Creek, La Honda Creek, Russian Ridge, Skyline Ridge, Long Ridge, and Mills Creek (yet to be formally named, planned, and opened for public use). These preserves feature steep, forested ravines; deeply incised canyons that hold fast-flowing streams; and grassy ridge tops. Here too are coast redwood and Douglas-fir forests, and hillsides cloaked with coastal scrub. Two of the northernmost preserves in this group, Purisima Creek Redwoods and El Corte de Madera Creek, were intensively logged from the mid-nineteenth to the early twentieth centuries. Fog often pushes in from the San Mateo coast and pours over Skyline Boulevard, especially in summer. When fog condenses on leaves and branches of the forest canopy, it falls to the ground and provides water for trees, shrubs, and other plants during the dry season. This process is called fog drip, and it provides an important source of irrigation for the forest. Because they are connected to relatively undeveloped lands along the San Mateo coast, the west-facing preserves provide important wildlife habitats and corridors for wildlife movement.

East-facing from Skyline Boulevard

Teague Hill, Thornewood, Windy Hill, Coal Creek, Los Trancos, Foothills, Monte Bello, and Saratoga Gap. Oak woodlands, large areas of grassland, and fingers of mixed-evergreen forest that follow creeks and streams characterize these preserves. Where there are oaks, there are acorns, providing food for animals (such as deer, squirrels, and acorn woodpeckers). The varied terrain creates transitional edges between habitats, and these edges attract wildlife. Although affected by coastal fog, the east-facing preserves enjoy plenty of sunshine when the fog burns off.

Valley Edge

Pulgas Ridge, Rancho San Antonio, Picchetti Ranch, and Fremont Older. Located near heavily populated areas, these islands of open space represent prime agricultural lands that were saved from development. Prior uses of these preserves include grape growing and wine making, fruit growing, grazing, ranching, and haying. Today hikers, joggers, equestrians, mountain bicyclists, and picnickers enjoy a respite from the frenetic life in Silicon Valley by visiting these preserves, which contain oak woodlands, extensive grasslands, and lovely displays of wildflowers. The District and community partners have worked to preserve historic features here, including the Picchetti winery complex, the Fremont Older house, Deer Hollow Farm, and Grant Cabin.

Steelhead Trout and Coho Salmon

Steelhead and salmon are anadromous fish, breeding in fresh water but spending part of their lives in the ocean. Coastal creeks draining District lands have runs of Coho salmon and steelhead, both federally listed as threatened species. Spawning areas in these creeks are easily damaged by too much sediment, which may be caused by logging, road building, and even improperly sited trails or excessive erosion from roads and trails. Diversion for agricultural and human uses also degrades creeks by reducing the flow of cold, fresh water. Steelhead also spawn in the upper reaches of Guadalupe Creek, which they enter after migrating through San Francisco Bay and downtown San Jose. At one time, salmon and steelhead were abundant on the Pacific coast, but the damming of major rivers and loss of spawning areas have drastically reduced their numbers. Within the past ten years, steelhead have been sighted on seven District preserves in the higher elevations of the Santa Cruz Mountains. The District currently protects steelhead habitat at El Corte de Madera Creek, La Honda Creek, Long Ridge, Mills Creek (an interim name designation), Purisima Creek Redwoods, Russian Ridge, and Sierra Azul Open Space Preserves.

Lexington Basin to Loma Prieta

Bear Creek Redwoods, El Sereno, St. Joseph's Hill, and Sierra Azul. This vast, mostly undeveloped area contains the District's southernmost preserves, which are also its most wild and remote. Steep, chaparral-cloaked slopes alternate with riparian areas to form a biologically rich and diverse zone, which is home to a wide variety of plants and animals. Where present, fog drip provides irrigation for conifers and other large trees. Mountain lions use the area's ridge tops to roam into nearby state and county parks. District lands that may in the future have a trail-to-the-sea connection, and lands managed by other agencies, provide an important ecological connection between the Santa Cruz Mountains and the Diablo Range to the east. Periodic fires sweep through this seasonally hot, dry terrain, rejuvenating the flora.

San Francisco Bay Shoreline

Ravenswood and Stevens Creek Shoreline Nature Study Area. Much of the original San Francisco Bay shoreline has disappeared, a victim to diking and filling for industrial and residential development, transportation, and salt production. Gone, too, are most of the salt marshes that once ringed the Bay, providing habitat for birds, fish, and small mammals. These two preserves recapture some of the Bay's ecological past. Ravenswood is a former salt pond, recently restored to tidal action. Stevens Creek Shoreline Nature Study Area was probably never used for salt production, but was the location of the original Bay margin. Both preserves feature salt marshes that attract shorebirds, waterfowl, and wading birds, mostly during fall, winter, and spring.

Watershed Protection

District preserves encompass key watersheds that drain both sides of the Santa Cruz Mountains. Within these watersheds are major year-round creeks, their tributaries, and assorted seasonal streams. On the San Francisco Bay side, the major creeks that drain District lands are Cordilleras, San Francisquito, Adobe, Permanente, Stevens, Los Gatos, and Guadalupe. On the San Mateo and Santa Cruz coast side, they are Purisima, Lobitos, Tunitas, San Gregorio, Pescadero, Soquel, and San Lorenzo. Many District preserves—Bear Creek Redwoods, Coal Creek, El Corte de Madera Creek, La Honda Creek, Purisima Creek Redwoods, and Stevens Creek Shoreline Nature Study Area—take their names from creeks within or on their borders, reflecting the importance of these water resources. The District's goals in protecting water resources include maintaining pure, healthy water for people and wildlife, recharging groundwater supplies, and protecting rare, threatened, or endangered species.

USING THIS BOOK

This book is intended as a guide to the District's twenty-five preserves, twenty-four of which are currently open to the public. The preserves are ordered in the book alphabetically, and there is a preserve locator map on page 22. Each preserve is introduced with historical, cultural, and anecdotal material. At the end of each introduction is a table specifying the trail uses for that preserve as they apply to bicycles, dogs, and horses. All of the trail routes described stay within the preserve where they begin, except the "Grand Loop," which takes you through Monte Bello, Coal Creek, Russian Ridge, and Skyline Ridge Open Space Preserves. Long-distance hikers, mountain bicyclists, and equestrians can devise their own combinations of routes that traverse multiple District preserves, or utilize adjoining state or county parks. This trail guide is an introduction to District lands and not a comprehensive listing of each trail in every preserve. Please do wander to your heart's content, and modify (or ignore altogether) my suggested routes.

I hope to have captured something of the excitement and spirit of adventure that I felt when setting out to explore the District's varied and beautiful preserves. A good guidebook should do more than just lead you along a specified route. I have scattered throughout the route descriptions what I hope are useful and interesting tidbits of natural and human history. Small details often turn enjoyable hikes into memorable ones. Hopefully this book will be a knowledgeable, but not an overbearing, companion. When using a guidebook, it is helpful to know something about its author. In the interest of full disclosure I hereby confess to certain biases: I prefer loops to out-and-back routes. As a photographer, I love to climb high for great views, but as an aging hiker, I look for the easiest way down; I am fascinated by native plants, especially chaparral shrubs and colorful wildflowers, and I am an avid birder. During the year that it took to research this book, I hiked each of the thirty-eight routes, some more than once. Each day in nature is different, so your experience of a particular preserve or trail will probably be different from mine. I have tried to indicate this variability in two ways. First, by liberally using the word *may* in the text, as in "During the rainy season, you may come upon seasonal waterfalls and water-loving creatures, such as banana slugs and California newts." Second, by being as specific as possible about when things that vary by season, such as the blooming of wildflowers or the migration of birds, are most likely to occur.

Names

One of the hardest tasks of a guidebook author is to figure out what to call things. Names are sometimes slippery things, when you try to pin them down. Over the course of time, spellings get altered, apostrophes get dropped, and the people who gave their names to the land pass on. Two excellent books helped me in this regard, *California Place Names,* by Erwin G. Gudde, and *California's Spanish Place-Names,* by Barbara and Rudy Marinacci (further information regarding these books, and others mentioned in the text, may be found in the list of suggested reading material on pages 372–73). When in doubt, I follow District names and spellings as they appear on District maps and other District documents.

District Preserves

District preserves are generally named for some aspect of the landscape, such as Russian Ridge Open Space Preserve or St. Joseph's Hill Open Space Preserve. Most of the time, I use Preserve (for Open Space Preserve) when referring to District preserves. This is to avoid confusion and make it clear that I am writing about the preserve rather than the ridge or creek for which it was named.

Flora

The common names of plants are fickle. The same plant may have two or more names, and the same name may apply to different plants. For example, a violet of the coast redwood forest, *Viola ocellata,* appears in one plant guide as "two-eyed violet" and in another as "western heart's-ease." My solution for this book was generally to follow the names used in *Plants of the San Francisco Bay Region,* by Kozloff and Beidleman. Where it would not cause confusion to do so with plant names, I removed some hyphens and dropped some modifiers, such as "California" and "western."

Fauna

For the common names of birds, I rely on the American Ornithologists' Union (AOU) checklist for birds of the continental United States and Canada. In this checklist, old friends such as rufous-sided towhee and scrub jay have new names—spotted towhee and western scrub-jay.

Favorite Hikes

Here are some of my favorite hikes on District lands, places I'd return to and share with my friends:

PRESERVE	ROUTE	HIGHLIGHTS
El Corte de Madera Creek	Tafoni Loop	Rock formations
Fremont Older	Hunters Point	Flora, views
Long Ridge	Long Ridge	Exercise, views
Los Trancos	San Andreas Fault Trail	Geology
Monte Bello	Black Mountain	Exercise, views
Picchetti Ranch	Zinfandel Trail	Flora, wine tasting
Purisima Creek Redwoods	Purisima Canyon	Redwoods, views
Rancho San Antonio	Duveneck Windmill Pasture	Exercise, flora
Russian Ridge	Borel Hill	Exercise, wildflowers
Sierra Azul	Limekiln–Priest Rock Loop	Flora, views
Skyline Ridge	Ridge Trail	Exercise, flora, views
Windy Hill	Spring Ridge	Exercise, views

Selecting a Route

People visit District lands for a variety of reasons, such as exercise, scenery, nature study, or just to escape from the hustle and bustle of civilization. Selecting a route involves several factors, including season, time available for the outing, level of difficulty, and personal interests, such as the desire to see wildflowers, birds, or scenic vistas.

Length measures round-trip distance from what I designate as the trailhead, which is almost always adjacent to the parking area. **Time** is the estimated duration of the hike, including a few stops, based on my average hiking pace of 1.5 to 2 miles per hour. **Rating** indicates whether the route is easy, moderate, or difficult. For this book, "Easy" means that the route is mostly flat and can usually be completed in an hour or less. "Moderate" indicates a more challenging, hilly hike that will probably take two to three hours. "Difficult" means a hike is more than six miles in length and involves a significant elevation gain. Under **Highlights**, you can learn the type of route—loop, semi-loop, out-and-back—and the names of the trails you will use. You can also see at a glance the main attractions of the route, such as wildflowers or great views. **Directions** gets you to the parking area from the nearest major roadway. **Facilities** lists amenities that may be near the trailhead, usually just a vault toilet. Finally, **Trailhead** tells you where to start your trip. For almost all the routes in this book, I designate the point at which you leave the parking area as the trailhead, and I measure the round-trip mileage from that point.

Most of the routes on District lands follow dirt roads and single-track trails. Within the route descriptions themselves, the subjective terms *gentle, moderate,* and *steep* are used to indicate the grade of ascent and descent. A gentle grade, if you are reasonably fit, is one that is almost imperceptible and requires no change of pace. A moderate uphill grade requires a bit more exertion, but should not interfere with regular breathing or conversation. Climbing steeply uphill forces concentrated effort, and is best done by maintaining a slow but measured pace coordinated with deep breathing. Moderate and steep downhill grades (especially over loose, rocky ground) require caution—a walking stick or a trekking pole is invaluable here. Distances given in the route description are approximations, and always refer to the start of the hike. Thus, "After a rolling, winding descent, you arrive at a fork near the 1-mile point," means that the fork is about one mile from the trailhead.

Maps

Each route description in this book is accompanied by a map. When I refer to a map in a route description, the map is the one produced by the District for the public. You can generally obtain these maps at or near the trailhead for each trip, except at El Sereno, Foothills, and Stevens Creek Shoreline Nature Study Area. La Honda Creek and Bear Creek Redwoods require a permit for entry, which comes with a map of the preserve. You can download District maps and preserve descriptions from the Web site at *www.openspace.org.* Maps can also be obtained from the District office: (650) 691-1200.

The maps included in this guidebook show existing trails and facilities available at the time of production of the book. As a result, be aware that due to additional acquisitions, natural changes, or improvements made over time, the maps included in this book may become outdated. Visitors are encouraged to obtain the most current District maps.

Respect Private Property

Many of the District preserves are bordered by private property, and some of the roads and driveways within the preserves lead to private residences. Please respect the private property boundaries, and help the District be a good neighbor by adhering to signs posted by the District and staying on designated preserve trails.

Appendixes

This book contains three appendixes with reference information. Appendix A is a bibliography of suggested reading material about the Midpeninsula area, natural history, and other topics. Appendix B is a list of information sources, including government agencies and other organizations. Appendix C is a list of District preserves that are near or adjoin non-District parks and open space areas.

Comments

Comments, corrections, and suggestions are certainly appreciated. Please send them to: Midpeninsula Regional Open Space District, 330 Distel Circle, Los Altos, CA 94022, or info@openspace.org.

REGULATIONS AND TRAIL ETIQUETTE

Please be courteous to other trail users. Always yield to equestrians and allow other trail users to pass. When in a group, avoid blocking the trail. Prevent injury to yourself and avoid damage to natural resources by using only designated trails. Bicyclists, please announce your presence when approaching hikers and equestrians from behind. Control your speed at all times and obey the District speed limits. Visitors with dogs should follow "Dog Access Guidelines," a pamphlet available from the District. Littering is prohibited on District preserves. Visitors should carry out any materials brought in.

Abuses of trail etiquette should be brought to the attention of a District ranger, or reported to the District office: (650) 691-1200.

Regulations

For their own safety and that of others, and for the protection of District preserves, visitors are responsible for knowing and obeying District ordinances. Below is a list of some basic regulations that will help to ensure a safe, enjoyable visit. A complete list of all District ordinances is available at the District office. Information about seasonal and other trail closures is available at the Web site, *www.openspace.org*, or from the District office: (650) 691-1200.

Hours

Preserves are open from dawn until one half-hour after sunset.

Bicycles

Bicycles are allowed on selected District preserves and trails as noted in this book. Helmets are required at all times. Please observe the following speed limits: 15 mph on trails, 5 mph when passing. Ride only on trails designated on the District map for bicycle use. Trails designated for bicycle use may be closed seasonally to prevent trail damage and erosion.

Dogs

Dogs are allowed on selected District preserves and trails as noted in this book. Dogs must be controlled on a maximum six-foot leash (retractable leashes must be locked in a position not to exceed six feet) at all times. The only exception is when the dog and its owner are within the off-leash area at Pulgas Ridge Preserve. In this area, dogs must be under voice control. Call the District office for guidelines on retractable leashes, and please clean up after your dog.

Horses

Horses are allowed on selected District preserves and trails as noted in this book. Trails designated for equestrian use may be closed seasonally to prevent trail damage and erosion.

Fires

Fires are prohibited on District preserves.

Smoking

Smoking is prohibited on District preserves.

Weapons

All weapons are prohibited on District preserves.

Plants and Wildlife

Please leave plants and animals undisturbed. If you are fortunate enough to encounter wildlife during your visit, do not approach, startle, or feed it. Although wild animals are generally fearful of humans and will run away, some wildlife can be dangerous.

Facilities

Improvements on District lands are generally limited to facilities for low-intensity recreational uses. Low-intensity recreation avoids concentration of use, significant alteration of the land, and significant impact on the natural resources, or on the appreciation of nature.

In keeping with a wilderness ethos, District improvements often consist only of gravel or dirt staging areas, trails or patrol roads, occasional vault toilets, and a minimum of signs. Drinking water is not available at the preserves; visitors should be sure to bring an adequate supply of drinking water.

Be aware that cellular telephones may not have reception on the preserves. District rangers and other field staff are equipped with radios, and can assist in case of emergencies. In the event that you experience an emergency on District lands (fire, accident, or other immediate threat to life or property), contact the District's 24-hour emergency dispatch number for District rangers at (650) 968-4411. This phone number is for emergency use only; for any other District business, call (650) 691-1200. This number is answered during regular business hours, and voice mail is available outside of regular hours. E-mail can also be sent to info@openspace.org.

For Your Safety

While visiting the open space preserves, visitors may encounter wildlife and poison oak, or other natural or manmade hazards. Some trails are rugged and steep, and some lead to rugged and remote parts of a preserve. Such risks are a natural part of the preserve and visitors must be aware of and willing to accept these risks, a few of which are listed below.

- *Rattlesnakes* are native to this area, and are especially active in warm weather.
- *Poison oak* grows on most preserves; learn to identify and avoid it in all seasons.
- *Ticks* are active in this area and may carry disease. Stay on designated trails, and check yourself frequently for ticks.
- *Mountain lions* are occasionally sighted in the open space preserves. The Department of Fish and Game has published recommendations for dealing with chance encounters with mountain lions. For more information, visit the District's Web site at *www.openspace.org,* or the Department of Fish and Game's Web site at *www.dfg.ca.gov.*

Be Prepared

The weather in the Santa Cruz Mountains can be unpredictable. No matter what season it is, be prepared for rain, wind, fog, or sun. Dress in layers (T-shirt, long-sleeved shirt, sweater and/or jacket). Wear boots or sturdy walking shoes appropriate for rugged trails. Bring sun protection (hat, sunscreen) and insect repellent. Carry adequate drinking water and a snack.

Trail around seasonal pond at Picchetti Ranch Open Space Preserve

THE PRESERVES
& TRAILS

Barn at Coal Creek Open Space Preserve;
a reminder of the area's ranching and farming past

COAL CREEK
OPEN SPACE PRESERVE

~

Visitors to this preserve may find themselves on Crazy Pete's Road and wonder about the origin of the name. Was there really a Crazy Pete? According to some sources, he was a tall, unkempt Irish hermit who lived alone in the Santa Cruz mountains and hired out as a woodchopper, helping local farmers and ranchers clear their land. In a privately published memoir, Emma Stolte Garrod says that her father, Ferdinand Stolte, employed a man named Peter O'Shaunessey to help clear land and chop cordwood for a farm on upper Black Road. She describes him as having "piercing black eyes, a high-bridged nose and coal-black hair and beard always too long and uncombed." She also says his mind was "not right."

After years of working for the Stolte family, the itinerant Irishman nick-named "Crazy Peter" left the area to take a job some miles away. His new neigh-bors apparently were not as welcoming or as tolerant as the Stoltes, and they had Crazy Peter committed to the Agnews State Hospital in Santa Clara, California, where he died on the morning of the 1906 earthquake. Although Garrod weaves a great story, was the road actually named for her father's woodchopper? The fact is, no one knows for sure.

Here are some other versions of the story. The road may have been built in the 1890s by Pete Martinez or Peter Feliz—these may have been the same person—who got his nickname because the construction was so difficult people thought he was crazy to attempt it. Or perhaps Crazy Peter was an ornery logger who controlled the comings and goings on "his" road, which provided access via Alpine Road to Portola Valley. Finally, "Sunny" Jim Rolph, a governor of California who owned nearby Skyline Ranch in the 1930s, may have made up the story of a mythical, unseen hermit to amuse his children on the journey up Alpine Road. Legend has it that when their coach stopped, Rolph would fire his pistol a few times to frighten away "Crazy Pete."

Although Coal Creek Preserve is only around five hundred acres, there is much here to enjoy. A forest of oak, bay, madrone, and Douglas-fir clings to the steep, northeast-facing slopes above Corte Madera Creek and its tributaries, one of which is Coal Creek. In spring, wildflowers decorate the trailside meadows, and rolling grasslands frame expansive views of San Francisco Bay and nearby urban communities. During the rainy season, you may come upon seasonal waterfalls and water-loving creatures, such as banana slugs and California newts. Other wildlife that call this preserve home include coyotes, rabbits, bobcats, and even mountain lions. Acquisition by the District saved this area from being turned into a residential subdivision.

Coal Creek Trail Use

Bicycles   Allowed on all trails
Dogs   Leashed dogs allowed on all trails
Horses   Allowed on all trails

COAL CREEK OPEN SPACE PRESERVE

Trip 1. Hidden Meadow

Length: 4.8 miles
Time: 2 to 3 hours
Rating: Moderate

Highlights: This athletic, semi-loop trip uses Crazy Pete's and Alpine Roads, and the Valley View and Meadow Trails to explore one of the District's smaller but surprisingly varied preserves. Along the way, visitors will wander through a forest lush with oak, Douglas-fir, and bigleaf maple, cross a ravine that holds a seasonal waterfall, and then climb through a secluded meadow decorated with spring wildflowers.

Directions: From the junction of Skyline Boulevard and Page Mill/ Alpine Road, take Skyline Boulevard northwest 1.7 miles to a roadside parking area on the right, just before Crazy Pete's Road.

Native Americans gathered and ground acorns and other seeds here, according to Janet Schwind, a longtime resident of the South Skyline area who serves as its historian. "People in these days are pretty quiet about Native American sites, but there are a lot of mortars in this area," she says. "I found one myself one day. It was really a thrill. I was walking along a trail in Coal Creek, I won't be any more specific, and I looked down and there was just this circle of leaves. And I thought, that's very round. So I just dug up a little bit of the weeds and there was a deep mortar. I told Patrick Congdon [former District ranger] where it was, and he went down and said he thought it was part of a very large bedrock mortar. And if you find some oak trees with a rock on a nice viewpoint you're apt to find some grinding holes."

This preserve is a close neighbor of Russian Ridge, Skyline Ridge, and Monte Bello Open Space Preserves, and you can devise longer routes than the two

Facilities: None

Trailhead: At the junction of Skyline Boulevard and Crazy Pete's Road

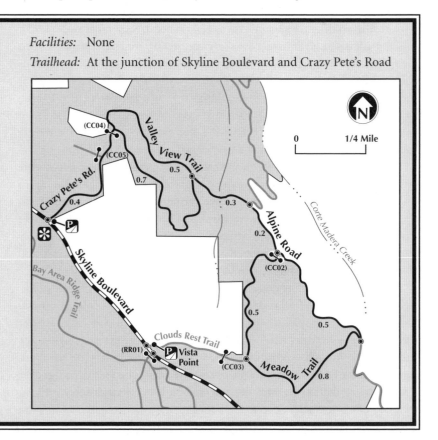

described below by using these adjoining preserves. The section of Alpine Road that runs along the preserve's east side is closed to vehicles, but open to bicyclists, equestrians, and hikers. The approximately five miles of multiuse trails at Coal Creek Preserve provide important trail connections between Alpine Road and Skyline Boulevard.

The map for Coal Creek Preserve is part of the District's South Skyline Region map.

Trip 1. Hidden Meadow

From the trailhead, just north of the roadside parking area, follow Crazy Pete's Road, a paved route closed to all vehicles except those of residents and District staff. A moderate descent winds through a forest of canyon oak, California bay, buckeye, and Monterey pine. Shrubs beside the road include hazelnut, blue elderberry, thimbleberry, and poison oak. Although the ridge top is frequently windy and fogbound, the tall and stately trees soon provide shelter.

The grade eases and the road passes several driveways leading to private homes. After about 0.25 mile, the pavement changes to dirt and gravel. The road bends right and descends to a junction. Here a driveway heads left, but you turn right and follow Crazy Pete's Road a short distance to a fence and a metal gate. Passing through a gap in the fence, you'll see two District information boards and a map holder on the left. Just beyond the information boards is a junction. Here the Valley View Trail goes straight, and a road signed CRAZY PETE'S ROAD turns right.

You go straight, now on a rough and rocky track that soon curves left. Coyote brush, yerba santa, and berry vines form a screen that blocks the view, but in places it gives way to reveal a splendid scene, including Palo Alto, Mountain View, and the southern reaches of San Francisco Bay. Large, beautiful madrone trees frame this vista with their orange trunks and bright green leaves. You wander through a dense forest that includes Douglas-fir, tanbark oak, coast live oak, and black oak, with an understory of toyon, oceanspray, snowberry, and ferns.

After a rolling, winding descent, you arrive at a fork near the 1-mile point. Here, the Valley View Trail ends and connects with Crazy Pete's Road via two short trail segments, one veering left, the other right. You bear left and after about 100 feet join Crazy Pete's Road. Now the route narrows to a single-track and wanders through a possibly wet area lush with thimbleberry, hazelnut, and giant chain fern. Descending on a moderate grade, you reach a bridge over a rocky ravine that, in wet weather, may hold a lovely waterfall formed by a tributary of Corte Madera Creek. Look for the thorny stems and delicate pink flowers of wood rose beside the trail.

Curving right and climbing on a moderate grade, the trail soon reaches a fence marking the preserve boundary. You pass through a gap in the fence and reach Alpine Road, managed by San Mateo County and here closed to vehicles. Turning right, enjoy a gentle climb on a well-graded dirt road that is heavily used by bicycles. At a junction ahead, a trail you will use later departs to the right. But for now, continue straight, accompanied by power lines overhead. Gaining elevation via S-bends, Alpine Road passes beautiful stands of bigleaf maple, madrone, and valley oak. Corte Madera Creek is hidden in a deep ravine to the left.

Just shy of the 2-mile point is a junction with the Meadow Trail, right. A District information board, also right, marks the boundary of the preserve. Turning right, you climb on a gentle grade to a switchback angling left. A grassy meadow, right, is bisected by an unofficial trail leading to the top of a low hill. Look beside the trail for spring wildflowers, including California buttercup, hound's tongue, lupine, purple owl's-clover, milkmaids, and woodland star. A much larger meadow lies straight ahead, and the trail passes through a corridor of coyote brush. A moderate climb over rocky ground puts you back in the trees. The trail widens at a possibly wet area and soon increases in slope to steep.

A magnificent view awaits when you finally reach level ground. On a clear day, the scene extends from the San Mateo Bridge to Mt. Diablo, and also takes in much of the peninsula, including Palo Alto and the Stanford campus. A vast,

View of grasslands at Coal Creek Open Space Preserve

Coal Creek Trail Use

Bicycles   Allowed on all trails

Dogs   Leashed dogs allowed on all trails

Horses   Allowed on all trails

COAL CREEK OPEN SPACE PRESERVE

Trip 2. Valley View

Length: 2 miles

Time: 1 to 2 hours

Rating: Easy

Highlights: This semi-loop, using Crazy Pete's Road and the Valley View Trail, is perfect for a 1- to 2-hour easy stroll through a beautiful forest. Along the way, you pass a few coast redwoods near a tributary of Corte Madera Creek. This preserve is a great place to practice "birding by ear," the art of identifying birds by their songs, notes, and calls.

Directions: Same as for "Hidden Meadow" on pages 52–53

Facilities: None

Trailhead: Same as for "Hidden Meadow" on pages 52–53

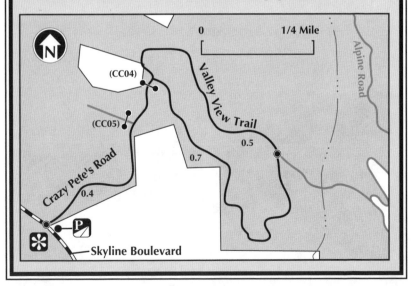

open meadow dotted with coyote brush is right, and just ahead is a junction. Here, the Clouds Rest Trail (not listed on the trail sign) climbs left to Skyline Boulevard, but instead veer right and descend steeply through the meadow. With power lines overhead, the road continues to lose elevation, now on a moderate grade. Entering a forest, you soon reach a gate marking the preserve boundary. About 100 feet ahead is Alpine Road, where you turn left.

Now retrace your route along Alpine Road to the junction with Crazy Pete's Road, where you turn left. Listen as you walk through the forest for the sharp cry of a northern flicker, a member of the woodpecker family. These large, boldly patterned birds are found throughout the United States. This species of flicker was formerly considered two species, red-shafted and yellow-shafted. (The "lumping" together of species—and also the "splitting" that sometimes occurs when a single species is divided in two—illustrates the fluid nature of biological classification.) Returning to the junction with the Valley View Trail, you bear left at the first fork and left again after about 100 feet. From here, follow the route description in "Valley View" on page 56 back to the parking area.

Trip 2. Valley View

Follow the route description for "Hidden Meadow" on pages 52–53 to the fork near the 1-mile point. Here, you bear right and after about 100 feet reach Crazy Pete's Road. Climbing on a gentle grade, the dirt road makes several swerves and then begins to climb, passing a few coast redwoods, reminders of the ancient giants that once dominated our coastal mountains. Emerging into a brushy area, you pass under a set of power lines and then ascend on a moderate grade.

A shady forest with dense underbrush is the favored habitat of many songbirds, including California towhees and dark-eyed juncos, both of which may be found here. Like other members of the Emberizid family, including sparrows, these two species feed on insects during summer and seeds in winter. California towhees are drab, gray-brown birds, slightly smaller than a robin. Juncos are sparrow-size with a black cap and a pink bill. Towhees are usually seen singly or in pairs, whereas juncos travel in noisy flocks.

Several property fences on the left adjoin private homes. To the right, the oak-framed view stretches all the way to Mt. Diablo on a clear day. Not done yet with its ups and downs, the road descends and then rises on a moderate grade, passing a grove of poison oak, colorful in fall, on its way to the junction with the Valley View Trail. Once there, turn left and retrace your route uphill to the parking area.

Dark-eyed junco; photo taken at Rancho San Antonio Open Space Preserve

PRICELESS OPEN SPACE

What is the value of open space? Can we calculate its scenic and recreational value, or its importance to the protection of rare, threatened, or endangered species? Can we quantify the benefits of preserving forests, grasslands, salt marshes, and watersheds? Like beauty, the value of open space is often in the eye, heart, or mind of the beholder. Here are some thoughts from people who use, manage, and enjoy District lands.

Nonette Hanko is a District founder and board member: "When I first moved to Palo Alto, I was looking for places to just get away and recharge my internal batteries. So I'd get in my car and I'd drive up Page Mill Road. . . . I'd start up Page Mill Road, and everywhere I'd go there would be NO TRESPASSING signs. Every place that was open space was NO TRESPASSING. So I finally got up to what is now Los Trancos Open Space Preserve, and there was a place where the road comes around, and there was an old walnut orchard. And it wasn't fenced, not very well anyway. So I would go down there and sit in that walnut orchard. I never knew, you know, as time went along that that would be one of the first acquisitions that we would make."

Steve Salveter is a District volunteer docent: "It sure has been a godsend for our general well-being and our health. I think if it weren't for the District there would be development and pollution and all kinds of problems. This is one of the most populated areas in the world. Los Altos didn't have any vacant lots, even in the '70s. We would have had rows of houses up there, and crowded highways and polluted streams and smog like Los Angeles. But now we can look up there and see wilderness. It's pretty nice to be able to walk from your front door to Black Mountain, and come back in the same day."

Jane Huber is a District volunteer crew leader: "Having grown up on the East Coast, with the whole megalopolis between Boston and D.C., there's very little open space. And there hasn't been open space for such a long time that you just take it for granted. Out here there is significantly more open space, and people don't always see it, until it's gone. It's reassuring to know that you're not going to go up there one day and see giant palatial estates where there was just beautiful land. It's going to be there, and the next generations will still be able to enjoy it. I think the District and their supporters were lucky that they started preserving open space when they did. Other counties haven't been so lucky, and now they're seeing their mistake."

Marc Auerbach is a former volunteer with the District's Preserve Partners program who also helped with modifications to the design of the District

Web site: "I think there are just the aesthetic reasons—it's just nice to look up and see a green hillside. As a backdrop for the city, it's much prettier than a hillside full of homes, which it easily could be. It's nice to have these kinds of places where you can go back and reconnect to nature and see what the world around us really looks like. I also think of it in a philosophical way—when is enough, enough? I mean how much raw land, open land, do we have to consume? It's unfortunate that we always seem to be in a position where we have to put its economic value against its aesthetic value. We should just be able to say as a species that we really value nature and we really like this big, green space, and we just want it and we don't have to justify how much it costs."

Herb Grench is the District's former general manager: "I take different kinds of hikes. Sometimes I'll want to be in the out-of-doors for the out-of-doors experience, and yet I want to do something that's aerobic. And so I'll work at my hiking. Other times I just want to be out there, seeing every little thing along the trail. But mainly for me, hiking is getting in touch with nature, and unplugging from the hustle and bustle of urban life. I think the connectedness is particularly important to me."

Craig Britton is the District's general manager: "I live in Los Altos, and I can walk out my front door and look up and see the foothills. I consider that enjoying open space, you don't have to touch it. And so I always appreciated the fact that open space was also rest to the eyes. I appreciate the visual aspect of what the District's trying to preserve, which is lost on some people. It wasn't lost on Wallace Stegner though."

Wallace Stegner was a writer, teacher, and conservationist who founded the creative writing program at Stanford and served on the faculty from 1946 until 1971. A memorial bench in Long Ridge Preserve dedicated to Stegner carries his words on the value of open space: "To try to save for everyone, for the hostile and indifferent as well as the committed, some of the health that flows down across the green ridges from the skyline, and some of the beauty and refreshment of spirit that are still available to any resident of the valley who has a moment, and the wit, to lift up his eyes unto the hills."

Panorama of El Corte de Madera Creek Open Space Preserve

EL CORTE DE MADERA CREEK OPEN SPACE PRESERVE

~

Encompassing over 2,800 acres and boasting approximately thirty-six miles of multiuse trails, this preserve has become a mecca for mountain bicyclists, but hikers and equestrians also will enjoy the steep, forested canyons that once echoed to the sound of the logger's ax and saw but are now preserved for public recreation. Listen for the flutelike note of a varied thrush or the scolding cry of a Steller's jay as you wander beneath towering coast redwoods and Douglas-firs, whose outstretched limbs form a protective canopy through which rays of sunlight play on the fern-filled forest floor below.

The stumps of giant old-growth redwoods mark this as one of the places in the Santa Cruz Mountains where sawmills feverishly tried to keep pace with the growing demand for lumber in San Francisco following the Gold Rush. The timber-rich headwaters of El Corte de Madera and nearby Harrington creeks had the most mills in San Mateo County, according to Ken Fisher, longtime area resident. At least eight and perhaps as many as fifteen different mills operated here during the late 1800s, and with a sharp eye you may be able to pick out former mill or cabin sites, or even rusty artifacts from that bygone era. The last serious logging ended around 1900, but selective logging by private landowners continued until 1988, shortly after the preserve was created.

The Santa Cruz Mountains are known for their changeable weather, and especially for the fog that blows in from the Pacific Ocean and curls over the ridgecrest. At an elevation of around 2,000 feet, the highlands along Skyline Boulevard also get snow from time to time, as one outdoor enthusiast discovered to her delight. Jane Huber, a District volunteer crew leader, said, "When it snowed a few years ago, I was able to go up there that day, only for a short time, and it was amazing to see this landscape completely transformed. Near El Corte de Madera Creek

Tafoni Sandstone Formations

One of the highlights of this preserve is a visit to the sandstone formations located just off the Tafoni Trail. Geologists use the term *tafoni* to describe the cavelike indentations and delicate honeycomb structures formed on the surface of sandstone by just the right combination of weather and atmospheric conditions. The sandstone boulders here came from undersea sediments originally located off the Southern California coast. Movement northwest along the San Andreas fault over millions of years, combined with mountain-building action that formed the Santa Cruz Mountains, placed the boulders where they are today. Acidic rain during the winter and evaporation during the summer has eroded the sandstone and broken through its hard outer layer. It takes hundreds of years for *tafoni* to form. Please admire these fascinating features from the nearby observation deck, and do not climb on the boulders.

Preserve, the Douglas-firs were heavy with snow, and [I was] driving along and having the snow go 'boom' on the hood of the car as it would fall. And I went for a little walk at El Corte de Madera, and there were little raccoon footprints in the snow. And I wondered what they thought about all that. It's something that hardly ever happens in their lifetime. Or ours even, here. And that was totally beautiful. . . . That was really an unforgettable experience. I'm lucky I got to see that. . . . I grew up on the East Coast, and I really miss the snow."

The preserve takes its name from the creek that flows through its midst on the way south to a rendezvous with San Gregorio Creek, a major drainage on the San Mateo coast. *Corte de Madera,* and the abbreviated form *Corte Madera,* are Spanish for "a place where wood is cut." In addition to its fame as a wood-producing area, Kings Mountain has a tragic side as well. San Mateo County's worst aviation disaster took place here on October 29, 1953, when a fogbound DC-6, "The Resolution," on approach to San Francisco Airport slammed into a ridge west of Sierra Morena, killing eight crew members and eleven passengers, among them world-renowned American pianist William Kapell. But the tragedy might have been much worse. The plane was headed toward the newly opened Kings Mountain Elementary School on Swett Road, which is about one mile north of the crash site. The time was 8:43 A.M., and school was in session.

The land suffered years of misuse, which the District is working hard to overcome. The former landowner allowed a motorcycle club to use the property as an off-road riding area, and the motorcyclists created an extensive network of trails.

Erosion and creek sedimentation, which jeopardize already-threatened fish habitat, as well as frequent illegal trail use have resulted in a regulation that you must stay on the official trails in this preserve or face a stiff fine. This is the first time the District has ever instituted such a regulation, which some feel goes against the concept of open space. The issue is not merely cosmetic or aesthetic. The San Francisco Bay Regional Water Quality Control Board, the California Department of Fish and Game, and the National Marine Fisheries Service are concerned about degradation

Tafoni sandstone caves at El Corte de Madera Creek Open Space Preserve

Henry Pastorelli is a former president of Responsible Organized Mountain Pedalers (ROMP): "Like many kids growing up in the Bay Area, I experienced my first real sense of freedom when I learned how to ride a bike. As an adult, I often rediscover my childhood joy, freedom, and exhilaration through mountain biking. In simple terms, riding a bike on a trail in a natural environment is just plain fun. The unencumbered feeling of flowing movement through redwood forests, oak forests, and grasslands, while experiencing the smells, temperature changes, and challenges of the terrain is wonderful. It puts a smile on my face. It makes me feel like a kid again. When we, the local residents, voted to create the Open Space District in 1972, we sent a message to the community that we value open space. We value it not only for its intrinsic value, but for the enhanced quality of life it provides."

El Corte de Madera Creek Trail Use

Bicycles: Allowed on all trails except the short trail from the Tafoni Trail to the sandstone formations

Dogs: Not allowed

Horses: Allowed on all trails except the short trail from the Tafoni Trail to the sandstone formations

EL CORTE DE MADERA CREEK OPEN SPACE PRESERVE

Trip 3. Redwood Loop

Length: 8.4 miles

Time: 3 to 5 hours

Rating: Difficult

Highlights: This strenuous loop uses the Sierra Morena, Methuselah, Giant Salamander, Timberview, and Gordon Mill Trails to explore a hidden realm of towering redwoods and massive Douglas-firs. Dropping almost all the way to the preserve's namesake creek, the route then rises to visit one of the few remaining old-growth redwoods on District lands. Not yet complete with this pilgrimage, you drop once more to a lush, creekside canyon before steadily climbing back to Skyline Boulevard.

Directions: From the junction of Skyline Boulevard and Highway 84 in Sky Londa, take Skyline Boulevard northwest 3.5 miles to roadside parking areas on both sides of the road.

to the property. The area is a headwater for one of the best Coho salmon and steelhead spawning creeks on the coast. Any silt that comes down has an effect on their breeding, and they're both federally threatened species on California's Central Coast." The District is currently implementing a comprehensive plan to reduce erosion in the preserve by upgrading the roads and trails to an engineered standard. In addition, District staff, board members, and representatives from the mountain bicycling community are working together to educate visitors about the preserve's ecological sensitivity. Among the groups that the District has enlisted to fight illegal trail-building and off-trail riding are the International Mountain Biking Association (IMBA), Responsible Organized Mountain Pedalers (ROMP), and Team Wrong Way.

Facilities: None

Trailhead: Gate CM02, on the southwest side of Skyline Boulevard.

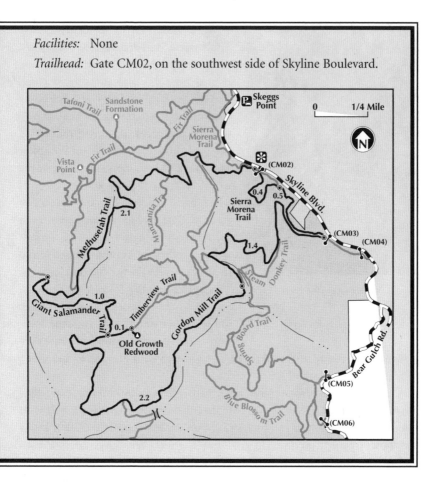

Trip 3. Redwood Loop

The Sierra Morena Trail, going left and right, and two District information boards with a map holder are just beyond the trailhead. Turn right and walk about 100 feet to a junction with the Methuselah Trail, a dirt road that descends through a dense forest of coast live oak, tanbark oak, Douglas-fir, madrone, and California bay. This is a lush area full of ferns, berry vines, and nonnative French broom. A few second-growth coast redwoods grow tall beside the road, giving you the opportunity to crane your neck upwards. Most of their ancestors were reduced to stumps during the redwood logging boom of the nineteenth and twentieth centuries, which began in the Santa Cruz Mountains and then spread throughout California's central and northern coastal mountains.

Methuselah tree near
El Corte de Madera Creek
Open Space Preserve

At a junction in a clearing, the Timberview Trail departs left, but instead continue straight on the Methuselah Trail, named for a Biblical ancestor of Noah said to have lived for 969 years. The name Methuselah is often used in conjunction with ancient trees, including one about 100 yards from the trailhead on the opposite side of Skyline Boulevard. But in the world of coast redwoods, the oldest of which had a life span of more than 2,200 years, Methuselah himself would have been considered a youngster. Besides coast redwood, another interesting conifer found in this preserve is the Sargent cypress. This species ranges from Mendocino to Santa Barbara counties and is most often found on serpentine soil. In some locations, Sargent cypress grows no larger than a shrub, but here it thrives as a tall, straight tree with gray bark, dull green foliage, and small, round cones.

Climbing on a moderate grade and perhaps serenaded by birdsong, you follow the road as it makes a sweeping curve to the left, then a sharp bend to the right. At a four-way junction, you continue straight on the Methuselah Trail, now losing elevation over rough ground. The grade here alternates between gentle, moderate, and steep, as you follow a tributary of El Corte Madera Creek downhill. Evergreen huckleberry, gooseberry, and blue blossom are some of the shrubs growing beside the road. When you reach a clearing, note the towering Douglas-fir nearby, and examine it more closely, especially if you have binoculars. This is a "granary tree," so called because acorn woodpeckers stash their namesake food supply in holes bored in its trunk. A communal effort, this process involves many birds and hundreds, perhaps thousands, of acorns.

A mature forest is the perfect habitat for band-tailed pigeons, another bird often found in flocks. This species is a larger, more attractively decorated relative of our urban pigeon, or rock dove. When startled, a flock of band-tailed pigeons will often take wing noisily in groups of three or four birds.

Still descending, but now on a gentle grade, you pass the Fir Trail, right, at about the two-mile point. The next junction is with the Giant Salamander

Trail, and here you leave the Methuselah Trail by turning left. Now on a rough, eroded single track, you descend through a junglelike area of red-woods, huckleberry, ferns, and berry vines. El Corte de Madera Creek is to your right, but hidden from view. This stretch of trail (for which the District is planning a major repair project) may be very muddy during wet weather. During wet conditions or predicted wet weather, this trail may be closed to bicyclists and equestrians.

Curving left and then beginning to climb, you turn away from the creek and follow a tributary upstream on a rolling course. Soon you cross a culvert hold-ing the tributary. Now you begin a snaking climb on a grade that alternates between moderate and steep. A splendid assortment of ferns, including giant chain fern, adds to the magical quality of the forest here. A plank bridge takes you across a seasonal stream, and climbing beyond it, you enter an area of Douglas-fir and tanbark oak. The trail curves sharply left and reaches a junc-tion with the Timberview Trail, a dirt road.

To visit one of the preserve's remaining old growth redwoods, turn left here and go about 0.1 mile to a clearing, right, marked by a sign that reads: TO OLD GROWTH REDWOOD, NOT A THROUGH TRAIL. Turn right into the clearing, and then find a trail on its left-hand edge that leads about 100 feet to a massive coast redwood, approximately fifty feet in circum-ference at its base. The tree is so tall that you barely have enough room in the overgrown area to step back and appreciate its height. When you have finished paying your respects to this monarch of the forest, return to the junction with the Giant Salamander Trail.

*Acorn woodpecker;
photo taken at Rancho San
Antonio Open Space Preserve*

Here you continue straight on the Timberview Trail, descending moderately along a ridge top. The road leaves the ridge with a sharp left-hand bend, and now you give up all the hard-won elevation gained on the previous trail, plunging on a grade that alternates between gentle, moderate, and steep. The Timberview Trail ends at a junction near another tributary of El Corte de Madera Creek. Here, at about the 5-mile point, the Lawrence Creek Trail heads right, but you go straight on the Gordon Mill Trail, a dirt road, and begin to climb. This road was the primary haul road when logging was active here. Red alder and hazelnut thrive in this moist environment, adding color to the scene in autumn. Several fractured rock faces left of the road hold beautiful hanging gardens of ferns and mosses. In the rainy season, the sound of rushing water rises delightfully from the deep canyon to your right.

At a junction with the Spring Board Trail, right, you continue straight. A short distance ahead, your route passes a steep and eroded connector to the Timberview Trail, left, and then curves right. Now following the shape of the landscape, the road continues gently to gain elevation, passing stands of manzanita and bigleaf maple, two species that usually do not share the same habitat. If you see a bird that looks like a robin, look again. It may be a varied thrush, in the same family as our American robin, but sporting a patterned head and wings. The call of the varied thrush—a single, flutelike note—echoes eerily through the forest.

Passing a short connector to the Steam Donkey Trail, right, you may begin to hear traffic noise from Skyline Boulevard, perhaps the first unnatural sound

El Corte de Madera Creek Trail Use

Bicycles: Allowed on all trails except the short trail from the Tafoni Trail to the sandstone formations

Dogs: Not allowed

Horses: Allowed on all trails except the short trail from the Tafoni Trail to the sandstone formations

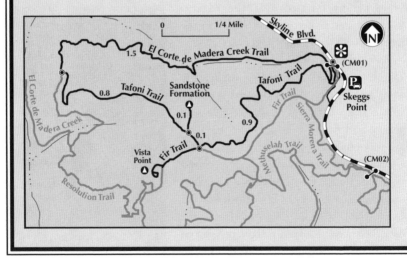

in hours. Now the road curves sharply right and climbs to a four-way junction. Ahead, the Gordon Mill Trail ends at gate CM03 and Skyline Boulevard. The Sierra Morena Trail, a dirt road, angles right, passing a District information board on its way to gate CM04. Your route is the single-track branch of the Sierra Morena Trail, which heads left. You cross a grassy area dotted with coyote brush and then return to forest, traveling on a magic carpet of redwood duff that covers the trail and cushions your steps.

On a rolling course, you reach a junction with a trail veering right and climbing steeply. Ignoring this shortcut back to the trailhead (unless you feel in need of further exertion), you stay on a narrow ledge notched from a hillside that drops to the left. The trail curves around a promontory jutting out from the end of a ridge, and here you have another opportunity to admire the preserve's fine trees, in this case massive Douglas-firs. After the shortcut merges sharply from the right, you go another 100 feet or so to return to the trailhead.

EL CORTE DE MADERA CREEK OPEN SPACE PRESERVE

Trip 4. Tafoni Loop

Length: 4.7 miles

Time: 2 to 3 hours

Rating: Moderate

Highlights: An unusual sandstone formation called *tafoni* is the main attraction of this invigorating loop, which uses the Tafoni, Fir, and El Corte de Madera Creek Trails at the north end of the preserve. Along the way, you visit Vista Point, a scenic overlook with terrific views of the Pacific Ocean and the coastal hills. Towering Douglas-firs and coast redwoods, a sea of chaparral, and a lush riparian corridor near the headwaters of El Corte de Madera Creek are some of the other attractions visitors will enjoy here.

Directions: From the junction of Skyline Boulevard and Highway 84 in Sky Londa, take Skyline Boulevard north 3.9 miles to the Caltrans parking area at Skeggs Point.

Facilities: Picnic tables, vault toilets

Trailhead: Gate CM01, on the west side of Skyline Boulevard, about 100 yards northwest of the parking area.

Trip 4. Tafoni Loop

A metal gate and a wood fence mark the trailhead. A narrow gap in the fence allows hikers to pass through, and a wider one with a low barricade of logs accommodates bicyclists and equestrians but is designed to keep motorcycles out. Two District information boards with a map holder, an open space preserve sign, and a trail sign are just past the gate.

From here, you follow the Tafoni Trail, a dirt road that soon begins to climb on a moderate grade past towering Douglas-firs. These magnificent trees dwarf their companions such as coast live oak, tanbark oak, and blue blossom. The road then levels and curves right, bringing you to a junction. The return part of this loop, the El Corte de Madera Creek Trail, joins from the right, but for now you continue straight. California bay, madrone, and a few coast redwoods add to the dense forest. The hillside on your right falls steeply right into the canyon holding the headwaters of El Corte de Madera Creek. Ferns, berry vines, and mosses accentuate the rainforest feeling.

Hummingbirds

Hummingbirds are among the wonders of the avian world. Their small size, delicate construction, fearless demeanor, and nearly constant movement are a source of amazement and delight. Hummingbirds are attracted to the flowers of many different plants, most notably flowers that are red or orange. However, these tiny aviators also visit plants not known for producing colorful flowers, including various species of manzanitas. On wings beating so fast as to be invisible, hummingbirds will negotiate through dense thickets of manzanita, probing each pea-sized, urn-shaped flower in search of nectar. The species found most often on District lands, Anna's hummingbird, is about 4 inches long, has a wingspan of a little more than 5 inches, and weighs about 0.15 ounce. This tiny bird was named by French naturalist Rene P. Lesson for Anna de Belle Massena, the wife of Prince Francois Victor Massena. The prince, like many other well-to-do Europeans, was a natural-history enthusiast and a collector of specimens. His collection contained the specimen on which the first description of *Calypte anna* was based. Anna's hummingbirds live mainly in low-elevation areas along the West Coast, and may breed as early as mid-December.

As you descend on a moderate grade, listen for some of the birds that live in this forest, including Steller's jays, ravens, and hawks. Their vocalizations run the gamut from plaintive to quarrelsome, adding to the rustling of leaves and the eerie groaning of trees rubbing against each other on a breezy day. The forest is dark and cool, with only occasional patches of sunlight hitting the road or lighting up tree trunks and foliage. The rocky track snakes along on a rolling course, bordered by evergreen huckleberry and early blooming wildflowers such as hound's tongue and Douglas iris. The road swings sharpy left to a T-junction. The left branch is a closed trail, so here you turn right.

Climbing on a gentle grade, you travel parallel to a ridge top that is uphill and left. At about the 1-mile point, you come to a saddle and a four-way junction in a small clearing. Here, the Fir Trail is left and straight, and the Tafoni Trail is to the right. Before continuing on the Tafoni Trail, you can make an easy excursion to Vista Point, where views of the San Mateo coast and the Pacific Ocean await.

To do so, go straight on the Fir Trail, a rocky and eroded dirt road that descends to a fork marked by a sign reading VISTA POINT. Now bear right and make a short, steep climb on a dirt road that bends left and forks again. Staying right, you come into the open and are suddenly surrounded by a sea of chaparral, including chamise, manzanita, yerba santa, and coffeeberry. From here, the road bends left and loops back on itself across the top of a rise. This rise, called Vista Point on the District map, makes a great picnic spot.

When you have finished relaxing at this enjoyable spot, retrace your route to the junction of the Fir and Tafoni Trails. Here, turn left on the Tafoni Trail, a dirt road, and

Bridge crossing at El Corte de Madera Creek Open Space Preserve

descend on a gentle grade. At a junction signed SANDSTONE FORMATION, turn right on a single-track trail that is closed to bikes and horses. Passing through a fenced entrance, wind your way downhill through stands of coast redwood, Douglas-fir, madrone, and tanbark oak. Soon you come to an observation deck and a sign explaining the process that creates *tafoni,* the eroded sandstone formations you can see from the deck. The large sandstone boulders just ahead were formed from undersea sand deposits originally located off the coast of what is now southern California. These marine sediments moved northwest along the San Andreas fault and were thrust upwards millions of years ago during the formation of the Coast Ranges.

Weathering by slightly acidic rain has eaten away the sandstone and created a fascinating array of caves, depressions, pockmarks, and honeycomb patterns in the rock. Because it takes a combination of factors—massive, unbroken sandstone boulders, and alternating wet and dry seasons—for the structures to form, *tafoni* is not common. These formations are fragile and need to be protected so they can be enjoyed by future generations. Please do not climb or carve into the rock. The terrain around the formations is very steep: please stay on the trail or the observation deck at all times. When you have finished enjoying this unusual area, return to the Tafoni Trail and turn right.

The following is an excerpt about *tafoni* from Moore & De Pue's *Illustrated History of San Mateo County, California. 1878:*

> *Aside from the many beautiful and varied scenes of mountain, hill, plain, ocean and bay that abound in this county, there is one almost unknown secluded gem, of rare beauty and picturesque form, and also a geological curiosity. Situated three miles south and west of the Summit Springs House, on the side of a cañon known as the head of Deer Gulch, nearly 2,300 feet above sea level, there stand two enormous sand rocks, like lone sentinels of the forest. They are covered with nature's hieroglyphics, consisting of several large alcoves and arches winding through and down among boulder-like formations, studded with columns of curious designs. Along the sides of the rocks is a perforated mass of different sizes and depths, from one inch to over a foot, no two alike, all varying in form; some resembling the shape of a diamond, the square, the ellipse, the egg, and numerous other irregular shapes. Among these perforations may be seen several column-shaped formations, free from perforations and resembling somewhat the masonry of man. The oak, the pine, the redwood and madrona cling to the sides and top of these rocks.*

We have gazed in wonder upon the granite walls of the Yosemite Valley, but with all of its varied scenery and massive combination of rock, tree and waterfall, none will surpass this little gem in beauty at our own doors.

The road curves and descends on a moderate, then gentle, grade. The madrones here are competing with redwoods and Douglas-firs for light, so instead of trying to outgrow them, which would be futile, they bend toward openings in the forest canopy. Some madrones exceed the limits of their stability and topple over, perhaps aided by the wind. Now on a ridge top, you follow a rolling course, which soon leads to a long, moderate descent. While passing through a rocky road-cut, look to your right to see a huge Douglas-fir that has wrapped its roots into the rock cliff for stability. The road bends, climbs for a while, and then descends along a ridge. A fenced restoration area will force you to turn right, as the Tafoni Trail becomes a single track carpeted with tanbark oak leaves and redwood duff.

Beside the trail are huge redwood stumps surrounded by family circles of second-growth trees, remnants of the area's logging past. At about the three-mile point, you merge with the El Corte de Madera Creek Trail, which joins sharply from the left. Continuing almost straight, you follow the single-track trail gently uphill through one of the District's densest forests. Soon the trail curves right. El Corte de Madera Creek lies at the bottom of the steep drop to your left. Serenaded by the sound of rushing water, you descend and follow the trail as it bends sharply left. Passing through a stand of young redwoods, you come to a bridge across El Corte de Madera Creek. This refreshing stream contributes its water to San Gregorio Creek, which joins the Pacific at San Gregorio State Beach.

Once across the bridge, you reach a T-junction with the El Corte de Madera Creek Trail, a dirt road. The road is closed a couple of hundred feet to the left, so you turn right and walk upstream beside the creek, which is to your right in a narrow gully. Ferns and redwood sorrel grow beside the road. As you climb steadily in a shady, steep-walled canyon, the creek wanders back and forth under the road through culverts. This is an enchanting place! All too soon, however, the sound of cars on Skyline Boulevard reminds you of your proximity to civilization. The road now bends right and brings you to the junction with the Tafoni Trail, where you began this loop. From here, turn left and retrace your route to the parking area. When walking back to the parking area, carefully cross Skyline Boulevard and use the wide dirt shoulder on the east side of the road.

KINGS MOUNTAIN

The view from Ken Fisher's office off Skyline Boulevard looks southwest over the forested ridges and canyons of Purisima Creek Redwoods Preserve. Fisher is a longtime area resident. "If you looked at this view as we sit right here 5,000 years ago you wouldn't have seen a tree there," says Fisher, gazing out of his window. "Not one. If you went off a little to the south of here where we have redwoods, it would have been redwood trees, full grown. But where you have the firs on the north end like this, that would have all been burned off." Fisher says a combination of fire (some of which was intentionally set by Native Americans) and cattle grazing during the Spanish and Mexican eras helped maintain wide-open grasslands. "The early Americans started changing the landscape," he says. In fact, according to Fisher, the surrounding terrain looks today more like it did before the arrival of Native Americans. It was the concentrations of coast redwoods, of course, that brought the early Americans (the first European settlers) to Kings Mountain, as the 2,000-foot-high ridge extending southeast from Highway 92 to Bear Gulch Road is called. Logging was the main activity on Kings Mountain for

King family photo (Frank King back row and center;
Honora King front row and fourth from the left)

Grabtown Gulch (a long-term logging camp), looking southeast

many years. Fisher says Kings Mountain was named for Frank and Honora King, who ran the Kings Mountain Brow House, a boarding house and hotel located on the ridge where the current Kings Mountain Road and Skyline Boulevard meet.

In an article written for the November, 1990 issue of *La Peninsula*, the journal of the San Mateo County Historical Association, Fisher recounts "Kings Mountain's Colorful History." Two settlements, long since vanished, were established on the mountain: Grabtown and Summit Springs. Grabtown, a long-term logging camp, was the first stop for wagon teams en route from the mountain's sawmills to the port at Redwood City. The origin of the name Grabtown is uncertain, but perhaps was based on the rapacious nature of its inhabitants, or maybe on the fact that the wagon drivers "grabbed" new teams of horses there. Summit Springs was "the cultural center of 19th-century life on Kings Mountain," with a hotel, a school, a livery, a store, a saloon, and the Kings Mountain Brow House. The wagon route linking San Gregorio with Redwood City ran through Summit Springs, allowing it to prosper while Grabtown faded. In 1866, the wagon road became the Redwood City and San Gregorio Turnpike, a toll road. It followed the alignment of the modern Kings Mountain, Tunitas Creek, and Star Hill roads.

Fisher's article is full of rough-and-tumble characters and incidents straight out of the Wild West. One of the best stories concerns Nathan Comstock, a pioneer who arrived on the mountain in 1850, perhaps its first permanent resident. A hermit, Comstock worked in several lumber mills but somehow managed to save enough money to buy 140 acres of prime land. In 1892, a woodchopper named Steve Perkins found Comstock trapped under a fallen tree. Perkins came to his aid and freed him, receiving Comstock's gratitude and a promise to be remembered in Comstock's will. Twenty years later, on Christmas Eve, Perkins received what Fisher describes as "a yellow, age-worn letter bearing a new stamp and a San Francisco postmark." Perkins read the following words: "Dear Friend: From the westerly end of Frank King spring on the Grabtown road you will measure 25 feet toward the sun when it sets over bald Mount. There dig into the ground and three feet from the surface you will find reward for your kind service to me. Let it help you in your old age as you helped me. Nathan Comstock." The letter was dated Christmas Day, 1892. Comstock had been dead for sixteen years. Following the instructions in the letter, Perkins dug up a rusty tin can containing $500 in gold coins. Who mailed the letter? Fisher says no one knows for sure, but some attribute the good deed to "Uncle Nathan's ghost."

In the course of roughly sixty years, logging so decimated the coastal canyons on the western side of Kings Mountain that the only redwoods left standing were either too inaccessible or too deformed to bother cutting. "In the 19th century the cost of transportation was so high," Fisher says, "that you'd want to reduce the log as much as you could as close to the standing stumpage. And so you had little mills in the trees, which is why we had the mills here. But as more and more efficient milling came to pass, that wiped out all the inefficient ones. And as the cost of transportation diminished, because transportation became more efficient, trucks became better—the nature of what you would do in a mill changed." Fisher says logging on Kings Mountain hit its peak in the 1880s, and except for periodic spurts when lumber prices rose, declined steadily and then died out around 1920. The mountain's other major commercial activity, dairy ranching for cheese production and buttermilk, disappeared around 1930 because of increased competition from other areas, made possible by improvements in refrigeration and transportation. At the same time, cars were becoming more popular and roads were improving. For example, Skyline Boulevard was built in the 1920s. This led to a new type of enterprise on Kings Mountain.

What Fisher calls the "Summer Cabin Era" began around 1910, with the fading of the sawmills and the dairies and the beginning of vacation-home development. "There were a lot of people who were building a summer cabin," Fisher says. "They found this place when they took the scenic drive, and they bought a small lot, and they built a summer cabin. And this gets into the period that I like to refer to as the period of the hermits and the reclusives and the people who were trying to get away." After World War II comes the rise of "peninsula suburbanism," says Fisher. "People are prepared to drive longer distances to get to a job someplace over on the Bay side." As they had done during the logging era a hundred years ago, economic factors once again determined the fate of Kings Mountain.

"In the 1960s," Fisher says, "real estate had been relatively inexpensive, and there were still a lot of summer cabins from the earlier era. And so you had a lot of people who were living here year-round, renting a summer cabin that somebody had built in the 1930s, let's say. And they're renting the cabin for $100 a month and they're living kind of a neo-hippie lifestyle. So you can envision a world with a lot of incense and candles." The euphoria and the cheap rents were short lived. "In America generally and here specifically," says Fisher, "you had a continuing wave of inflation and rapidly rising real estate prices. The rising real estate prices started driving those people out, because the guy that owned the rental built in the 1930s heard he could get $300,000 for it, he said, 'Wow, I'll sell because I can go do something else with the money.'"

This was the situation, Fisher says, when the District started buying land on Kings Mountain to preserve as open space. "You've got a mixture of people. You've got some of the higher-income people, but not many. You've got a great many of the hippie people. You've got the rednecks. The hippie people are sympathetic with the concept but don't much like the government—you know, 'I want to grow my marijuana out on that property.' The rednecks are hostile to the District because there is this fear, which is articulated in all kinds of ways, that ultimately what they're going to do is try to turn this into one big park and drive all the locals out. There's a sense that this is an encroachment of government into the woods. And we came up here to get away from the government." Today, the District is well-established on Kings Mountain, with two of its most important redwood forest holdings, El Corte de Madera Creek and Purisima Creek Redwoods Preserves. As you visit these beautiful preserves, try to imagine the landscape as it was in earlier times, when enterprise was the order of the day, and the canyons echoed with the sounds of men and machinery engaged in extracting wealth from the soil.

View of El Sereno Open Space Preserve
from Kennedy Road in Los Gatos

EL SERENO
OPEN SPACE PRESERVE

~

More than 1,400 acres of chaparral, wooded canyons, and hidden meadows make up this preserve, which is perched on a steep hillside west of Los Gatos and Highway 17. The headwaters of Trout Creek and San Tomas Aquinas Creek are within the preserve's borders, as is a 2,500-foot summit named El Sereno, which is Spanish for "the serene one." The trails here are dirt roads, and as they wind downhill from the slopes of El Sereno, you have terrific views of the Santa Clara Valley, Mt. Umunhum, Loma Prieta, Mt. Hamilton, and Lexington Reservoir. Native-plant enthusiasts will enjoy the preserve's rich collection of shrubs, including chamise, manzanita, buckbrush, toyon, silk tassel, yerba santa, mountain mahogany, chaparral pea, and leather oak.

Preservation of the land has also preserved memories for people who grew up nearby. "I was raised in Los Gatos right at the base of what is now El Sereno," says Jay Thorwaldson, editor of the *Palo Alto Weekly*. "My sisters had horses, and I learned to ride when I was three-and-a-half. I got my own horse when I was four, and by the time I was seven or eight, I was riding on my own to the top of the mountain on property that was the Charles Moore estate. There were two meadows near the top. One on the side of the ridge that gave a stunning view down into Los Gatos and into the beginning of the Santa Cruz Highway. The upper meadow was just a magical place. It was pretty much level. At one end it had a great big oak tree with branches that came down and rested on the ground. Even when I was a kid, it was all covered with initials, but we could take our horses up there and tie two of them together and they could wander all around this meadow. When we first went up there the wild oats were up to our stirrups, three feet high, and over the years we

El Sereno Trail Use

Bicycles: Allowed on all trails

Dogs: Not allowed

Horses: Allowed on all trails

EL SERENO OPEN SPACE PRESERVE

Trip 5. Chaparral Traverse

Length: 6.3 miles

Time: 3 to 4 hours

Rating: Difficult

Highlights: This out-and-back route high above Highway 17 and Los Gatos is sure to please anyone interested in the fascinating plant community called chaparral. These hearty shrubs have adapted to California's cycle of wet and dry seasons, and to the periodic fires that sweep across the state's wildlands. Using a network of unnamed dirt roads, the route climbs a bit at first, but then loses about 1,000 feet of elevation as it skirts the canyon holding the headwaters of Trout Creek. The turn-around point is at a beautiful meadow, perfect for picnicking.

Directions: From Highway 17 southbound, take the Bear Creek Road exit south of Los Gatos. After 0.1 mile, you come to a stop sign at a four-way junction. Continue straight for 0.3 mile to the junction of Black and Montevina Roads. Go straight, following Montevina Road, for another 4.1 miles to limited roadside parking on the right.

From northbound Highway 17, take the Bear Creek Road exit south of Los Gatos. After 0.1 mile, at a stop sign, turn left, cross over the

pretty much ate up the wild oat crop and gave the California native plants a chance to come back. But from there, you could see all of the Santa Clara Valley. We spent a lot of time up there."

The preserve was acquired in 1975, and gave the District an early opportunity to protect land in the Los Gatos/Monte Sereno area. Access to the preserve is via steep and winding Montevina Road, and there is limited parking. No loop hikes are available.

highway, and at the next stop sign turn right. Continue straight for 0.3 mile to the junction of Black and Montevina Roads, then follow the directions above.

Facilities: None

Trailhead: Gate ES03, about 200 feet past the roadside parking on Montevina Road

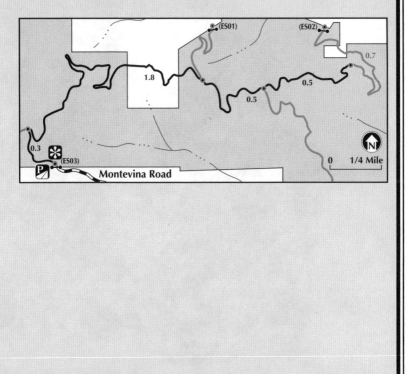

Trip 5. Chaparral Traverse

Passing the gate on the right and stepping over a low barricade of logs designed to block motorcycles, you continue climbing, now on the dirt-and-gravel continuation of Montevina Road. The grade is moderate, and the open, rolling terrain is cloaked in chaparral. The shrubs beside the road are mostly chamise, but you will also find manzanita, buckbrush, toyon, and silk tassel. This route starts high, about 2,300 feet, and you have fine views east to

Coast live oak

the Santa Clara Valley and southeast to Mt. Umunhum and Loma Prieta. A selection of extraordinary homes are perched on nearby hillsides. In autumn, migrating hawks may soar overhead.

The first part of this route, mostly devoid of tall trees, is nevertheless rich with plant life, including interior live oak, scrub oak, blue elderberry, coffeeberry, yerba santa, coyote brush, and poison oak. At a T-junction with a dirt road, you turn right and soon stroll on a mostly level grade past stands of California bay, mountain mahogany, chaparral pea, sticky monkeyflower, and several varieties of ceanothus. Look beside the road for hummingbird sage, one of the six "true sages" (genus *Salvia)* found in the Bay Area. This low-growing plant has rough-textured green leaves, and red flowers that attract its namesake bird.

As you proceed, improving views to the northeast take in Mt. Hamilton and the East Bay hills. Crossing a low rise, you descend to a clearing and then follow the road as it bends left and continues to lose elevation. A dense grove of oak and bay trees, accompanied by tangles of berry vines and wild roses, is on your left. Now climbing on a moderate grade, and then contouring across the steep southeast flank of El Sereno, you have Highway 17 and Lexington Reservoir far below and to your right. Entering a cool and shady forest presided over by madrones, tanbark oaks, canyon oaks, and bay trees, you make a 180° bend to the right and then begin to descend.

Now on a chaparral-covered hillside, you soon come to a clearing, where the road turns sharply left. In this type of open, scrubby habitat, oak trees often provide oases of food and shelter for songbirds, including chestnut-backed chickadees and goldfinches. Descending continuously, the rocky and eroded track drops below 2,000 feet and passes a solitary coast live oak. Black sage, another *Salvia,* grows beside the road here. Downhill and right is a deep canyon forming the headwaters of Trout Creek.

At about the 2-mile point, you reach a junction with a dirt road joining sharply from the left and signed NOT A THROUGH TRAIL. Here you continue straight, following the road through several gentle bends. Now the road curves left and drops steeply for a short distance. Back on easier ground, you soon come to a junction, where a dirt road departs to the right. You follow the advice of an arrow on a trail post and go straight. The gray-green chunks of rock on the road are serpentine, California's state rock. Soil containing serpentine is inhospitable to many plants, but certain ones thrive in it. One of these, found nearby, is leather oak, usually a compact shrub with small, prickly, downward-curved leaves.

On a gentle downhill grade, you follow a ridge crest topped by a lone Douglas-fir into a beautiful meadow, with a fine view of Mt. Umunhum and Loma Prieta directly ahead. From here, the road descends about 250 feet in approximately 0.5 mile to the preserve boundary at gate ES02. This meadow makes a great rest stop and a good place to turn around. After you have finished enjoying this lovely spot, retrace your route back to the parking area.

View of chaparral at Foothills Open Space Preserve

FOOTHILLS OPEN SPACE PRESERVE

~

When the District was formed in 1972, it was a year or so before funds were available to buy land. So the general manager at the time, Herb Grench, sought out people who were willing to make gifts of land to the District to get the ball rolling. One such gift, made in 1974, was this small parcel tucked between Hidden Villa and Foothills Park south of Palo Alto. Later, this gift was used to obtain a matching grant for the purchase of Stevens Creek Shoreline Nature Study Area. In the world of open space preservation, sometimes the whole really is greater than the sum of its parts.

The 211-acre preserve's steep, chaparral-clad slopes and forested ravines form part of the Adobe Creek watershed. A short trail from the limited roadside parking on Page Mill Road leads to a hilltop with great views of the San Francisco Bay communities from San Jose to San Francisco. Mt. Hamilton, Mission Peak, and the East Bay hills are beautifully revealed on a clear day. Along the way, you pass groves of coast live oak and stands of toyon, scrub oak, chamise, coffeeberry, and silk tassel.

Trip 6. A Short Walk in the Santa Cruz Mountains

Passing through a gap in a wood fence marking the preserve boundary, you ignore an unofficial trail, right, and instead go straight on an unnamed single track that climbs on a moderate grade. Coast live oak, toyon, and scrub oak are some of your companions here, and you may be serenaded by the "Chi-ca-go" call of a California quail. This trail, though short, passes through an area rich in plant life. Some of the other shrubs growing nearby include chamise, coffeeberry, California sagebrush, silk tassel, and sticky monkeyflower. According to District staff, a number of the

Foothills Trail Use

Bicycles: Not allowed

Dogs: Leashed dogs allowed on all trails

Horses: Allowed on all trails

FOOTHILLS OPEN SPACE PRESERVE

Trip 6. A Short Walk in the Santa Cruz Mountains

Length: 0.5 mile

Time: 1 hour or less

Rating: Easy

Highlights: Although it is only 0.25 mile long, this short trail passes through several distinct plant communities, including oak woodland and chaparral, before depositing you atop a knoll with stunning views that take in much of the Bay Area. This route wins the prize for the most scenery per calorie expended on District lands.

Directions: From I-280 in Los Altos Hills, take the Page Mill Road/ Arastradero Road exit, and go south 3.7 miles to a roadside parking area on the left with space for two cars.

Facilities: None

Trailhead: Gate FO01, on the east side of the roadside parking

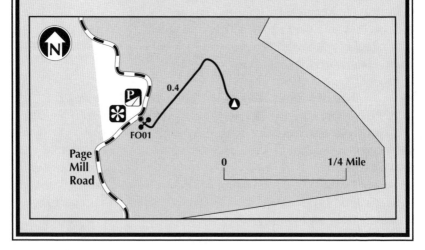

oaks in this preserve appear to be hybrids between scrub oak, Oregon oak, and blue oak.

After briefly touring a shady grove, the trail levels, curves right, and then finds open ground. Now a short, moderate climb puts you atop a hill where 360° views await. From San Jose northward to San Francisco and Oakland, the scene on a clear day is stunning, especially with the aid of binoculars. To the east, Mt. Hamilton, topped by the white domes of the Lick Observatory, towers above the Santa Clara Valley. Northeast are Mission Peak and the East Bay hills. Here the District trail ends, but a very steep and difficult unofficial trail continues down to Hidden Villa Ranch. When you have finished enjoying this fine vantage point, retrace your route to the parking area.

California quail; photo taken at Rancho San Antonio Open Space Preserve

Bicyclists descending from Hunters Point at Fremont Older Open Space Preserve

FREMONT OLDER
OPEN SPACE PRESERVE

~

This is one of the District's urban preserves, located on the outskirts of Cupertino and Saratoga. Bordering Stevens Creek County Park, the preserve has more than 700 acres of flower-fringed grasslands, sunlight-dappled canyons, and chaparral-covered ridges to enjoy via nine miles or so of multiuse trails. Spring and fall are the best times to visit. Native Americans may have used the hilltop now called Hunters Point to survey the surrounding region for game. Later, homesteading families grazed the land, cultivated vineyards, and planted orchards of apricots, plums, and walnuts. The Garrod family bought land here in 1910 and used it for pasture, orchards, and hay growing. The land remained in the Garrod family until purchased by the District in 1980. The Garrod family still owns a ranch next door with a commercial stable and a vineyard.

Also in the early 1900s, Fremont Older and his wife, Cora, bought part of what was to become his namesake preserve, and in 1914 they completed the ranch house they called "Woodhills." Older was a crusading newspaperman, who some say was the most influential editor in the West. Born in Wisconsin and named for John C. Frémont, Older lost his father and all his uncles in the Civil War. With only three years of school, he became a printer's apprentice and moved to California in his teens. Taking Horace Greeley as his model, Older worked his way up from printer to editor of a Redwood City paper. In 1895, Older was hired as editor by the San Francisco *Bulletin,* and he rejuvenated that paper using many of the tactics still employed by journalists today, including sensationalism, advice columns, and attention-grabbing headlines.

Cora Older, a prolific writer, was responsible for overseeing the building of the house and gardens, including the innovative flat roof and large picture windows. The Olders entertained frequently, and the Woodhills guest book has the signatures of many influential thinkers of the day, including writers Max Eastman, Carl Sandburg, and Lincoln Steffens; educator John Dewey; composer Henry Cowell; and politicians Hiram Johnson and James Rolph. Cora died in 1968 at the age of 93. Woodhills was heavily mortgaged, and the bank sold the property. The new owner planned to subdivide the property and invited friends to take what they wanted from the house, which was in a state of disrepair. When the District began acquiring the property in 1975, the plan was to demolish the house. The El Camino Trust for Historic Preservation objected but had no money available to fund restoration.

At the eleventh hour, Mort and Elaine Levine stepped forward. Mort, a newspaper publisher himself, was president of the El Camino Trust for Historic Preservation. "We came up with four or five rather fancy alternatives, including a youth hostel or little retreat building for conferences, various things like that," he says. "Finally at one meeting I suggested the idea of a private party entering into a venture with the District to restore the building in exchange for a long-term lease. The idea was to restore the building to what it was like in the World War I period, when it was built. They said, 'Well, who would possibly do that?' And I said, 'Well, possibly I would.' And then I went home that night and mentioned this to Elaine.

Fremont Older house and garden, "Woodhills"

It all came as quite a shock, but that's how it evolved."

When the Levines finally took a close look at the house, they were somewhat taken aback, to put it mildly. "The porch had fallen away from the front by a foot or two," says Mort. "The living room had settled in one corner to the point where the floor was sloped, the floorboards were all warped—there was a hole in the ceiling because there had been a fire set by some squatters, and then the rain warped all the oak boards in the floor. The vines and other plants had so taken control that you had to hack your way through. It was an astonishing thing, like coming upon a Mayan ruin in a Central American jungle." But like their predecessors, Fremont and Cora, the Levines pos-

Leashed dogs are welcome at Fremont Older Open Space Preserve. Bring plenty of water for your pooch.

sessed a dedication born in the world of journalism, and an ability to imagine beauty as expressed in architecture and gardening.

That the Levines went ahead with the restoration is a testament to their determination and their commitment to historic preservation. "I think it's important to demonstrate that preservation works," Mort says. "That you can do something, and after it's accomplished it serves as a model for others. That was really one of our goals and still is in the whole preservation movement." The Levines found a retired contractor who was willing to take on the project, and they funded the entire restoration themselves, in exchange for a long-term lease that would allow them to live in the home. Longtime neighbors who remembered what the house was like offered advice. Evelyn Wells, a protégé of Fremont Older's and his

Fremont Older Trail Use

Bicycles: Allowed on all trails except the Creekside Trail

Dogs: Leashed dogs allowed on all trails

Horses: Allowed on all trails except the Creekside Trail

FREMONT OLDER OPEN SPACE PRESERVE

Trip 7. Hunters Point

Length: 3.1 miles

Time: 2 to 3 hours

Rating: Moderate

Highlights: The varied terrain found in the northeast corner of this preserve, and the superb views from Hunters Point, make this semi-loop route a favorite among South Bay hikers. In spring, the grasslands visited on the Cora Older and Hayfield Trails come alive with wildflowers, while the secluded canyon traversed by the Seven Springs Trail offers shady respite on a warm day. Remnants of walnut and apricot orchards harken back to Santa Clara Valley's heyday as an agricultural paradise.

Directions: From Highway 85 at the Cupertino–San Jose border, take the De Anza Boulevard exit, go south 0.5 mile to Prospect Road, and turn right. After 0.4 mile you come to a stop sign, where you stay on Prospect Road by turning left and crossing a set of railroad tracks.

When you reach the junction of Prospect Road and Rolling Hills Road, follow Prospect Road, as it bends sharply left. At 1.8 miles, you reach the preserve entrance and the parking area, which is left. (The

biographer, supplied the Levines with photographs showing details of furniture, fabrics, and decorative items that had once graced the interior of Woodhills. And best of all, people began showing up on the Levines' doorstep with items they had taken from the house when it was slated for demolition.

Restoration lasted about two years. In 1980, the house was listed on the National Register of Historic Places. The Levines continue to lease and reside in the home. You can visit Woodhills during the annual house and garden tour, which usually takes place in the spring. Call the District office for details: (650) 691-1200.

parking area is adjacent to Saratoga Country Club, and a sign here warns you to beware of flying golf balls and to park at your own risk.)

Facilities: Vault toilet

Trailhead: On the north side of Prospect Road, across from the parking area

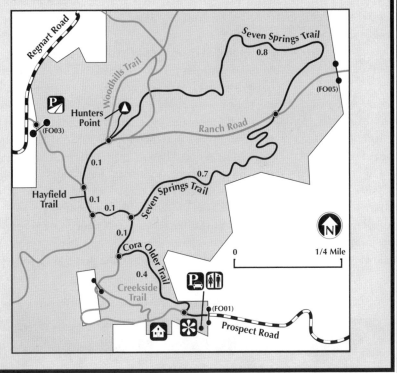

Trip 7. Hunters Point

From the trailhead, which has two District information boards and a map holder, you follow the Cora Older Trail uphill and right. After about 100 feet, the single-track trail switchbacks left, then winds uphill and crosses several culverts draining seasonal creeks. The landscape here alternates between open slopes and wooded canyons. Coast live oak and California bay preside over the woodlands, whereas chamise, coyote brush, toyon, and California sagebrush dominate the open areas. Hollyleaf cherry and mountain mahogany, often found in chaparral, are also nearby.

Identifying birds by their calls and songs is called "birding by ear." As you follow the trail, you may be able to identify some common birds found here. Listen for the sharp cry of the northern flicker, the rapidly repeated notes of the wrentit, and the harsh, descending call of the Steller's jay. Turning left and crossing an open hillside, where you enjoy views southeast to Mt. Umunhum and Loma Prieta, you pass a firebreak and soon reach a T-junction. Here, you go right on a dirt road and after several hundred feet arrive at another junction. From this junction, the road curves left, but you angle right on the Seven Springs Trail, a single track.

With a ravine holding a seasonal creek on your left, you cross a firebreak and then suddenly enter a cool and shady forest. Here, California buckeye and western chokecherry join coast live oak, with an understory of blue witch, oceanspray, manroot, and poison oak. Soon the ravine widens to a valley, whose north-facing slope holds the remnants of an orchard. Winding your way downhill, you pass stands of walnut trees and then meander through a brushy area of willows, berry vines, and dogwood. The trail turns left, crosses a culvert draining the seasonal creek, and then reaches a four-way junction.

Here, Ranch Road joins from the left, and a road signed STOP, DO NOT TRESPASS goes right. Your route, the Seven Springs Trail, continues across the junction and then angles right. Now climbing on a gentle grade, you pass a few tall eucalyptus trees and more walnuts. Power lines span the valley you've been following, which is downhill and right. Approaching the preserve boundary,

Open grassland slopes at Fremont Older Open Space Preserve

*Great views of Silicon Valley and the South Bay
reward visitors to Hunters Point.*

the trail curves left and then ascends via switchbacks to a ridge top. Veering off
the ridge top, you cross a firebreak and then find shade, welcome on a warm
day, in a grove of coast live oak. After another firebreak, you traverse a scrubby
hillside dotted with old apricot trees and then climb moderately toward Hunters
Point, one of the preserve's high points.

A level stretch and then a gentle descent bring you to two junctions. At the
first, a fork, you bear left. At the second, where a connector to Ranch Road joins
from the left, you continue straight. The steep hillside, left, is home to several
large valley oaks. Hugging the east side of the hill beneath Hunters Point, which
is decorated with sticky monkeyflower and yerba santa, your trail soon merges
with Ranch Road, coming sharply from the left. Now you bear right and just
ahead meet the Hayfield Trail, a dirt road winding its way uphill. Turning right,
you soon come to a fork where the Woodhills Trail goes left. Here, you veer
right and, after about 100 feet, find yourself atop Hunters Point.

The sweeping 360° views from this fine vantage point take in San Jose, the
Santa Clara Valley, Mt. Hamilton, Mt. Umunhum, and most of the southern end
of San Francisco Bay, the East Bay hills, and Mt. Diablo. On a clear day, you can
even see Mt. Tamalpais and the San Francisco skyline. After enjoying a rest and
the superb scenery, retrace your route to the junction with the Woodhills Trail,
and then to the next junction, just west of where the Seven Springs Trail and

Fremont Older Trail Use

Bicycles:　Allowed on all trails except the Creekside Trail

Dogs:　Leashed dogs allowed on all trails

Horses:　Allowed on all trails except the Creekside Trail

FREMONT OLDER OPEN SPACE PRESERVE

Trip 8. Maisie's Peak

Length:　3.7 miles

Time:　2 to 3 hours

Rating:　Moderate

Highlights: Reaching Maisie's Peak is just one of the attractions of this aerobic loop, which uses the Cora Older, Hayfield, Coyote Ridge, Toyon, and Creekside Trails to explore the southern part of this preserve. Along the way, visitors will enjoy grasslands dotted with colorful spring wildflowers and learn about some of our hearty native shrubs, such as toyon, mountain mahogany, and hollyleaf cherry.

Directions: Same as for "Hunters Point" on pages 96–97

Facilities:　Vault toilet

Trailhead: On the north side of Prospect Road, across from the parking area

Ranch Road merge. Here, you follow the Hayfield Trail as it angles right and descends on a moderate grade. You next pass two dirt roads, both to the right. The first is unsigned, but the second is signed REGNART ROAD, 0.2 MILE.

Continuing straight, you follow a rolling course through open habitat that is perfect for western meadowlarks, a songbird found throughout the West and also in the Great Plains. Meadowlarks have a lovely, liquid song and often travel in large flocks. (Look for a bird about the size of a robin sporting a yellow breast, a brown, striped back, and white feathers along the outside of its tail.) When you arrive at a junction with a trail signed PROSPECT ROAD PARKING, 0.8 MILE, you turn left. After several hundred feet, you reach the junction with the Seven Springs Trail, where you began this loop. Now you turn right and retrace your route to the parking area.

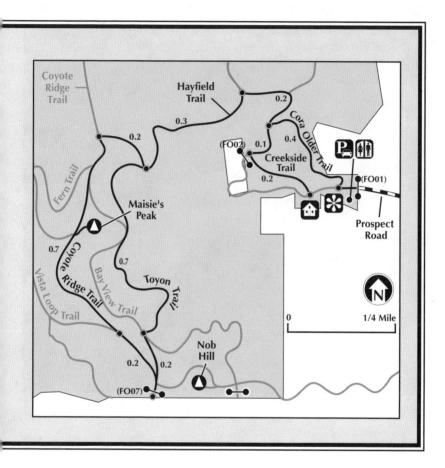

Trip 8. Maisie's Peak

Follow the route description for "Hunters Point" on pages 96–97 to the junction with the Seven Springs Trail, about 0.5 mile from the trail-head. Here you turn left and go several hundred feet to a T-junction with the Hayfield Trail, a dirt road. Turning left, you descend, curve right, and then find level ground amid stands of walnut trees, some riddled with woodpecker holes. Coast live oak, toyon, coyote brush, and poison oak are some of your other companions. The preserve's grasslands sport a stunning selection of spring wildflowers, including blue-eyed grass, Ithuriel's spear, blue-dicks, California poppy, mule ears, lupine, and owl's-clover. Soon the road bends left and climbs to a junction, left, with the Toyon Trail, at about the 1-mile point.

A hiker pauses to snap a wildflower photo at Fremont Older Open Space Preserve.

You stay on the Hayfield Trail as it switchbacks right and becomes steep. The views of the preserve, including the area around Hunters Point, improve as you gain elevation. Winding your way uphill, you reach a T-junction with the Coyote Ridge Trail. Turning left, you spy your goal, Maisie's Peak, ahead. An unofficial trail that climbs to a viewpoint joins sharply from the left, and then you come to a junction with the Fern Trail, right. Staying on the Coyote Ridge Trail, you cling to a ridge top that climbs and bends left. Chamise, California sagebrush, and scrub oak grow nearby, marking this as an area of chaparral.

The next junction is with the Bay View Trail, left, but you remain faithful to the Coyote Ridge Trail on your quest to reach Maisie's Peak. A large row of eucalyptus trees dominates the hillside downhill and left, and some of these nonnative trees are also on your right. Just past a junction with the Vista Loop Trail, right, you turn sharply left and climb steeply to the preserve's highest point, named for Maisie Garrod.

A screen of trees and low shrubs circles the summit, but a few gaps offer views to other parts of the preserve, including Hunters Point, which is several hundred feet lower in elevation. After spending some time enjoying this airy perch, retrace your route to the previous junction. Here, you turn left on the Coyote Ridge Trail and descend moderately, rewarded with fine views (to the left) of the Santa Clara Valley, Mt. Hamilton, and the East Bay hills. Now in the shade of coast live oaks and eucalyptus trees, you meet the Vista Loop Trail joining sharply from the right, but you continue straight.

A vineyard and a few valley oaks cling to a hillside on your right. Leaving the shade behind, you soon reach a junction with the Bay View Trail, which departs sharply left. A fence ahead marks the preserve boundary. Beyond it is the entrance to privately owned Garrod Farms. Turning left onto the Bay View Trail, a dirt road, you next come to a four-way junction with the Toyon Trail, right. Angling slightly right to get on the Toyon Trail, you pass a fence with a gate that prevents access by bikes and horses during wet weather. (When the gate is closed, hikers can pass through a narrow gap in the fence.)

Topping a low rise and starting to descend, you have a fine view of the open grasslands south of Hunters Point. Toyon, the trail's namesake plant, is abundant nearby, bearing bright green leaves and, in fall, red berries. Again shaded by eucalyptus and coast live oaks, you follow a rolling course through a wet area drained by culverts. Blue elderberry and California bay grow beside the trail. Passing another seasonal gate, you arrive at a junction where a short connector jogs left to the Bay View Trail. You stay on the Toyon Trail, descending gently past stands of Monterey pine, mountain mahogany, and hollyleaf cherry. Traversing a hillside of chaparral that falls away to your right, you soon find yourself back at the junction with the Hayfield Trail.

Now you turn right and retrace your route to the junction with the Cora Older Trail (where bikes must turn left). From here, stay on the dirt road, following it downhill and right to a junction with the Creekside Trail, a single track. Turning left, you soon enter a lovely forest of oak, bay, and California buckeye. The Fremont Older house is uphill and right, hidden from view. An unsigned trail that descends left via wood steps leads to the Older's pet cemetery, where you will find markers for some of their pets, including Gretel, Melitta, and Sylvie. Fremont Older himself was buried here until the death of his wife, Cora.

Now descending on a moderate grade, the trail winds its way down to a bridge over a creek. After crossing the bridge, you soon reach a fence with a gap, and then paved Prospect Road. When you come to the road, turn left and follow it about 0.1 mile back to the parking area.

TRAIL BUILDING

When you explore the District's many preserves, you travel mostly on dirt roads and single-track trails. The dirt roads are primarily fire roads, ranch roads, and logging roads that have existed for many years. The single-track trails, with few exceptions, were built more recently by District crews working with trail-building contractor Gene Sheehan, who is a legendary figure among District staff. "On most of the single-track trails here, he was the person that laid them out and was the one that built the trails," says David Topley, the District's support services supervisor. The District supplied crews, equipment, and materials, and Sheehan provided specialized tools and a steel-tracked mini-backhoe called a Morrison Trailblazer. "He had his way of doing it, and if you did it any other way it was the wrong way. And he would joke about it and give you a hard time. Gene would always say that 'You either got an eye for dirt or you don't.' Which means they could look at a trail, look at the grade, and be able to use that piece of equipment to get a finished product that looks like a trail. The people that had an eye for dirt, he would teach them how to run the trail machine. Gene's saying, which he would always say to me when we were building a trail, is that people hiking on the trail shouldn't have to look at their feet. They should be able to walk on the trail and enjoy the vista, the view, without having to worry about looking at their feet."

Topley says that Sheehan usually worked with a District planner to map and then lay out a new trail. Laying out a new trail meant flagging the route with pieces of colored tape tied to a tree limb or a branch of brush. "They'd have a starting and finishing point, and they'd have a grade," Topley says. "Ten percent grade would be his maximum. They'd take into consideration the property lines. And they would flag the trail. So Gene would stand here and often he'd take somebody like me or someone else to do this. The other person would crawl on their hands and knees through the poison oak, get to where [Gene] would want that trail to be in fifteen yards. And when that person was where he would want that trail to be, he would say, 'Okay,' and they would put a piece of tape on the poison oak bush or whatever. And then you would crawl through the poison oak, or climb over trees, or go through brush to the next twenty or thirty feet. He would get the grade and the spot that he wanted you. And you'd put another piece of tape there."

After the trail was laid out, District crews cleared the route of all brush— often poison oak—and forest debris so that Sheehan's trail machine had a firm surface to follow. Frequently, the work took place on steep hillsides

Lead Open Space Technician Michael Bankosh and
trail building contractor Gene Sheehan work to realign the
Toyon Trail at Fremont Older Open Space Preserve

in the heat of July or August. A two- or three-mile trail might take all summer to build. The crew used chainsaws and industrial-strength hedge clippers to do battle with the brush. Following the flag line laid out by Sheehan, the crew cleared a path for the trail machine.

Operated by Sheehan, the trail machine chugged along, breaking up the dirt ahead with a miniature backhoe arm, and smoothing out the resulting path with a narrow blade. Often the flagged route would have to be altered slightly to account for impediments such as large rocks and trees. Once the mechanized work was done, trail crews followed behind with an array of finishing tools, including a Sheehan invention called a bent shovel. Former District ranger Patrick Congdon, now general manager of the Santa Clara County Open Space Authority, says that everyone who worked on trails with Sheehan learned a lot. "Many of us would not be as skilled or have the knowledge of trail construction, maintenance, and design that we do, if it wasn't for him. I think that we owe him a great deal of gratitude. Because even though he was, at times, a little ornery and difficult to work with, he had a vision of how he would like to see trails laid out and built." So the next time you are admiring the view from a particularly scenic stretch of trail, take a moment to thank the District staff and contractor Gene Sheehan for getting you there.

The Bent Shovel

A bent shovel, as its name implies, is a shovel whose blade is set at an angle. Bent shovels make it easier for the trail crew to achieve sloping uphill and downhill banks to the trail, thus alleviating erosion problems.

View west from the Vista Point across the coastal hills toward the Pacific Ocean

LA HONDA CREEK OPEN SPACE PRESERVE

∼

Located at the head of La Honda and Harrington creeks just west of Highway 84, this 2,078-acre preserve offers visitors about three miles of secluded ranch roads that wander amid sky-scraping coast redwoods and Douglas-firs, but also cross open grasslands where spring wildflowers frame stunning vistas toward the San Mateo coast. Wildlife sometimes seen here includes bobcats, coyotes, and deer, along with songbirds and raptors. The preserve contains a massive old-growth redwood that is certainly worth a visit. This giant was reportedly spared the logger's saw because it was a former owner's favorite tree. And the view of the coastal valleys in the San Gregorio Creek watershed from a vantage point on the preserve's south edge is not to be missed.

The District acquired the property from the Dyer family. On the day the property changed hands, David Sanguinetti, superintendent of the District's Skyline office, listened to the Dyers reminisce. "Mr. Dyer was an airline pilot for United Airlines back in the 1940s," he says. "He flew a route from New York to Hawaii, and he would fly over the coast as he went across, and he'd look down on this piece of property and say, 'You know, I want that piece of property!' So one day, while he was in San Francisco, he went up to the property, saw it, got a hold of a real estate agent and bought the property."

When Dyer told his wife about the purchase, she was thrilled. So thrilled, in fact, that she loaded a Diamond T pickup truck with all their belongings and drove alone across the country to surprise her husband, who was staying on the property. "So he's asleep at night," says Sanguinetti, "and he's in the house, and all of a sudden he hears this noise. And he looks out the window, and here she comes up the driveway with the Diamond T and all their belongings. She loaded the whole truck up, drove all the way across the United States to surprise

La Honda Creek Trail Use

Bicycles: Not allowed

Dogs: Not allowed

Horses: Allowed on all trails

LA HONDA CREEK OPEN SPACE PRESERVE

Trip 9. Big Tree and Vista Point

Length: 2.7 miles

Time: 2 to 3 hours

Rating: Moderate

Permit: **A special permit is required to access La Honda Creek Open Space Preserve.** To obtain a permit, call the District office: (650) 691-1200.

Highlights: You can wander the old ranch roads in this secluded preserve, marveling at tall coast redwoods and enjoying flower-framed views of the San Mateo coast. The semi-loop route uses several unnamed dirt roads to visit a magnificent old-growth redwood tree, and then heads south to enjoy a breath-taking vantage point on the divide between La Honda and Harrington creeks.

Directions: From the junction of Skyline Boulevard and Highway 84 in Sky Londa, take Skyline Boulevard northwest 2.3 miles to Bear Gulch Road West. Turn left, go 0.6 mile to Allen Road, marked by a metal gate, and turn left. Go 1.1 miles to a locked gate. Open the lock using the combination on your District permit. Be sure to close and relock the gate. Go another 0.2 mile to a roadside parking area on the right.

Facilities: None

Trailhead: At the entrance to the roadside parking area

him at the house. So he didn't have to fly out and help her. I thought that was a pretty amazing story."

A compound with several homes and farm buildings is still on the property, including a historic barn with hand-hewn beams and uprights that may date from the turn of the last century. The preserve consists of two parcels, the former

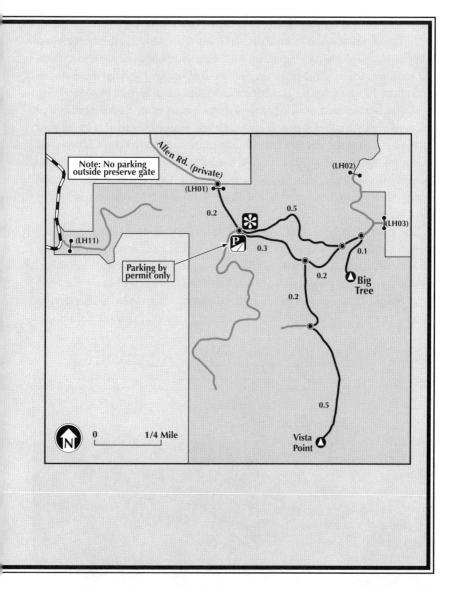

Dyer ranch, open by special permit, and the former McDonald ranch to the south, which is currently closed to the public. A master planning process is currently scheduled for this entire preserve. Preserve access and use will be addressed in the master planning process. For permit information, call the District office: (650) 691-1200.

Trip 9. Big Tree and Vista Point

Two dirt roads diverge from the paved entrance road just slightly northwest of the roadside parking area. One heads southwest, the other east. Your route is the road heading east. You find it by walking back on the entrance road about 100 feet from the parking area and then turning right. Now you are in a coast redwood forest, traveling over a magic carpet of twigs and needles that cushions your steps. Judging by the size of a few nearby stumps, this forest must have contained some magnificent old-growth trees. (Later on this hike you will visit one of these ancient giants.) Coast live oaks, tanbark oaks, madrones, and Douglas-firs join the redwoods to preside over a kingdom that also contains Douglas iris, tarweed, redwood sorrel, miner's lettuce, redwood violets, ferns, and berry vines.

The road stays level as it crosses a hillside, which drops steeply left to a canyon holding the headwaters of La Honda Creek. Occasional bird songs are the only sounds that interrupt the stillness. Evergreen huckleberry, thimbleberry, wood rose, and poison oak are some of the shrubs found along the road. After about 0.5 mile, you reach a junction, where another dirt road joins sharply from the right. Now atop a ridge, you continue straight for another

Rolling hills at La Honda Creek Open Space Preserve

0.1 mile to a junction with a very over-grown dirt road that departs to the right. Here, you turn right. (If you miss this junction, you will soon reach a more obvious one, where the road you are following curves left, and another road veers right toward gate LH03. From this junction, turn around and retrace your route to locate the correct road.)

Manzanita, toyon, and French broom are prevalent beside the grass-covered road, which descends on a gentle grade. Look left through the verdant screen to catch a glimpse of your first goal on today's walk, a towering ancient redwood. After several hundred yards, your road becomes too overgrown to travel, but another road joins from the left. You turn left and follow it for about 100 feet to the base of a massive redwood, shown on the District map as BIG TREE. In fact, this is a *very* big tree. The bare lower limbs, which themselves are the size of ordinary trees, radiate like spokes from the hub of a wheel. At a height where most trees reach their apex, this giant is just starting to show its evergreen foliage. From near the tree's enormous, nearly fourteen-foot-diameter base, you have to crane your neck just to sight upward along its trunk. A few logs strewn about provide places to sit, rest, and contemplate this awe-inspiring living thing.

When you are ready to leave, retrace your route uphill to the main dirt road. When you reach it, turn left and retrace your route for about 0.1 mile to a fork. Here, you bear left on a dirt road that rises on a gentle grade. As you enjoy an easy stroll, look left from time to time to see if you can spot the giant redwood you visited only a few minutes ago. Along the way, don't ignore the beautiful coast live oaks and colorful madrones that line your route. Soon you reach open grassland and then a compound with several homes and farm buildings. At a four-way junction, you turn left on a paved road that, after about 125 feet, turns to dirt and grass.

Climbing gently through a landscape dotted orange with California poppies, you crest a low rise and are suddenly confronted with a fabulous view of the Pacific Ocean—when it is not hidden by fog. Rolling hills and wooded canyons form an artistic foreground to this stunning scene. Spring wildflowers abound here, and you may find checker bloom, blue-eyed grass, Ithuriel's spear, lupine, mule ears, and owl's-clover beside the road. Losing a bit of elevation, you pass an unofficial single-track trail heading right. Just beyond this junction is an open gate and a ramshackle fence.

A line of trees to the left provides shade for a lovely collection of wild irises, which can vary in color from rich blue to pale lavender. Descending steeply over rough, rocky, and eroded ground, you follow a ridge top

Solitude greets visitors to secluded
La Honda Creek Open Space Preserve.

through a forest of mostly redwood and Douglas-fir. An abrupt transition to grassland heralds your approach to Vista Point, a vantage point at the edge of a very steep drop-off. The views here extend from west to east, and take in the Pacific Ocean, many of the District's preserves along Skyline Boulevard, and the East Bay hills topped by Mt. Hamilton. When you have finished basking in this terrific scenery, retrace your steps to the four-way junction in the building compound.

Turning left on a paved road, you pass a residence on your right and then begin to descend through a shady corridor of trees and shrubs, including manzanita and coffeeberry. Coming into the open again, you soon reach the roadside parking area where you began this hike.

Views of the Pacific Ocean from the junction of Peters Creek Trail and Long Ridge Road at Long Ridge Open Space Preserve

LONG RIDGE
OPEN SPACE PRESERVE

~

Twelve miles or so of multiuse trails await visitors to this nearly 2,000-acre preserve, located near the District's geographic center. From atop Long Ridge, near a memorial bench honoring writer and environmentalist Wallace Stegner, you can look out over the Pescadero Creek watershed and gaze westward upon thousands of acres of forested canyons, rolling hills, and grass-covered ridges. Much of this land is protected by state and county parks, including the adjoining Portola Redwoods State Park, which connects to Long Ridge Preserve via a hiking-only trail. Heading north, the Bay Area Ridge Trail provides easy access to Skyline Ridge Preserve. Upper Stevens Creek County Park and Saratoga Gap Preserve lie just across Skyline Boulevard with connections to other District preserves and also to parks in Santa Cruz County (approximately 650 acres of Long Ridge Preserve are within Santa Cruz County). A new 1.7-mile hiking and equestrian trail, the Achistaca Trail (named for a small subgroup of the Ohlone Indians that inhabited the upper end of the San Lorenzo River watershed) is also available at this preserve, providing a key connection between Long Ridge Preserve and California State Parks' Skyline-to-the-Sea Trail.

The preserve has fine examples of mixed-evergreen and riparian forests, and also contains an apple orchard along Peters Creek that blossoms beautifully in spring and bears fruit in fall. There is a long history of ranching and farming here worth noting. According to Janet Schwind, a longtime resident of the South Skyline area and its historian, perhaps the first property owner on Long Ridge was Winston Bennett, who lived in a spot known then as Pot Hollow. Bennett was born in Georgia, came West in the 1840s, and, like many others of his time, caught gold fever and headed for the Sierra foothills. After a career as a trader, a constable, and a deputy sheriff, Bennett sold his ranch to John Fatjo in 1884.

The Fatjos, a Spanish family, came to San Jose in 1849 from Chile. When you pass the apple orchard on Peters Creek Trail, you are passing the site where the Fatjo ranch house once stood. After many years, the Fatjo family began selling parts of their land. Among the buyers were the Barnett and Wyant families of Saratoga, who wanted to build a weekend retreat in the Santa Cruz Mountains. Their complex, consisting of a cabin and a small barn, was named the Bar-Why Ranch. In the early 1960s, a group of families from the Palo Alto area bought the remaining 390 acres of the Fatjo ranch for private recreational use and to preserve as open space. Their plan to build cabins, campsites, stables, and trails fell through, but they did manage to create a pond for swimming and fishing by damming Peters Creek.

In 1965, the group transferred thirty acres of land to Pacific High School, an alternative boarding school for students dissatisfied with conventional education. The students built their own dwellings, including a variety of geodesic domes. They constructed classrooms and workshops, and brought in barns, chicken coops, and storage sheds. The school was loosely affiliated with Peninsula School in Menlo Park and had about fifteen faculty members. Schwind says the students showed great spirit at first, but as the years went by, things deteriorated. Regularly scheduled classes disappeared, and drug use intensified. Eventually, the school became just another commune, and an albatross around the landowners' necks.

This was the state of affairs in the late 1970s, when the District became interested in the property. The Palo Alto group was willing to sell (at half the market value), but what to do about the remnants of Pacific High School and the people living there? In a complex transaction, the District found a Buddhist group in Mountain View that was interested in buying the school site and turning it into a retreat and meditation center. General Manager Craig Britton, who was the District's land acquisition manager at the time, remembers what happened next.

"They did an interesting thing," Britton says. "They took over the property on a shoestring. And they went in there and gathered all the people together and said, 'We're going to create a Buddhist retreat here, and we're going to put in some gardens and tear down some of these buildings. Here's our plan for the property in the long run. What we'd like to do is have you experience us over a year or two. And then you make a decision whether you want to join us or you want to move on.'" Britton says that after two years only a couple of "hangers-on" remained. "So they sat them down and said, 'Well, the time has come for a decision.' And those people moved on. So all the animosity just kind of melted away over that two-year period, as people realized this was a serious group, they were serious about their meditation and their program up there." The meditation center is called Jikoji, and if you ascend the Peters Creek Trail to Long Ridge Road, you pass the Jikoji property as you cross the dam.

Jay Thorwaldson, editor of the *Palo Alto Weekly* and Long Ridge neighbor, remembers the area of Peters Creek called Devils Canyon as being another magnet for the counterculture in the 1960s. In fact, the canyon, which is at the north end of the preserve, was known locally as Aquarian Valley, in honor of the counterculture types it attracted. "As you get to the Portola Heights area, there's Devils Canyon down below, and there's a significant waterfall with a cave behind it," says Thorwaldson. "The hippies would go up there and hike down to this cave. There were some permanent residents of the cave, and the weekenders, part of their admission fee was to bring in bags and boxes of groceries."

Thorwaldson says the homeowners in the area were not happy about the hippies, especially the young girls they saw hiking down to the cave. "So we decided to go do this investigative hike down there. An assistant city editor and I went down, and they were just all laid back you know, and it was an interesting group. I hiked a little bit out and came through some brush, and there was this young guy totally nude with a short blonde beard and short blonde hair sitting there watching the sun go down. He sort of glowed and he was sitting cross-legged as far out on the edge of a rock without falling off this thousand-foot canyon as he could get and still have gravity holding him on the rock."

Another part of Long Ridge Preserve was acquired from the Panighetti family, who were prominent in Los Gatos. According to Patrick Congdon, one of the District's early rangers, the Panighettis had a cabin and a couple of other buildings located on a flat near the current Ranch Spring Trail. "There was just this beautiful little flat," he says, "which now has a couple of cypress trees at the entrance to the flat that identify the site, but that's all that remains. But at one time that was the hub for that area." The Panighettis ran cattle on the property for many years before selling the land to the District. Congdon says that there was a lot of cattle ranching in the South Skyline region during the first half of the last century, but by the time the District acquired the Panighetti property in the mid 1980s, it was the last real working cattle ranch in the area.

Long Ridge contains the old Summit Road alignment, which is now part of the Peters Creek Trail. Summit Road was the route that ran partway along the spine of the Santa Cruz Mountains before Skyline Boulevard was built. Long Ridge was the first District preserve to have wild turkeys, a game bird introduced by the California Department of Fish and Game. Wild turkeys are now found in a handful of District preserves, and the males can be very aggressive, especially during spring mating season. The

Long Ridge Trail Use

Bicycles: Allowed on all trails

Dogs: Leashed dogs allowed under a special permit on the Peters Creek Trail, Ridge Trail, and the firebreak that parallels Skyline Boulevard. Permits are available on-site at the Grizzly Flat parking area.

Horses: Allowed on all trails

LONG RIDGE OPEN SPACE PRESERVE

Trip 10. Long Ridge

Length: 4.6 miles

Time: 2 to 3 hours

Rating: Moderate

Highlights: Superb views are the reason to wander uphill from the shady confines of Peters Creek to the dramatically situated Wallace Stegner memorial bench high atop Long Ridge. On a clear day, the scene extends westward over the Pescadero Creek watershed, taking in thousands of acres of protected lands, truly a living monument to the open space movement. This semi-loop route uses the Ridge, Peters Creek, and Long Ridge Trails, along with Long Ridge Road.

Directions: From the junction of Skyline Boulevard and Page Mill Road/Alpine Road south of Palo Alto, take Skyline Boulevard southeast 3.1 miles to a roadside parking area on the left. This parking area, sometimes called Grizzly Flat, serves both Long Ridge Preserve and Upper Stevens Creek County Park.

Facilities: None

Trailhead: At the entrance to the roadside parking area

preserve was also where sudden oak death, a disease that affects oaks and other forest trees and shrubs, was first identified on District lands. In addition, Long Ridge has been one of the the sites in a trapping program to control feral pigs. Sempervirens Fund provided critical support for acquisition of part of this preserve.

The map for Long Ridge Preserve is part of the District's South Skyline Region map.

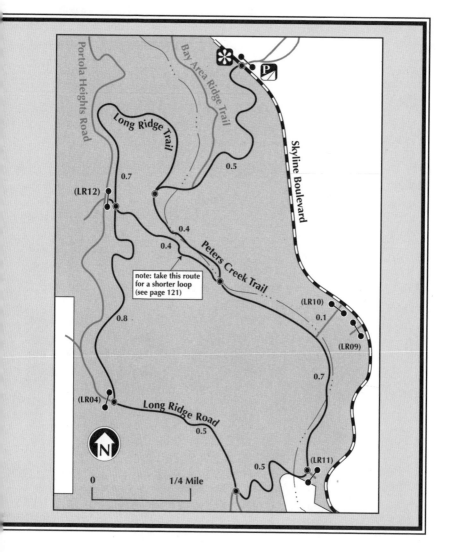

Trip 10. Long Ridge

At the trailhead is a fence with a gate that prevents access by bikes and horses during wet weather. (When the gate is closed, hikers can pass through a narrow gap in the fence.) About 50 feet beyond the fence are two District information boards and a map holder. From here, you follow the Peters Creek Trail, a single track, as it wanders across a hillside that falls away to the right. Coast live oak, canyon oak, and madrone are your arboreal companions, and the grassy slope may be colorfully decorated with wildflowers in spring. Soon the trail swings left and descends into a cool, dark forest of mostly Douglas-fir and California bay. These trees tower over an understory of toyon, blue elderberry, hazelnut, buckbrush, snowberry, ferns, and berry vines. Also nearby is interior live oak, one of California's three common "live," or evergreen, oak species.

At a junction, a trail merges sharply from the right. This is the Ridge Trail, which heads north to Skyline Ridge Open Space Preserve. The Ridge Trail and the Peters Creek Trail (from this point on) are both part of the Bay Area Ridge Trail. Dogs are prohibited beyond this point on the Peters Creek Trail. You continue straight and after several hundred feet cross the trail's namesake creek on a bridge. This is a lovely area, shaded by stands of big-leaf maple and tanbark oak. Another couple of hundred feet ahead is the next junction, where the Long Ridge Trail joins from the right. Again you continue straight, passing an amazing fern garden in the creek bed to your left. Now in the open, you enjoy a level walk past willow thickets that line the creek, and the remains of a still-prolific apple orchard that blooms beautifully in spring and is often heavily loaded with several varieties of apples in fall.

Just shy of the 1-mile point, you meet a dirt road that connects to the Long Ridge Trail heading sharply right. *(For alternate directions, see sidebar on page 121.)* From here, you continue straight on the Peters Creek Trail, now a dirt road. Soon you reach an open field with a line of willows guarding the trail's namesake creek. A dense forest of Douglas-fir, California bay, tanbark oak, and bigleaf maple is to your right. Coffeeberry, buckbrush, and wood rose border the road. Look here for spring wildflowers such as hound's tongue, milkmaids, mosquito bills, mission bells, fairy bells, and a violet called western heart's-ease. At an unsigned junction, a dirt road heading to gate LR10 forks left and crosses a bridge over a wet area. Several hundred feet ahead, another dirt road angles left and joins the road to gate LR10.

Passing an old fence where a gate once stood, you soon cross Peters Creek, which flows under the road through a culvert. The tall trees here are red alders, told by their doubly serrated oval leaves with deeply impressed parallel veins. This moisture-loving species is often found beside rivers and creeks. Where a gated dirt road angles left to the preserve boundary, you turn right and cross an earthen dam. Built in the 1960s, this 200-foot-long dam turned part of Peters Creek into the cattail-fringed lake on your left. Since 1979, the lake has been the property of the Buddhist group, now known as Jikoji, that runs the nearby meditation center. On the far side of the dam, Peters Creek drains water from the lake, and you cross the creek on a wooden bridge.

Now the trail zigzags uphill through forest to a fence with a gate that prevents access by bikes and horses during wet weather. (When the gate is closed, hikers can pass through a narrow gap in the fence.) Just beyond the gate is a four-way junction atop Long Ridge, at about the two-mile point. Here, you meet Ward Road, a dirt road, just where it makes a sharp bend and nearly doubles back on itself. On the outside of the bend, Long Ridge Road, also dirt, heads right, along the ridge top. From here, you have a fabulous view that extends westward across the Pescadero Creek drainage to the Pacific Ocean. You turn right and follow the spectacularly situated road, which is bordered by coast live oak, canyon oak, and interior live oak.

Leaving the ridge top, you enjoy a rolling course through mostly open terrain that brings you in about 0.5 mile to the Wallace Stegner memorial bench, which is just left of the road. Stegner, one of California's best-loved writers and a tireless advocate for land preservation, lived from 1909 to 1993. In the 1960s, Stegner and others bought about 400 acres of land that later became the genesis of this preserve. The bench was built and dedicated to Stegner's memory by the District in 1996. This is certainly a fine place for the appreci-

---

To shorten this route, turn right, climb gently for 0.4 mile, and veer right on the Long Ridge Trail near gate LR12. Your route, now a single track, meanders and climbs through stands of black oak, a deciduous species told by its deeply lobed, bristle-tipped leaves that turn yellow and orange in autumn. Emerging abruptly onto a southwest-facing hillside, you find a dense grove of gorgeous manzanita thriving on the often sun-drenched slope. Crossing a private driveway and now back in the woods, you continue straight on a level track that soon begins to curve to the right. Topping a low rise, the trail now starts a winding descent on a moderate and then steep grade. When you reach the junction with Peters Creek Trail that you passed earlier, turn left and retrace your route to the parking area.

ation of open space, as you are surrounded by thousands of protected acres, including District lands of the South Skyline Region; San Mateo and Santa Clara county parks; and state parks such as Big Basin Redwoods, Castle Rock, Portola Redwoods, and Butano. Just past the Stegner bench, the road reaches gate LR04 and private property. Your route, the single-track Long Ridge Trail, veers right from the road.

After about 100 feet you come to another seasonal-closure gate. Once past it, you enter dense forest and contour across a hillside that falls away to the right. Joining the massive Douglas-fir trees here are beautiful madrones with orange bark and bright green leaves, and canyon oaks carpeted with thick tufts of moss. Crossing a saddle, you begin to descend via curves and switch-backs, soon reaching a junction in a clearing. Here, your trail crosses a dirt road that runs between gate LR12, which is just across the clearing and

The old orchard still has apple trees that bloom in spring and make fruit in fall.

The Wallace Stegner memorial bench, just off Long Ridge Road

slightly left, and the Peters Creek Trail, which is about 0.4 mile to your right. You find the continuation of the Long Ridge Trail on the other side of the clearing. From here, follow the directions for the shorter version of the hike (see sidebar on page 121) beginning near gate LR12.

DISTRICT RANGERS

District rangers are based in two regional offices—the Foothills office, located at Rancho San Antonio Preserve, and the Skyline office, located at Skyline Ridge Preserve. David Sanguinetti is superintendent of the District's Skyline office. He was hired as a ranger in 1980. "There were eight rangers and one supervisor, and that's all there was," he says. "There were no technicians, there were no seasonals, there were just the nine of us. And the operations supervisor was rarely in the field. We did everything from foot patrols to vehicle patrols. In those days, we were so small, and people hadn't discovered us yet, so there was little use of the preserves. At Rancho San Antonio we would be assigned an eight-hour foot patrol, and we would carry a backpack with a radio, and wear our ranger hat. We would walk the trails of the preserve and see if we could find visitors. I would spend an eight-hour day on a Saturday in the middle of summer and see maybe three visitors in Rancho San Antonio and that was it." Now, of course, Rancho San Antonio Preserve is the District's busiest preserve, with the large parking areas on weekends often full before noon.

The original District patrol vehicle was a 1974 Volkswagen Thing, which Sanguinetti said was hilarious. "I used to patrol in that," he says. "I would put the top down, drop the front window down, and drive through Rancho with my ranger hat on, and it was a kick." At that time the District logo resembled a leafy green plant known for its mood-elevating properties. The Thing wore one proudly, as did the rangers on their uniforms. The Thing also had a big bullhorn on the left front fender, red and yellow emergency lights on the back, and a siren. "It was a very user-friendly vehicle," says Sanguinetti. "One of the things I like is to connect with the public—that's why I got this job. I really like to help the public enjoy the preserves, and I love to hear the stories they have to tell. I find when I'm in a patrol truck, it's very standoffish. People don't want to come up to you when you're in this patrol truck with a light bar—it stands up real big, you're up in it, you've got this fire pumper on the back. They just kind of stay away from you. When you came up in the Thing, they came to you like it was a magnet."

Protection of District land is a ranger's most important duty. This can encompass law enforcement, fire prevention, public education, understanding of usage patterns at existing preserves, and preparing newly acquired preserves for public use. There are two qualifications for being a successful ranger, Skyline office Supervising Ranger Dennis Danielson says. "I think number one is just to know the District lands. To know the trail systems. To know the boundaries. To be able to interpret the maps. To know what is actually owned by the public and what you are responsible for. I think second is high interpersonal communication skills. Being able to talk to

Education is an important part of a ranger's job. "Back then, a lot of it was educating people about the District," says David Topley, support services supervisor and former ranger, "for example, about how the District started from a group of people meeting in their living rooms with an idea to preserve the open space. It was put on the ballot, and it was voted on by the people. I'd start telling this story, that it was an agency created by the people, so you can use this land and not have it developed into homes or into shopping centers. We rangers saw the people out there that had some appreciation for open space." Topley says that one of the biggest challenges the District faced at its inception, and still faces today, was to regulate use yet preserve public access, and balance the needs of various user groups.

Over the years, District rangers have amassed a treasure-trove of stories, some of which become folklore. Sanguinetti tells a classic from Monte Bello Preserve: "I was on patrol one day, and I was driving down Canyon Trail. I saw something moving, and it looked like a dog with its head in a log. So I get out and I walk over, and sure enough, this dog has got its head stuck in this hollowed-out log. And I can't get it out and he can't get it out, and he's backing up all the time, dragging this log. And the dog really looks distressed, like he's been there for awhile. So I ended up using a screwdriver and picking away at the log. I eventually was able to break the log apart. The dog had been bitten by termites and carpenter ants that were in there. He had his tags, and we were able to locate his owner. Apparently, he'd been gone for three days, and they couldn't figure out what happened. Chances are he had that thing on his head for a couple of days and was just stuck there off in the brush. I just happened to see him. So that was an interesting rescue. You don't see a dog's head in a log every day."

people. To explain a feature of the land. Or, if it's an enforcement situation, 90 percent of our enforcement is a verbal warning. Even if somebody is getting a citation or a written warning, you should be able to explain why the rule exists. So we certainly take an educational and interpretive approach to rule enforcement."

Danielson says he finds public contact a rewarding part of his job. "I always enjoy meeting people on the trail or in the parking lot, explaining the natural history, the geology, or the Native American history, or even some of the other local history. And also sharing the District's mission."

David Topley is the District's support services supervisor. In 1980, he was hired as a ranger. "The role of the ranger back then was patrolling District land," he says. "At that time, a lot of it was newly acquired, and a lot of it was not known to the public. Much of the use was from people that were using the lands before the District acquired it. It was mostly motorcycles and shooting practice." In the early days, Topley says, there were no open space technicians, so the rangers also spent part of each year building trails. "We used to build a few small parking lots and a lot of trails, and then just open up the lands to people. There were no bathrooms, no benches, and very few parking lots. When I first started working here the District didn't even own a tractor. Now we have tractors and dump trucks. A lot of the work was done by hand and a lot of hard work without mechanization."

Ranger Ken Miller was hired in 1992. "Even then, we were starting to spend a lot more time interacting with the public and doing less of the maintenance, which the open space technicians do now," he says. "The majority of our time is spent responding to people contacting us. How do we get to [Deer Hollow] Farm? What's a good trail to go on? Where can I ride my bike? Where can I take my dog? What are the other areas in the District we can go to? Is there a campground in the District? Mostly just basic questions. We give out maps to people. Redirect them when they want to take a dog where dogs are not allowed. We give them lots of different options of places they can go. Just trying to get all the user groups to interact in a positive way."

Former District Ranger Tom Randall and Supervising Ranger Brendan Downing carry out an injured preserve visitor on a straight backboard as part of a training exercise.

Rangers participate in a variety of District programs that involve volunteers from the community. "Through the years, I have really come to enjoy working with the volunteers," says ranger Ken Miller. "I've realized that they're a great resource and you can get a lot of work done with them. Specifically with nonnative, invasive plant removal, but even with maintenance and fence building projects." Miller says he finds working with young people especially rewarding. "We don't get as much accomplished as you would with adults, but I think it's very important to instill a sense of stewardship in children and teenagers as early as possible. A lot of times we're contacted by school groups that have to complete service projects to graduate from high school. That's something I didn't have to do in school, but I think it's great."

Rangers are trained at the National Park Service's seasonal law enforcement academy in Santa Rosa, and are well versed in federal, state, and local laws. Rangers are sworn in as peace officers by the District Board of Directors under the California penal code. By direction of the board, they do not carry firearms, but are trained in their use. In addition to law enforcement training, rangers go through a basic wildland fire-fighting class, and classes in first-aid and CPR. About half of the rangers and many open space technicians are also emergency medical technicians (EMTs), although this is not required.

Some interactions with the public involve law enforcement situations, Miller says. "Law enforcement—in our training we're told it's a management tool. It's just another tool of the trade. Trying to get people to respect the resources, just straight-out education. Even if it's law enforcement, we're stopping people and just talking to them, letting them know what the rules and regulations are and also letting them know why we have certain rules. We're just trying to get all the different groups to get along together and be more respectful of other people. I tell people if everybody was courteous to each other, we wouldn't have rules and you wouldn't have rangers. And everybody would get along just fine. Unfortunately, it's maybe five percent or less of any user group that gives the rest of the user group a bad name. So most of the people we do interact with are very positive and very supportive of the District."

Among the most common enforcement situations rangers deal with are speeding mountain bicyclists and people with off-leash dogs. "We're always striving to use law enforcement as an educational tool," says ranger Carrie

Sparks-Hart. "But we do enforce infractions and misdemeanors. I'm always trying to use the lowest level of enforcement to gain compliance. I think over time you just get experience on whether the individual might do it again or if giving a verbal warning is good enough. If I have a dog off leash or a speeding bicyclist, I'm going to use the facts to make up my mind if the individual will receive a citation or not. But even if I do give a dog-off-leash ticket, I always want to explain to the people why I'm doing it. Sometimes people don't care and sometimes they disagree. The thing to remember is that even though I do this every day, for the individual walking down the trail, it may be the first time they've ever been to an open space preserve."

In addition to their law enforcement duties, District rangers are always on call to respond to medical emergencies and wildland fires, working closely with the California Department of Forestry and air-ambulance services. "That's something that takes precedence," Sparks-Hart says. "We always have to be ready to drop what we're doing and be available to respond. I've responded to equestrian accidents. A lot of bicyclists with broken clavicles or head injuries, because more than likely where they're going to go is over the handlebars. So you see a lot of dislocated shoulders and a lot of broken clavicles. The priority is the patient, obviously. Get to the patient first. And call in—usually the local firefighters and paramedics come. If it's a place where we can drive, we'll load up the paramedics in our truck and take them to the patient. After we evaluate them, if that's what their needs are, we strap them to a backboard and put them in a patrol truck. Sometimes you have to carry them on a straight backboard. And that's very, very labor intensive. We've used a wheel-litter. It's basically like a cup-shaped backboard with a wheel. Those are nice because we can wheel them out rather than carry them."

Each ranger is assigned a truck equipped with maintenance tools, safety and first-aid equipment, and fire-fighting gear. Personal equipment consists of law enforcement tools such as handcuffs, a baton, and pepper spray, and first-aid supplies and equipment. Additionally, rangers may carry natural-history field guides to answer questions from preserve visitors about the flora and fauna they encounter on the trails. At the District, both rangers and open space technicians perform maintenance work. Among the maintenance duties rangers perform are clearing trails of fallen trees, digging ditches across trails to channel water and help prevent erosion, building and repairing fences, putting up trail signs, and resource management projects.

Sparks-Hart describes her daily schedule. "We have an early shift, a middle shift, and a late shift," she says. "The early shifts and the middle shifts are consistent. But the late shift changes with the time of year. In the summertime we'll be working later. I report to the Foothills office, and usually it starts off with some administrative duties like looking at my mail, my in-box. We have preserves that are considered our area of responsibility. Each ranger has two or three preserves. So what that means—area of responsibility—is I try and spend more time in those preserves. And if there's a work order, which is a maintenance detail assigned to me, that's the other stuff I do. I take care of those—fencing projects or cleaning out culverts or whatever. But really, the beauty of what I do is the flexibility and my own sense of what I feel needs to be done. I can prioritize what I need to do, unless my supervisor wants something done immediately. So I can go through and make my own decisions as far as the timelines that I have for those projects."

Each day is different, Sparks-Hart says, but she likes to spend as much time in the field as possible. "This morning I took care of my administrative duties," she says. "Then I was headed for Fremont Older to go on foot patrol, because it's been awhile since I'd been out on the Seven Springs Trail. But I got called back to Rancho San Antonio County Park, because somebody had locked their dog in their vehicle when they went for a run. So I had to come back and make sure the dog was okay and not overheated. Luckily, the person had cracked the windows and parked in the shade, so the dog was fine." Rangers patrol on foot, on mountain bicycles, in District vehicles, and on all-terrain vehicles during wet weather. "We have a list in our office of areas that are farther out," Sparks-Hart says, "or areas that are single-track trails that we need to monitor. So you glance at the board, and if nobody's been to the end of Stevens Canyon to hike up into Monte Bello for awhile, that would be something that I would look at and take the initiative to do."

What's the best thing about being a District ranger? That depends on whom you ask. "Getting to be outside," says Miller. "Being able to work outside in a natural environment. That's the perk that I really enjoy. Physical exercise. You have to be in good shape to do the job. That's something that means a lot to me. I really enjoy not having to deal with fee collection, picnic areas, trash, and parking lot problems. So for me it's getting out on the trails." Sparks-Hart says that flexibility is the best part of being a District ranger. "If I know Rancho San Antonio is busy, it's a great opportunity for me to be accessible to the public, whether on bike patrol or on foot. And if a drainage in Sierra Azul needs to be checked, it's a great opportunity to visit one of the District's more remote preserves. A variety of activities is encouraged."

Spring cumulus clouds puff high above Monte Bello Ridge.

LOS TRANCOS
OPEN SPACE PRESERVE

~

Wandering amid venerable oaks, fragrant bays, colorful bigleaf maples, and impressive Douglas-firs, you can complete two scenic loops in the headwaters of Los Trancos Creek. Open grasslands offer vantage points from which views extend northwest along the Peninsula to San Francisco and Mt. Tamalpais. The San Andreas fault also runs through the middle of this 274-acre preserve.

Part of the border between Santa Clara and San Mateo counties follows Los Trancos Creek, and thus Los Trancos Preserve is in two counties. According to Herb Grench, former District general manager, this presented something of a challenge prior to 1976, because the District had been approved only by Santa Clara County voters. "Well, the interesting thing was that it spanned two counties," he says. "And we hadn't even annexed into San Mateo County. But politically it was interesting, because it showed that a regional open space district, if it's going to do its job preserving these large expanses of natural lands and habitat, really can't be constricted by artificial political boundaries like a county line."

Near the start of the San Andreas Fault Trail is a memorial bench honoring Stan Norton, a District founder and its attorney from 1973 to 1994. The inscription on the bench, which sits atop a wildflower-fringed knoll, reads: "Still keeping an eye on Stanford and Palo Alto." District General Manager Craig Britton tells how that wording came about. "I got an option to buy some property from Stanford called Black Mountain Ranch, and it was the former Morell property. And there was an alumnus of Stanford that decided we weren't paying enough for it. And he was mad at us for reasons before my time. So Stanford tried to back out of the deal."

Riding on Sunday afternoon; Louis Oneal is leading on his favorite horse "Captain," a palomino. Photograph taken near the former Lori's Stables area of Monte Bello Open Space Preserve, which is located across Page Mill Road from Los Trancos Preserve.

Britton describes a high-level meeting with Stanford representatives, attended by himself and Norton. "Stan was a really incredible guy. He graduated from Stanford Law School. He was the editor of *The Chaparral*, the humor paper there. Anyway, at this meeting the Stanford representatives said they were going to back out of this deal, where we already had a binding contract. So they turned to us and said, 'Well, what is your response?' And Stan looked at them and said, 'We'll sue your ass.' They were kind of taken aback, but we finally did work it out. . . . Every once in a while I go to that bench and just sit there and remember Stan. A smile comes to my face every time. From a legal standpoint he was kind of a minimalist, he didn't like written opinions or lawsuits. If we just did our thing and didn't worry

about it too much, we'd be okay. And that served us well for a long time."

Once part of a 13,300-acre rancho in the nineteenth century, the land that was to become Los Trancos Preserve was purchased in the early 1900s by Louis Oneal, a San Jose attorney and state senator who raised horses and owned the nearby O & O Breeding Stables. Oneal also terraced some of the hillsides near Page Mill Road for vineyards. The property changed hands in the 1950s, and in the 1960s Palo Alto ran water and power lines to it, in anticipation of residential development. The Livingston–Blayney report detailing the high cost of providing city services to the foothills stopped a proposed subdivision. The District acquired most of the property in 1976. The preserve has about five miles of trails, approximately three miles of which are for hiking only.

Los Trancos Trail Use

Bicycles: Not allowed

Dogs: Not allowed

Horses: Allowed only on the Page Mill Trail

LOS TRANCOS OPEN SPACE PRESERVE

Trip 11. Double Loop

Length: 2.3 miles

Time: 1 to 2 hours

Rating: Moderate

Highlights: This route combines two scenic loops, the Franciscan Loop Trail and the Lost Creek Loop Trail, to explore a small, wedge-shaped preserve that is rich in geological and botanical interest. The San Andreas fault runs through the preserve. Oaks, bays, bigleaf maples, and Douglas-firs provide a protective canopy for an assortment of native shrubs and wildflowers. Along the way, visitors will descend to the headwaters of Los Trancos Creek (which forms part of the border between San Mateo and Santa Clara counties). You can easily combine this route with the self-guiding San Andreas Fault Trail, which is described next.

Directions: From I-280 in Los Altos Hills, take the Page Mill Road/Arastradero Road exit and go south on Page Mill Road 7.2 miles to a parking area on your right. This parking area is just a few hundred feet past the parking area for Monte Bello Preserve, which is on the left.

Trip 11. Double Loop

 From the two District information boards at the trailhead, you head north on the Franciscan Loop Trail. On a clear day, you are immediately rewarded with a sweeping view that stretches up the Peninsula to San San Francisco and takes in the hulking forms of San Bruno Mountain and Mt. Tamalpais. After about seventy-five feet, the single-track trail forks. The right-hand branch, an unofficial trail, climbs a low rise, offers additional views, and rejoins the Franciscan Loop Trail. Staying left, you cross a weedy field full of coyote brush, oats, and some thistle. The depression on your left, marked with white-striped posts to indicate minor fault breaks from the 1906 earthquake, is

From the junction of Skyline Boulevard and Page Mill Road/Alpine Road south of Palo Alto, take Page Mill Road north 1.4 miles to a parking area on your left. The parking area for Monte Bello Preserve is just a few hundred feet past this parking area, on the right.

Facilities: None here, but there is a vault toilet in the Monte Bello Preserve parking area across Page Mill Road.

Trailhead: At the northeast corner of the parking area

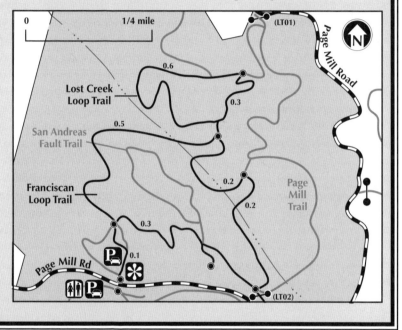

a sag pond. Sag ponds are found in fault zones and landslide areas, where the land has sunk because of earth movement. These ponds often fill with water during winter and become freshwater marshes.

Approximately 100 yards from the trailhead, you are joined sharply from the left by a trail that leaves the parking area's west side and passes the San Andreas Fault Trail's stations 1 and 2. Ahead another 150 feet or so is the next junction. Here the Franciscan Loop Trail goes both left and straight. The San Andreas Fault Trail, which for part of its length follows the Franciscan Loop Trail, is straight. The unofficial trail mentioned previously joins sharply from the right. Bear left and descend through a shady corridor of canyon oak, valley oak, black oak, tanbark oak, madrone, California bay, bigleaf maple, and Douglas-fir. The understory is lush with coffeeberry, hazelnut, poison oak, ferns, and berry vines.

Now on a rolling course, you cross a bridge and then follow the trail, which is lined with snowberry, gooseberry, and oceanspray, to a T-junction with the Lost Creek Loop Trail. Here you turn left and after about seventy-five feet pass the returning end of the Lost Creek Loop Trail on your right. Continuing straight, you climb a bit and then find level ground. Crossing under two sets of power lines, you now begin to lose elevation on a gentle grade. In a dense forest, you work your way down a ridge via switchbacks to the bank of Los Trancos Creek. In Spanish, *tranco* means stride or big step, and *tranca* is a bar or barrier. Gudde's *California Place Names* favors a corruption of the latter to explain this creek's name: perhaps there were barriers here at one time to prevent cattle from crossing it, or perhaps the creek itself formed a natural barrier.

The creek bed is rocky and full of fallen tree limbs and branches. Elk clover and thimbleberry thrive in this moist, shady environment. Walking downstream, you have the creek on your left. Soon, the trail finds a level course, but the creek cuts its way into an ever-deepening canyon. Hedge nettle, hound's tongue, milkmaids, Solomon's seal, Pacific starflower, and trillium are a few of the many forest wildflowers found in this preserve. Now your route curves right and follows a tributary of Los Trancos Creek (which may be dry) upstream. Just past the 1-mile point, you reach a junction. Here the Page Mill Trail goes sharply left and also straight, joining the Lost Creek Loop Trail for several hundred yards. You continue straight.

At the next junction, say goodbye to the Page Mill Trail by following the Lost Creek Loop Trail as it turns sharply right. Now you ascend via switchbacks into a brighter realm, where a short boardwalk helps you through a marshy area. Just past the raised trail is a good place to see bleeding hearts in spring. Reaching a T-junction where the two ends of the Lost Creek Loop Trail join, you turn left and retrace your route for about seventy-five feet. Here at the junction with the Franciscan Loop Trail, you continue straight, then curve right and begin to climb through an area of rock outcrops. Where a connector to the Page Mill Trail departs uphill and left, stay right, passing through another possibly wet area.

The trail now wanders through the hills that give rise to Los Trancos Creek, soon passing a very short trail to gate LT02 on Page Mill Road. At a T-junction with the San Andreas Fault Trail, right, you turn left and immediately confront a fork. Angling left is a short trail to the San Andreas Fault Trail's interpretive station 3. Here, during the 1906 earthquake, the ground opened along the San Andreas fault. Later, it filled in, forming the flat area, or bench, you see now. Bearing right at the fork to stay on the Franciscan Loop Trail, you climb via switchbacks between a line of trees, right, and open meadow, left. At the four-way junction where you began this loop, simply continue straight and retrace your route to the parking area.

*Entrance sign and information boards on the north side of the
Los Trancos Open Space Preserve parking area*

Los Trancos Trail Use

Bicycles:	Not allowed
Dogs:	Not allowed
Horses:	Allowed only on the Page Mill Trail

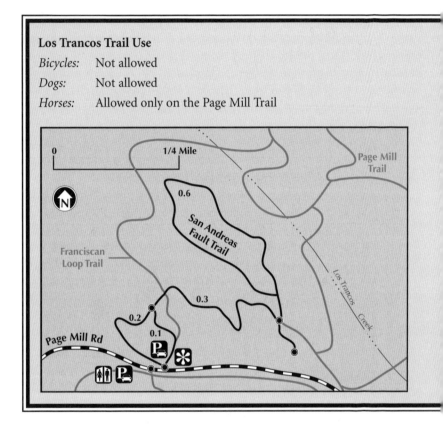

Trip 12. San Andreas Fault Trail

From the trailhead, you go through a gap in a low split-rail fence and get on a rocky single track that climbs through brushy terrain. As you gain elevation, the views northward up the Peninsula on a clear day are quite rewarding. From station **1** on this self-guiding trail, you can look southeast to Monte Bello Ridge, Stevens Creek Canyon, Mt. Umunhum, and Loma Prieta. The San Andreas fault, which divides the North American and Pacific plates, runs through Stevens Creek Canyon. The epicenter of the 1989 earthquake was not far from Loma Prieta, and geologists named the devastating quake for that peak.

Station **2** sits atop a hill, and from this elevated vantage point you have views northwest along the San Andreas fault to Crystal Springs Reservoir and San Andreas Lake. On a grassy slope dotted with California buttercup, blue-eyed grass, and purple owl's-clover is a stone bench honoring Stan Norton,

LOS TRANCOS OPEN SPACE PRESERVE

Trip 12. San Andreas Fault Trail

Length: 1.5 miles

Time: 1 hour or less

Rating: Easy

Highlights: This self-guiding trail was created in 1977 by former Foothill College geology professor Tim Hall, his father Nick Hall, and geology students from Foothill College, to illustrate features of the San Andreas fault, which runs through the preserve. **Boldface** numbers in the route description refer to numbered posts along the trail, which mark interpretive stations. The numbers are keyed to text in the District's Los Trancos Preserve map/ brochure, paraphrased in the following description. You can easily combine this route with "Double Loop," described on the preceding pages.

Directions: Same as for "Double Loop" on pages 134–35

Facilities: None here, but there is a vault toilet in the Monte Bello Preserve parking area, across Page Mill Road.

Trailhead: At the west side of the parking area

one of the District's founders and its attorney from 1973 through 1994. The inscription on the bench, "Still keeping an eye on Stanford and Palo Alto," refers to Norton's tireless efforts in support of open space and his role as a watchdog over public and private entities that often favored development over preservation.

Turning right, you descend on a gentle grade in the direction of the parking area. Joining the everpresent coyote brush here are gooseberry, blue witch, and a tangle of berry vines. Soon you merge with the single-track Franciscan Loop Trail, which leaves the parking area from its northeast corner. Bear left and wander past stands of canyon oak, coffeeberry, and blue elderberry. At a four-way junction, you go straight, following the conjoined Franciscan Loop and San Andreas Fault Trails. Curving right, the trail passes a grove of coast live oak and then crosses an open, grassy hillside. Several switchbacks help you lose elevation on a gentle grade.

This is how a fence built across the fault might have looked immediately after the 1906 earthquake. This fence has been reconstructed from century-old materials found on the preserve.

Although earthquake geology is the main attraction of this route, there is plenty here for plant lovers to enjoy, including trees, such as California bay and California buckeye, and many native shrubs, among them toyon, hazelnut, oceanspray, snowberry, and wood rose. After a final switchback, you come to station **3** and a junction. Sharply right is a trail that goes about 100 feet to a fence. Beside this trail are several wood posts with yellow bands. These posts mark the main fault break from the 1906 earthquake. (Posts with white bands mark the minor fault breaks.)

Just past station **3** is a junction. Here the Franciscan Loop Trail goes right, but you continue straight on the San Andreas Fault Trail. You have just crossed the San Andreas fault from the Pacific to the North American plate. Now in dense forest, you soon come to stations **4**, **5**, and **6**. When you come to station **7**, look just ahead to locate two oaks, one on each side of the trail, that sprout vertical limbs from horizontal trunks. The trees date from 1899, and the 1906 quake may have knocked them to the ground without destroying their roots, thereby causing their unusual growth pattern.

The trail snakes its way downhill to station **8**, indicating a small valley just left of the trail. At station **9**, the trail crosses the main fault again, and now you are back on the North American plate, enjoying the shade of bigleaf maples and Douglas-fir. After crossing a creek that drains through a culvert, you curve right and climb on a gentle grade. A sharp left-hand bend brings you to a T-junction and the end of the San Andreas Fault Trail loop. Here you turn left and retrace your route to the junction of the Franciscan Loop and San Andreas Fault Trails several hundred feet north of the parking area. From here, you continue straight to the parking area.

The San Andreas Fault

Los Trancos Preserve is an ideal spot to learn about earthquake geology. The San Andreas fault, one of the world's longest and most active faults, splits the preserve. The 1.5-mile self-guiding interpretive trail gives visitors a chance to learn more about the lead player on California's geological stage. The San Andreas Fault Trail was established in 1977 with volunteer assistance from former Foothill College geology professor Tim Hall and his students.

*Looking south, view of Monte Bello Open Space Preserve
and Stevens Creek Canyon*

MONTE BELLO
OPEN SPACE PRESERVE

~

The name of this preserve speaks of a time in the nineteenth century when Italian farmers and winemakers settled on the flanks of a ridge they named Monte Bello or "beautiful mountain." In earlier times, the Spanish called these hills *Sierra Morena,* meaning brown mountains. Dominating the skyline (as seen from Palo Alto to Cupertino) Monte Bello Ridge and its high point, 2,800-foot Black Mountain, form a scenic backdrop that is unsurpassed on the Peninsula. Stevens Creek, which empties into San Francisco Bay, gets its start in the shady, oak-filled canyons at the northwest end of the preserve. There are about fifteen miles of trails to explore at this 2,954-acre preserve. Stevens Creek Canyon, which you can visit on the self-guiding Stevens Creek Nature Trail, is a fine example of riparian habitat, complete with ferns, banana slugs, and California newts.

Coyotes, bobcats, deer, and even mountain lions roam the preserve's grasslands. Snakes and lizards may join you on the trail. Birding here is superb. The open fields attract aerial predators, such as red-tailed hawks. Rough-legged hawks, prairie falcons, and merlins are sighted occasionally, as are golden eagles. Scan the grassy meadows for lazuli buntings and western bluebirds. Woodlands are home to various species of owls, including great horned, barn, pygmy, and northern saw-whet. Virginia rails are sometimes found in the sag ponds. Mountain quail sometimes may be found here, usually in winter. Other notables include fox sparrow, sage sparrow, red crossbill, purple finch, and black-headed grosbeak.

From high atop Black Mountain, you have 360° views that take in most of the San Francisco Bay Area, including other summits, such as Mt. Tamalpais, Mt. Diablo, Mt. Hamilton, and Mt. Umunhum. San Jose, Santa Clara, and the southern shoreline of San Francisco Bay lie at your feet. The San Andreas fault runs along the base of Monte Bello Ridge and bisects the preserve, making this a particularly exciting place for those interested in Bay Area geology. Everything west of the fault is part of the Salinian formation, a chunk of southern Sierra Nevada granite that has slid northwest over millions of years. The Franciscan formation, which extends through the Bay Area to the Central Valley, is east of the fault. Black Mountain, which has rocks unlike any found in the surrounding area, is an anomaly. Research indicates that it may have been formed near the equator as a tropical island more than 100 million years ago.

Until the building of the Golden Gate Bridge provided easy access to Marin County, dairies in the Santa Cruz Mountains supplied much of the milk for San Francisco and the Peninsula. There was a large dairy near the preserve's main parking area on Page Mill Road. Cattle roamed the slopes of Monte Bello Ridge and grazed freely. Ranch buildings dotted the landscape. Winemaking was also an important part of life in these hills, and you can still find evidence of terraced vineyards where families grew and harvested grapes. Portuguese and Italian farmers provided much of the labor and expertise for both the dairy and the wine industry here. (The nearby Picchetti Ranch Preserve contains a fine example of an historic winery.)

During the counterculture era of the late 1960s and early 1970s, the area along what is today the Canyon Trail from Page Mill Road to Indian Creek and over to the Stevens Creek Nature Trail was the site of a commune called The Land. Possibly as many as 100 people took up residence, and built a variety of dwellings on platforms scattered over about 700 acres of oak woodlands and secluded canyons. There was a large ranch building used as a central dining hall, and other preexisting structures were used as a woodworking shop, a stained-glass workshop, and a food store selling bulk items. Commune members, many of them pacifists opposed to the Vietnam War, grew their own food in gardens, followed artistic pursuits, and gathered for holiday dinners and celebrations.

Unfortunately, the commune was within Palo Alto city limits, and none of the homemade dwellings complied with city building codes or zoning laws. The property, which at one time had been proposed for a residential subdivision and then a cemetery, was in the process of being sold, and the buyer and seller got into a squabble that resulted in mutual lawsuits. At one point, the seller tried to evict commune members and bulldoze their dwellings, but a mass protest stopped these actions.

The District, which had approached both buyer and seller, finally acquired the property in 1977. The commune and its members, who were reportedly happy that the land was being preserved as open space, were nonetheless dismayed at having to leave. The former owner eventually evicted the people, considered tres-passers, prior to District acquisition. The District then demolished the dwellings, and restored the area to its former state. The District had planned to preserve one or two of the dwellings, but they mysteriously burned down. For a long time after the District took possession of the property, someone repeatedly cut down District fencing along Skyline Boulevard. The trespassing situation connected with this acquisition was one of the District's most controversial to date, and the rancor surrounding the eviction lasted for several years.

Legends about gold and gold mining are part of California's history, and Monte Bello Preserve has its very own story, concerning a gentleman called Indian Joe and a "ledge of gold." District general manager Craig Britton picks up the tale: "In 1983, I got a call from a woman who said that her father knew the whereabouts of a ledge of gold," he says. "And he would show us where it is, if he could have half the proceeds from the sale of the gold. It was an incredible story, and I couldn't resist the offer to meet with him and his daughter and tape his testimony."

"Apparently, he used to bring provisions to an Indian who lived down there at Indian Cabin Creek," says Britton. "This was at the turn of the century. To pay for the provisions, he would pull out one of the turkey feathers in his head dress and tap gold dust out of the quill of the feather. Apparently, every one of his feathers was full of gold dust. So he followed the old Indian up the ravine, and found one of those underground aquifers bubbling up, and the gold dust would just accumulate around the edges. The old Indian would take his feather and just fill the hollow quill with the gold dust."

Britton arranged a ranger tour of Monte Bello Preserve in a District vehicle for the old man and his daughter, explained that the District would never remove the gold, so it wasn't necessary to reveal the location. The old man died not long afterward, and he took the secret of the ledge of gold with him. Britton says he heard later that members of The Land commune had combed the nearby hills looking for gold but had never found a speck. Names such as Indian Creek and Gold Mine Creek seem to suggest that the legend has some truth, and there are those who say Indian Joe struck it rich and buried his treasure somewhere in the hills below Black Mountain.

Monte Bello Preserve borders on Rancho San Antonio Preserve and Upper Stevens Creek County Park, and there are easy trail connections to other District preserves in the South Skyline Region, allowing for long-distance travel. Mountain bicyclists will especially enjoy the many challenging routes available in this and adjoining parks and preserves. The Canyon Trail follows

Monte Bello Trail Use

Bicycles: Allowed on all trails except the Stevens Creek Nature Trail

Dogs: Not allowed

Horses: Allowed on all trails except the Stevens Creek Nature Trail

MONTE BELLO OPEN SPACE PRESERVE

Trip 13. Black Mountain

Length: 6 miles

Time: 3 to 4 hours

Rating: Difficult

Highlights: This challenging but supremely rewarding loop gains and then loses about 1,000 feet on its journey from the riparian corridor along Stevens Creek to the windswept grasslands of Monte Bello Ridge.

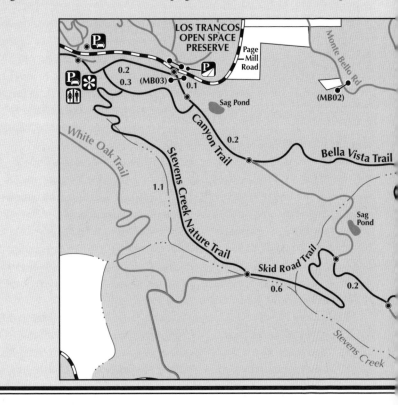

Using the Stevens Creek Nature Trail, Monte Bello Road, and the Canyon, Skid Road, and Indian Creek Trails, the route takes you across the San Andreas fault and then up the ridge that forms the scenic backdrop for Sunnyvale, Cupertino, and Mountain View. The views from Black Mountain (the summit of Monte Bello Ridge) are superb, and the descent along the Old Ranch and Bella Vista Trails offers some of the best hiking in the District.

Directions: From I-280 in Los Altos Hills, take the Page Mill Road/Arastradero Road exit and go south on Page Mill Road 7.2 miles to a parking area on your left. From the junction of Skyline Boulevard and Page Mill Road south of Palo Alto, take Page Mill Road north 1.4 miles to a parking area on your right.

Facilities: Vault toilet

Trailhead: At the southeast corner of the parking area

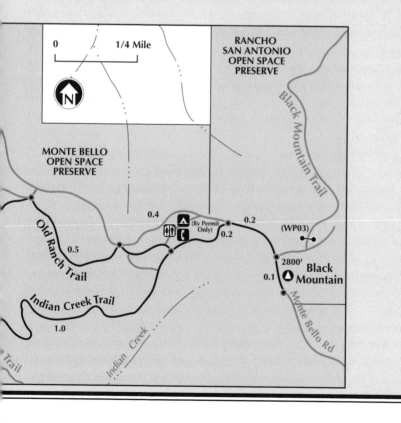

a historic ranch route connecting Stevens Canyon Road and Page Mill Road. Stevens Creek is named for Elisha Stephens, who in 1844 led the first wagon train across the Sierra Nevada. Born in North Carolina in 1804, Stephens became a blacksmith and went west, landing in Council Bluffs, Iowa. He captained the Stephens-Murphy-Townsend party and led its eleven wagons safely into California, via the Truckee River and the pass that now bears the name of a later, ill-fated party.

The first 500 feet of the Stevens Creek Nature Trail, beginning from the main parking area on Page Mill Road, can accommodate a wide array of physical abilities, although it is not officially designated an "Easy Access Trail." At the end of this short trail segment, visitors will find a rest bench on a vantage point overlooking the upper Stevens Creek watershed. The parking area has two handicapped parking spaces and a wheelchair-accessible toilet.

Black Mountain backpack camp, located on the site of the former Black Mountain Ranch atop Monte Bello Ridge, is the only place on District lands where visitors can spend the night under the stars. Four single campsites and one group site are available to the public by permit for one or two overnight stays throughout the year. The camp is approximately 1.5 miles and a 500-foot climb from Page Mill Road. A vault toilet and water for washing are provided. The water is nonpotable; campers must bring a water purifier or carry in their own drinking water. Campfires are prohibited. Visitors must obtain a permit in advance from the District office: (650) 691-1200.

Trip 13. Black Mountain

Follow the route description for "Stevens Creek Nature Trail" on pages 150–51 to the junction of the Skid Road and Canyon Trails, where you turn right. The Canyon Trail, a dirt road, angles left and almost immediately begins a steep climb. Soon, however, the road finds a rolling course through terrain that alternates between wooded and open. At a T-junction around the 2-mile point, the Canyon Trail turns right, but you switch to the Indian Creek Trail, also a dirt road, by veering left. Now you begin a long, steady climb up the side of Monte Bello Ridge. This massive feature, which trends northwest–southeast, parallels the nearby San Andreas fault, which runs through Stevens Creek Canyon. Monte Bello Ridge is topped by a summit called Black Mountain (one of many peaks in California with that name). Seen from the cities of Sunnyvale, Cupertino, and Mountain View, Monte Bello Ridge dominates the skyline.

View to the west from the Black Mountain Summit

On a mostly moderate grade, you ascend past several gorgeous valley oaks, their twisted and outstretched limbs draped with lace lichen. Young madrone trees, with bright green leaves and orange bark, stand out beautifully against a background of dark green foliage. Coastal scrub—California sagebrush, coffeeberry, sticky monkeyflower, and poison oak—soon gives way to chaparral vegetation, here consisting mostly of chamise, toyon, buckbrush, hollyleaf cherry, spiny redberry, and yerba santa. Gaining elevation, you have ever-improving views of the nearby headwaters of Stevens Creek, and also of distant summits, such as Mt. Umunhum and Loma Prieta.

A stand of poplars to the right of the road indicates an approaching respite from the unshaded climb. Just ahead is the Black Mountain backpack camp, the District's only campground. Aiming for a gap on the skyline, the road soon reaches two closely spaced junctions. At the first, a single-track trail leads left to Monte Bello Road, bypassing the backpack camp. At the second, a dirt road veers left. To reach the Black Mountain backpack camp and a well-deserved rest spot, turn left on this dirt road. After about 100 feet, you come to a T-junction with a gravel road where you turn left. On the right side of this road is a sign commemorating former property owner George F. Morell and his Black Mountain Ranch. Also right is a group campsite. There is a phone on the left side of the road. A little farther ahead on the right are four individual camp-sites and a vault toilet. The water available here is nonpotable.

To press on to the summit of Black Mountain, stay on the Indian Creek Trail as it curves right and climbs past the turnoff to the backpack camp. The Indian Creek Trail ends at the next junction, and you join Monte Bello Road by bearing right. This dirt-and-gravel thoroughfare winds uphill past stands of interior live oak, California bay, scrub oak, silk tassel, and buckbrush. Look here for serviceberry, a shrub with almost-round leaves that are toothed only near the tip edge. Power lines overhead and communication towers to your left herald the approaching summit. Before reaching it, you pass the Black Mountain Trail, a dirt road that descends steeply through the upper reaches of the Rancho San Antonio Preserve.

Monte Bello Trail Use

Bicycles: Allowed on all trails except the Stevens Creek Nature Trail
Dogs: Not allowed
Horses: Allowed on all trails except the Stevens Creek Nature Trail

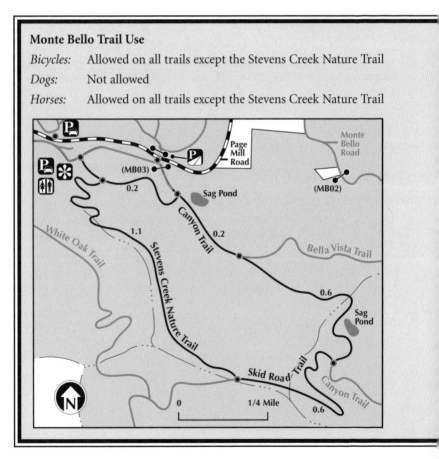

Continuing straight, you soon stand atop Black Mountain, marveling at the 360° views from the broad, rocky, and treeless vantage point. On a clear day, you can see most of the San Francisco Bay Area, bounded by Mt. Tamalpais, Mt. Diablo, and Mt. Hamilton. San Jose, Santa Clara, and the southern shoreline of San Francisco Bay lie at your feet. Once you have taken your fill of scenery, scan the sky for raptors, especially during spring and fall migrations. One of those on view may be a northern harrier, told by its long tail, white rump, and flight pattern, which is often low, skimming, and wobbly. This hunting bird was formerly called a marsh hawk, but its name was changed to more accurately reflect both its range and its hunting style. After enjoying this splendid summit, retrace your route to the backpack camp by turning left at the fork and following the trail directional sign to the camp.

MONTE BELLO OPEN SPACE PRESERVE

Trip 14. Stevens Creek Nature Trail

Length: 3 miles

Time: 2 to 3 hours

Rating: Moderate

Highlights: This delightful self-guiding loop uses the Stevens Creek Nature Trail, the Skid Road Trail, and the Canyon Trail to explore the north end of one of the District's larger and more fascinating preserves. Along the way, visitors will learn about some of the plants and animals that make the Santa Cruz Mountains such a complex and diverse place from a natural-history standpoint. Descending to densely forested Stevens Creek is a geological journey as well, because here you are crossing the San Andreas fault, at the junction where plates of the earth's crust collide.

Boldface text in the following route description refers to interpretive signs along the way. (During wet weather, it may be impossible to cross Stevens Creek, as is required on this trip).

Directions: Same as for "Black Mountain" on pages 146–47

Facilities: Vault toilet

Trailhead: Same as for "Black Mountain" on pages 146–47

Travel about 500 feet, swing right and continue 100 feet to join the gravel road. Turn left and walk through the backpack camp, which is nestled atop Monte Bello Ridge in a grove of coast live oak, Douglas-fir, and Fremont cottonwood. Just past the camp, you pass the single-track connector to the Indian Creek Trail, left. Continuing straight, follow the ridgetop between a screen of trees and shrubs, right, and open slopes on your left. At a four-way junction, Monte Bello Road joins sharply from the right, and continues ahead by veering right. Your route, though, is the single-track Old Ranch Trail, which angles left.

The trail contours through grassland and then winds its way gently downhill, offering superb hiking with terrific views. At the next junction, where a short connector goes right about 50 feet to Monte Bello Road, swing left onto the Bella Vista Trail, another single track. In places, the southwest-facing slope of Monte Bello Ridge is cut by gullies and ravines that carry rainwater to the upper reaches of Stevens Creek. These depressions are filled with trees and shrubs, including canyon oak, valley oak, and blue elderberry. When you reach the Canyon Trail, angle to the right and then follow the route description for "Stevens Creek Nature Trail" on pages 150–51.

Trip 14. Stevens Creek Nature Trail

Passing two District information boards and a map holder, follow the Stevens Creek Nature Trail, a single track, as it wanders through open grassland. After a couple of hundred yards, you reach **Vista Point**, marked by an interpretive sign, where you have a fine view of Stevens Creek Canyon, which formed along the San Andreas fault. Stevens Creek gathers water from the nearby hills and flows southeast through the canyon, then abruptly turns north on its journey to San Francisco Bay. In the distance are Mt. Umunhum, marked by the tell-tale building on its summit, and Loma Prieta, the flat-topped mountain to its right.

At a junction marked by a trail post and a rest bench, stay on the Stevens Creek Nature Trail by veering sharply right. The rest bench here honors the late Frances Brenner, a member of the Palo Alto City Council who was active in the conservation movement, especially with regard to protecting watersheds. Now descending via switchbacks across a hillside dotted with coyote brush and poison oak, you soon enter a forest of California bay, canyon oak, coast live oak, and madrone—a mixed evergreen forest. Four distinct plant communities are represented in this preserve: mixed evergreen forest, Douglas-fir forest, chaparral, and grassland. Factors such as soil type, sunlight, moisture, and wind, along with the effects of logging and fires, determine where different species of plants are found.

A **Bobcat** is a mostly nocturnal animal about twice the size of a house cat. Bobcats prey on rabbits, along with other small mammals and birds. Bobcats are fairly common on District lands, but these secretive and well-camouflaged predators may be hard to spot. A canyon, right, holds a seasonal tributary of Stevens Creek. Bigleaf maple, toyon, oceanspray, and ferns grow beside the trail. A sign marking a **Dead Tree** explains how nature finds a use for everything. As the wood decomposes, aided by bacteria, fungi, and insects, it supplies nutrients for other plants. Various animals, including woodpeckers, feed on insects that infest dead and dying trees. While still standing, such trees, called "snags," provide homes for birds, mammals, and reptiles.

Now the trail crosses several culverts, as it continues to drop into the canyon. Signs beside the trail indicate **Poison Oak**—"leaflets of three, let it be"—and **Edges**, the zones where two different plant communities merge. These zones are often good places to spot wildlife, including mammals and birds. Turning right, you cross a bridge over another seasonal tributary of Stevens Creek. Douglas-fir trees make their first appearance, and with them, perhaps a noisy Steller's jay or two. **Decomposers**, such as bacteria, fungi, and insects, are part of nature's recycling system. They break down dead plant materials and return nutrients to the soil. Dense growths of snowberry and wood rose line the route. One of our earliest seasonal wildflowers, milkmaids, may be plentiful here.

A sharp left-hand bend brings you to a set of wooden steps leading down to Stevens Creek. After crossing Stevens Creek on rocks (this may be impossible during wet weather) you climb an eroded bank to get back on the trail. The creek is a breeding area for the **California Newt**, a member of the salamander family. California newts are brown with an orange belly and a long, vertically flattened tail. Newts remain mostly hidden in rock crevices and under logs in summer, but during the rainy season they journey to their watery breeding grounds, often in large numbers. Newts are poisonous if eaten, and this apparently allows them to be active during the daytime when predators are about. If confronted with danger, a newt will arch its back, displaying its brightly colored belly.

Whereas newts are amphibians, the **Western Fence Lizard** is a reptile. Common in many habitats, including grassland, chaparral, and woodland, these small, brownish lizards are often seen sunning themselves on rocks, fence posts, and logs. (Medical research suggests that the ticks that feed on western fence lizards are incapable of transmitting Lyme disease.) A moderate climb that soon

Red-tailed hawk; photo taken at Skyline Ridge Open Space Preserve

Coyote looking through dried grass;
photo taken at Rancho San Antonio Open Space Preserve

Sag Pond at Monte Bello Open Space Preserve

levels brings you to a junction with the Skid Road Trail. Here you bear left on a dirt road, once traversed by teams of oxen dragging huge Douglas-firs and smaller tanbark oaks felled by loggers. To make the going easier, the road was inlaid with flat-topped logs called "skids," which were then periodically doused with water to reduce friction. In nineteenth-century Western towns, the neighborhood frequented by loggers, usually containing saloons, flop-houses, and brothels, was often called Skid Road or Skid Row.

Lush thickets of thimbleberry and a few currant bushes border the road. Your knowledge of **Animal Tracks** may help you identify the creatures that pass through the forest. Some common tracks, shown on a sign to the right of the trail, are those of raccoon, deer, bobcat, squirrel, and opossum. Just past the sign, a bridge takes you across a seasonal tributary flowing from right to left into Stevens Creek. Now cross Stevens Creek itself on a bridge, and then the route temporarily narrows to single-track width. Traversing a narrow ledge, you have the opportunity to admire a mass of western coltsfoot growing below in the creek bed. Coltsfoot is a streamside plant found in dense forests. It has large, almost-circular leaves cut with deep lobes. In spring and early summer, coltsfoot produces clusters of white-to-pink flowers rising atop a single stalk. It is reported that one group of Native Americans roasted the plant's deep green leaves on hot coals to produce salt.

A moderate climb brings you to a bridge over a tributary that falls from Monte Bello Ridge. Curving right and climbing steeply, the trail takes you across a precipitous hillside and soon returns to dirt-road width. Among the **Insects and Invertebrates** found nearby are buckeye butterflies, grass spiders, and—everyone's favorite—banana slugs. Now ascending via S-bends, you reach a fence with a gate that prevents access to the Skid Road Trail by bikes and horses during wet weather. (When the gate is closed, hikers can pass through a narrow gap in the fence.) In a clearing presided over by a large valley oak and several California buckeyes, you find a T-junction with the Canyon Trail, a dirt road. A sign here explains the concept of a **Food Chain**: plants take energy from the sun; small animals eat plants and their seeds; these animals in turn are preyed upon by larger animals.

Here you turn left and follow the Canyon Trail under the southwest-facing slopes of Monte Bello Ridge. The road passes a seasonally water-filled depres-sion called a "sag pond." Sag ponds are found in areas with earthquake and landslide activity, and with the San Andreas fault so close it is not surprising to find one here. Now the route curves left and climbs steeply through a dense forest of live oak, black oak, tanbark oak, and bay. After a curving ascent, turn sharply left, cross several culverts, and then find level ground. Passing an open, grassy slope on your right, you descend to a lovely grove of canyon oaks. Ahead is a rest bench and more open terrain. A moderate climb that soon eases brings you to the sign for **Coyote**.

The Coyote

The coyote is a California native member of the dog family that hunts and resides in most plant communities/environments found on District preserves. Although a rare sight to see, coyotes can be heard between the hours of twilight and dawn as they communicate with each other through high-pitched, yodel-like yelps. Coyotes are predators of small animals, including rabbits, mice, birds, and even young deer. Their diet is rounded out by feasts of seasonal fruits and berries.

Now you meet the Bella Vista Trail, which departs sharply to the right. Continuing straight on a level course, you pass stands of willows, dogwood, and cattails, indicating a wet area just ahead. To the left of the road is a swampy area, and on the right is another sag pond. This one formed along a curve in the San Andreas fault zone; as the Pacific and North American plates slipped past each other, a gap formed, creating a depression. Fed by a spring on Monte Bello Ridge, this sag pond is gradually becoming overgrown with cattails and pond lilies. In the future, it will fill with sediments, becoming first a wet meadow and then a forest. This process is called **Succession**.

After passing a rest bench, right, you come to a junction with a hiking-only trail on the left, not shown on the District map. Continue straight for about 100 yards and then turn left on the Stevens Creek Nature Trail, a single track also closed to bikes and horses. Now you pass through an old orchard of mostly English walnut trees, soon reaching a junction, left, with the previously mentioned hiking-only trail. Here bear right and leave the orchard behind, making a rising traverse across an open slope.

Raptors are carnivorous birds with hooked beaks and sharp talons, such as hawks, falcons, eagles, and owls. Common raptors here include red-tailed hawks, northern harriers, and American kestrels, all of which hunt over open grasslands. In spring and summer this hillside is decorated with colorful **Wildflowers**, including California poppy, checker mallow, purple owl's-clover, bluedicks, and blue-eyed grass. When you reach the junction where you started this loop, simply retrace your route to the parking area.

LIFE AT BLACK MOUNTAIN RANCH

Allan Lindh is a scientist retired from the United States Geological Survey in Menlo Park. In 1975, he was a graduate student in geophysics at Stanford. As part of a research project, he received permission to place geophysical instruments atop Monte Bello Ridge at Black Mountain Ranch, which Stanford had received as a gift from George Morell, a wealthy newspaper publisher. Expecting their second child, the Lindhs were looking for a new place to live. When Allan learned that Stanford needed a caretaker for Black Mountain Ranch, he applied and was accepted for the job. "We moved in January of 1975, and we lived there as caretakers for Stanford," he says. "We provided directions for people, and tried to keep the shooters, the hunters, and the four-wheel-drivers out." Lindh, his wife Julie, and their two children lived on the ranch for the next twenty years.

A collage of colorful wildflowers carpets the grasslands at many District preserves; photo taken at Russian Ridge Open Space Preserve.

Although privately owned for many years, Monte Bello Ridge has a long history of public use. "The Woodside horse people had it as part of their routine route," says Lindh. "It was private land all the way back to Page Mill Road or to Monte Bello Road at the other end. There's a through road there, a dirt road, and there was an understanding, which I think is probably correct, that it had once been a quasi-public road. But a lot of people hiked it, rode it on horseback. It was also at that point, however, used by motorcyclists, four-wheel-drivers, roughnecks looking for a place to shoot their guns, hunters looking for a place to poach deer. So life was fairly exciting. We got to know the county sheriffs pretty well, too."

After the District acquired the Stanford (Morell) property, the Lindhs stayed on as caretakers, reveling in the gorgeous sunsets, the waves of coastal fog pouring over the Santa Cruz Mountains, the storms, and the starry nights. "I'll probably start crying if I try to tell you," Lindh says. "It was the greatest place to live I've ever seen in the world. We had a 200° view of the

Pacific Ocean. We could see the Crystal Range above Lake Tahoe a few times a year on a really clear day. We had mountain lions in the front yard once or twice a year. Coyotes were daily companions right in the front yard. Coyotes singing at night were just part of our lives. Arguably we saw some of the greatest sunsets and sunrises in the world. Our nearest neighbor was a mile and a half away. We had wildflowers in the spring, and actually the wildflowers were better in those days, because Stanford was still leasing the land out for grazing. Oh, that's the other thing, there were still cattle on the land. And that actually helps the wildflowers because they graze the grass down in the spring. So the wildflowers show up much more prominently—you get much more prominent hillsides with color—if the cattle grazing goes just right and they work the grass down just a little bit."

Lindh describes their mountaintop home as primitive. "It was a Depression-era shack built as an outbuilding," he says. "The house we lived in was an add-on to a chicken coop. We heated strictly with wood. The wind blew right through the house. We had electricity because of all the radio facilities on top of the ridge. When we moved in, there was still a big ramshackle barn. People had carried off most of the nineteenth-century farm implements. The barn was at one time a working horse barn. It still had stalls with the horses' names carved into the posts. And we ran cows. I guess it was while Stanford still had it we started raising cattle and producing milk and meat for ourselves."

Life atop Monte Bello Ridge was a never-ending lesson in nature's power. "We had tremendous storms," Lindh says. "The barn blew away one time. We had hurricane-force winds. You couldn't stand up outside. And the barn roof—many, many tons of barn roof—lifted right off. A huge barn, maybe a hundred feet square, with an ancient corrugated-iron roof that lifted right off, and parts of it flew more than a hundred feet toward Los Altos Hills and landed in the top of an oak tree. We were lucky. The house was just twenty-five feet from the barn. If the wind had been a slightly different direction, all of that would have landed on top of us, and our fate would have been problematic." Lindh says summers were "hotter than hell," especially in a house with a flat, tar-paper roof. "So we lived outdoors in the summer." He describes winter as being "bitter cold," with regular freezes and occasional snow that brought cross-country skiers up from the valley.

"Our kids were educated at home," Lindh says. "I can't imagine a better place to be brought up." Deer paid daily visits, and the Lindh children gave each a name. Bobcats sauntered by occasionally. The days ended with a ritual visit to a hill just west of the ranch. "We'd go out there every evening to watch the sunset."

Rattlesnakes seemed to enjoy life at Black Mountain Ranch too, Lindh says. "There were rattlesnakes on the front porch in the spring. Rattlesnakes on the lawn. Rattlesnakes on the back porch. And they're pretty slow and dumb. One morning as I was leaving for work, I saw a red-tailed hawk. She was on the ground in front of me with something, and when I came around the corner she took off and here was a gigantic rattlesnake. She had it in the middle and was squeezing it. She was having a hard time lifting off."

Other birds of prey chose bigger targets. "Golden eagles would come over from the Hamilton Range in the spring and eat the fawns," says Lindh. Lindh's wife Julie was home on a spring day when she heard a pounding on the door. "People were banging at the door, and here was a middle-aged couple very, very upset. Sort of trembling. And they clearly had to talk to someone, and Julie's very comforting. So it turns out they had been coming up the Canyon Trail, and they had seen a doe with two fawns. And then all of a sudden a golden eagle came down out of the sky and grabbed one of the fawns. They can lift off with a small fawn. But before the eagle could get it together and lift off, the doe attacked. Does with fawns are not to be fiddled with. They attack you with their front hooves and it's serious. They could kill an eagle in one stroke. So the eagle dropped the fawn and took off. But while the doe was chasing the eagle, a coyote ran out of the brush on the other side and grabbed the other fawn and ran away into the brush with the fawn in its mouth. These people just couldn't get over it. This was too much nature in the raw for them!"

"Nature in the raw" is what led Mr. Morell to buy Black Mountain Ranch in the first place. Here is an excerpt from his essay, "History of Black Mountain and the Monte Bello Ridge," written in 1959:

> This is a very primitive area, kept so because of its inaccessibility either by road or trail. On the Morell, Winship, Johnson properties no destructive mark of fire or axe can be found. The land remains much as it was a century ago. Wildlife abounds. A magnificent coyote chorus greets the rising moon from a bald promontory. Coons, wild cats and foxes seem to be everywhere. Mountain lions have been in residence during most of the years since 1940, when I bought the ranch. Last year a female raised two cubs and exercised them almost daily within a quarter mile of the ranch buildings. Rattlesnakes are plentiful. We average fifteen killed yearly around the ranch buildings. It is to be hoped that the primitiveness of this core area, the Johnson, Winship, Morell ranches may be preserved. Wilderness areas such as this are becoming more rare and consequently more precious each year.

View of an orchard valley and wooded hilltop

PICCHETTI RANCH
OPEN SPACE PRESERVE

~

This lovely 308-acre preserve, with about four miles of trails to enjoy, takes visitors back to a time more than a hundred years ago, when vineyards, rather than silicon chips, were the area's most important resource. The name of this preserve honors an Italian family who settled here in the late 1800s. By 1900, there were more than a hundred wineries dotting the foothills on both sides of the Santa Clara Valley. As you leave the winery complex, you roam past terraced hills once planted with rows of grapes and old orchard trees whose branches still bear fruit. Along the way, you wander through oak groves that may be alive with the songs and calls of chickadees, flycatchers, and towhees. Exploring the Zinfandel Trail, which connects with Stevens Creek County Park, brings you to a secluded, shady realm of bigleaf maples, fragrant bay trees, and California nutmeg. A seasonal pond near the winery complex attracts California newts and frogs during the rainy season. From a hilltop above the pond, you can enjoy views of Silicon Valley, the southern reaches of San Francisco Bay, and the East Bay hills.

The Picchetti Ranch is historically significant because it represents Santa Clara Valley's rich agricultural heritage and the families who operated vineyards and wineries here. Vincenso Picchetti came to the valley around 1872 and worked in the vineyards and winery at Villa Maria, a Jesuit retreat attached to the College of Santa Clara. During his time at Villa Maria, Vincenso sent for his brother Secondo, who was still in Italy, to join him. Together they bought 160 acres of land above Cupertino on a ridge that they (and perhaps other nearby settlers) called Monte Bello, or "beautiful mountain." Their first house, a rough homestead with a steeply pitched roof, was built about 1882.

That same year, Vincenso returned to Italy, married his childhood sweetheart, Teresa, and brought her back to California. Upon his return, Vincenso stayed on as foreman at Villa Maria, while his brother and sister-in-law cleared land and planted grapevines on the recently acquired property. The Picchettis were among the first settlers to plant grapes on Monte Bello Ridge. In 1884, perhaps as the result of an unpleasant encounter with a bear, Secondo's wife convinced him to move to San Jose, and Secondo sold his half of the ranch to his brother. After they left, Vincenso moved his family, which now included a son, to the ranch. Vincenso and Teresa eventually had four more sons, one of whom died in childhood. They built a new, two-story wood frame house in 1886. Two years later, Teresa's sister came from Italy to join the family and help with child-rearing and household chores.

The Picchettis planted vineyards of zinfandel, petite syrah, golden Shasta, and other varieties. Once these began producing, they sold the harvest to nearby wineries. In 1896, Vincenso followed his wife's advice to withdraw their life's savings, some $8,000, from a bank in San Jose, and build a winery. The red brick winery building, with its rough wood roof beams and stone cellar—renovated by the District in the 1980s and funded by Proposition 12 Park Bond Act monies and a grant from the Santa Clara County Historical Heritage Commission—still stands on a low hill overlooking the Picchettis' two houses and other ranch

Winery building at Picchetti Ranch

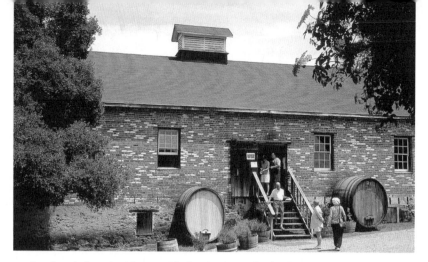

Sundays bring picnickers to Picchetti Winery for food, wine, and live music.

buildings. The winery was given bonding number 148, and produced wine under the "Picchetti Bros." label for more than sixty years. The wines produced under this label were considered distinctive, and sometimes outstanding.

Vincenso and Teresa's sons John and Antone lived on the ranch, raised families there, and eventually took over the winery following their father's death in 1904. By that time, the Picchettis owned about 500 acres of land surrounding their winery complex. There were orchards of apricots, pears, and prunes in addition to the vineyards. Orange, lemon, and pomegranate trees ringed the ranch house, and there was a bocce ball court nearby. A collection of animals, including horses, cows, hogs, peacocks, and other birds, delighted the Picchetti children. There was a large pond to play in, but after the 1906 earthquake it no longer held water during the dry summer months.

A phylloxera epidemic at the turn of the century, followed by Prohibition in 1919, took a heavy toll and forced the family to sell land to pay bills. Also, the Picchettis' terraced vineyards had been designed to work with horses, a technique that quickly became outdated in the era of mechanization and corporate farming. After Prohibition ended, the winery continued making wine for local sale, but stopped in 1963, a year after John's death. The family continued to make wine for their own use until the winery closed in 1971. In 1976, the Picchettis sold their land to the District, hoping to preserve it from development. (Today, only remnants of the fruit trees and about an acre of 100-year-old zinfandel vines remain.) Originally part of Monte Bello Preserve, Picchetti Ranch is now its own preserve.

The Picchetti winery complex is listed on the National Register of Historic Places and the Santa Clara County Heritage Resource Inventory. Restoration of the buildings was funded by the District, the Santa Clara

Picchetti Ranch Trail Use

Bicycles: Not allowed

Dogs: Not allowed

Horses: Allowed on all trails except the Zinfandel Trail south of its junction with the Orchard Loop Trail. There is no equestrian access from the main parking area.

PICCHETTI RANCH OPEN SPACE PRESERVE

Trip 15. Orchard Loop

Length: 1.5 miles

Time: 1 to 2 hours

Rating: Easy

Highlights: This easy semi-loop, using the Zinfandel, Orchard Loop, Bear Meadow, and Vista Trails, takes visitors through an old orchard and then up to a scenic vantage point with fine views of the surrounding countryside and the winery complex. Along the way, you'll pass a seasonal pond where you may find California newts and frogs during the rainy season. This route can be combined with the Zinfandel Trail, described next, to make a longer outing.

Directions: From I-280 at the Cupertino-Los Altos border, take the Foothill Expressway/Grant Road exit and go south on Foothill Boulevard. At 1.6 miles, this becomes Stevens Canyon Road. At 3.3 miles, turn right on Montebello Road. Go 0.6 mile to a parking area on the left.

County Historical Society, the California Office of Historic Preservation, and other sources. A private party leases the winery complex from the District and is currently producing wines under the Picchetti label. The winery is open daily from 11 A.M. to 5 P.M. On Sundays there is live music from 1 to 4 P.M. The winery offers tasting (for a small fee) and picnicking on the winery grounds, adjacent to the preserve trails, and is available for events, parties, and corporate meetings. The area within the winery complex has wide dirt roads that can be navigated by most wheelchairs. There is an accessible restroom and a wheelchair lift into the winery. The trails outside the winery compex are not improved for wheelchair access. For more information, call (408) 741-1310 or visit *www.picchetti.com*.

Facilities: None at the trailhead, but there are restrooms about 0.1 mile ahead, adjacent to the winery.

Trailhead: About 100 feet south of the parking area, on the right side of the dirt road to the winery

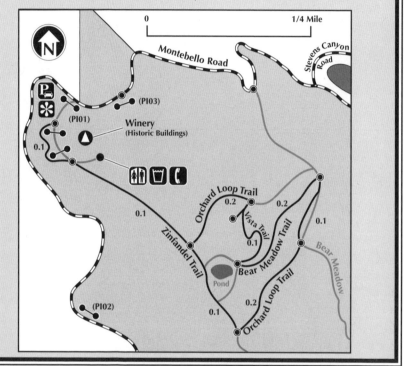

Trip 15. Orchard Loop

Pass through a gap in a wood fence just left of two District information boards and a map holder, and begin walking gently uphill on a single-track trail. The historic winery buildings, which are definitely worth a visit, are to your left across a lawn. To your right, coast live oaks and walnut trees are joined by a scrubby understory of coyote brush and berry vines. After several hundred feet, you cross a creek on a bridge. Brown dogwood and ninebark, both water-loving plants, grow beside the creek. Just past the creek, the trail follows a level, winding course and soon merges with a dirt road from the winery. Restrooms are to the left. Here angle right and follow the dirt road, which is called the Zinfandel Trail, past an old orchard. Plums, apricots, and

The seasonal pond near Picchetti Winery sometimes has birds and amphibians.

pears once flourished on this ranch, which also produced grapes for wine. (There are still some 100-year-old zinfandel vines growing on a hillside below Montebello Road.)

The appropriately named Orchard Loop Trail circles the high hill to your left, and you meet one branch of the trail just ahead on your left. Ignoring it for now, continue straight, passing the Bear Meadow Trail, which also departs left—you will meet this trail again too. Now the road descends and curves right, bringing you alongside a seasonal pond, which may contain a flock of mallards if there is water. Other birds you may see or hear nearby include spotted towhees, olive-sided flycatchers, wrentits, northern flickers, and chestnut-backed chickadees. Magnificent valley oaks add to the picturesque scene. The Vista Trail, left, wanders over to the pond. On a rolling course, you again meet the Orchard Loop Trail and this time turn left onto it. Descending in a corridor of coyote brush, blue blossom, and willows, you pass another unofficial trail heading left.

Now in a forest of coast live oak and California bay, you begin to see Stevens Creek Reservoir straight ahead. Soon you reach a four-way junction. Here the Bear Meadow Trail goes left and right, and the Orchard Loop Trail continues straight. Turn left and follow a single track for about 100 yards to where it rejoins the Orchard Loop Trail. At the next junction, turn sharply left onto the Bear Meadow Trail, a single track that climbs through thickets of poison oak, California sagebrush, and sticky monkeyflower. With the seasonal pond ahead and left, you come to another four-way junction. The Bear Meadow Trail continues straight, skirting the seasonal pond and then joining the Zinfandel Trail. The Vista Trail, left, also connects with the Zinfandel Trail. Your route, also part of the Vista Trail, turns sharply right and climbs.

After a switchback to the right, you arrive atop the high hill mentioned earlier, surrounded by stately coast live oaks. Just ahead is a T-junction. Here a short trail leads left about 100 feet to a viewpoint, where you can look out over the preserve, the old orchard, and the winery. A rock quarry to the northwest is the only jarring note in this otherwise scenic symphony. Back at the T-junction, continue straight on the remaining 150 or so feet of the Vista Trail, enjoying views of Silicon Valley, the southern reaches of San Francisco Bay, and the East Bay hills. At a T-junction with the Orchard Loop Trail, turn left. A short, moderate descent soon eases, and you find level ground amid old fruit trees. When you reach a T-junction with the Zinfandel Trail, turn right and retrace your route to the parking area.

Picchetti Ranch Trail Use

Bicycles: Not allowed

Dogs: Not allowed

Horses: Allowed on all trails except the Zinfandel Trail south of its junction with the Orchard Loop Trail. There is no equestrian access from the main parking area.

PICCHETTI RANCH OPEN SPACE PRESERVE

Trip 16. Zinfandel Trail

Length: 2.4 miles

Time: 1 to 2 hours

Rating: Moderate

Highlights: This out-and-back trip along the Zinfandel Trail takes you from the winery/ranch complex into the heart of a beautiful secluded canyon holding a tributary of Stevens Creek. The lush, shady environment along the steep-walled canyon is perfect for bigleaf maple trees, whose leaves turn yellow and orange in fall, and also for California nutmeg, an evergreen found in only a few District preserves. Elsewhere, the trail winds through thickets of chaparral, where you might find wind poppy, an unusual cousin of our state flower. This route can be combined with the "Orchard Loop," described previously, to make a longer outing.

Directions: Same as for "Orchard Loop" on pages 166–67

Facilities: None at the trailhead, but there are restrooms about 0.1 mile ahead adjacent to the winery.

Trailhead: Same as for "Orchard Loop" on pages 166–67

Trip 16. Zinfandel Trail

 Follow the route description for "Orchard Loop" on pages 166–67 to the second junction of the Zinfandel and Orchard Loop Trails. Where the Orchard Loop Trail curves left, you continue straight on the Zinfandel Trail, now a single track for hiking only. After about twenty-five feet, cross a

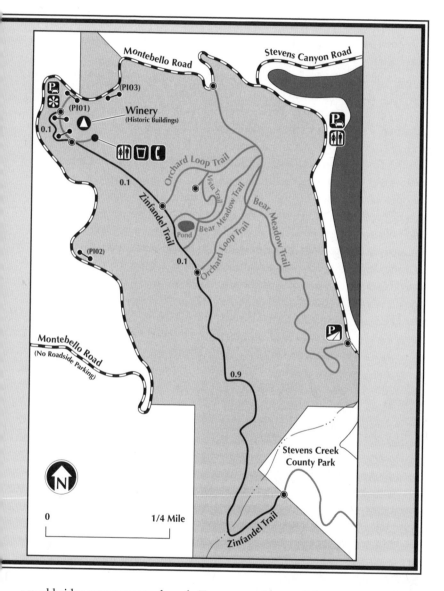

wood bridge over a seasonal creek. Toyon, snowberry, wild rose, and spiny red-berry are some of the shrubs growing beside the trail. Spring bloomers here may include blue-eyed grass, Pacific starflower, crimson columbine, and fairy bells. Hidden in the tangled understory of berry vines may be a family of California quail, clucking nervously to each other and getting ready to scurry away—their preferred method of evasion—at the last minute. After passing through a gap in a wooden fence, you follow a rolling course through a shady forest of coast live oak, California bay, and madrone.

Through gaps in the forest, left, you can catch glimpses of the urban sprawl that rings the southern end of San Francisco Bay, with Stevens Creek Reservoir providing the foreground. Beside the trail, look for canyon oak, similar in appearance to coast live oak, but with leaves that are dusted on their undersides with gray or gold. Shrubs found nearby include oceanspray, coffeeberry, sticky monkeyflower, and poison oak. In places, the slope you are traversing is cut by ravines that hold seasonal creeks. Your route emerges from the forest and crosses an open hillside dotted with California sagebrush, pitcher sage, and mountain mahogany. Adding to the interesting assortment of native plants are silk tassel and hollyleaf cherry, members of the chaparral community. Look here for the unusual wind poppy, which sports four bright orange petals spotted with purple.

Now descending on a ledge that has been notched from a steep slope, you enter a cool, shady forest of mostly bay trees. Ferns—and not much else—thrive on the slanting forest floor, which is dimly lit even during the day. Reaching a tributary of Stevens Creek set in a deep canyon, you cross it on a wooden bridge, then turn sharply left and begin to climb. The banks above the rocky streambed are home to such large-leafed plants as elk clover and thimbleberry. Above you tower bigleaf maples, colorful in fall. Also here is California nutmeg, an evergreen with spine-tipped needles, uncommon in the Bay Area. This tree resembles a young coast redwood, but one encounter with its sharp spines will quickly reveal its true identity. California nutmeg is a member of the yew family, and is not related to its namesake spice.

Visitors enjoy the Zinfandel Trail, the main route through Picchetti Ranch Open Space Preserve.

Climbing on a moderate and then gentle grade, the trail hugs a hillside that falls dizzyingly left. In places, wood reinforcements anchored by metal rods hold the slope in place. (Trail crews have dubbed these structures "The Great Wall.") Clinging to the steep slopes are delicate and delightful white globe lilies, each flower an almost-perfect sphere. California buckeye and scrub oak add to today's tree list. The route soon bends right and you regain your view of the reservoir. Impressive thickets of poison oak grow on both sides of the trail. At about 1.2 miles you come to the preserve boundary, marked by a District sign. Ahead, the trail enters Stevens Creek County Park and descends about 400 feet in 0.6 mile to Stevens Canyon Road. From here, simply retrace your route to the parking area.

PICCHETTI RANCH

Steve Tedesco is the great-grandson of Vincenso Picchetti, an Italian immigrant who came to the Santa Clara Valley in 1872 and established vineyards on the slopes of Monte Bello Ridge. Tedesco remembers regular childhood visits to the Picchetti Ranch and to the two-story house built by Vincenso in 1886. "We'd come up here pretty much every Sunday," he says, speaking of a period that began for him in the late 1950s. "The families would come up, so we would have Sunday lunch here. It was great to play up here, because at the time it was a real working ranch. We had great animals, and it was our own farm. There were always horses to ride, and after lunch we'd ride horses through the trails up into the mountains or just around the yard. Old Nugget and Bubbles were the horses." Other ranch animals included cows, sheep, chickens, and ducks; there were also peacocks and a cage full of canaries. There was a bocce ball court nearby, and Tedesco remembers watching his uncles play. "We'd sit in the lower winery or the cellar, particularly in the summer because it was so cool in there, and they'd be out playing a little bocce."

Tedesco says the tradition of Sunday visits dates back to when his mother, Irene Picchetti, was a child. "When my mom was young, people would come up on Sunday because they knew all the family was here," he says. "So you had a lot of people from down in the valley coming up here. They'd come up to buy wine, either a gallon or a case of four gallons. And they'd also come up here to get water, because the water to the house was spring water. It was great water, and I guess we were kind of the original Alhambra—we had bottled water. Right now we probably could sell the water for more than we were selling the wine for at that time." Wine sold for about a dollar per gallon, Tedesco says, and it was "pretty good wine." Families would come not only to buy wine, but also

Wind poppy; photo taken at Rancho San Antonio Open Space Preserve

to walk through the beautiful orchards of apricots, prunes, pears, and walnuts. The magic words for admission went something like this, according to Tedesco: "Well, Joe told me to tell you that Phil's a good friend of Aldo's, and that if I told you I was a friend of Phil's we could come up here."

Tedesco says he especially enjoyed learning about the natural world that surrounded the ranch. "We did a lot with my Aunt Tish, who still lives up the hill here," he says. Sundays in spring were not complete without a long hike to look for wildflowers. "This area was just loaded with wildflowers," he says. "I guess my favorite was the

Peacocks are a tradition at Picchetti Winery, delighting all with their antics.

The color of paintbrush is supplied by the flower leaf bracts rather than the flowers.

Wrentit; photo taken at Rancho San Antonio Open Space Preserve

Indian paintbrush, there were literally dozens of them. There were lots of California poppies up here, and we'd pick miner's lettuce out of the creek. When we were in school down in the valley and we had to do reports on flowers, we had the best pressed flowers. The variety of the wildflowers—the purple ones and the red ones and the pink ones. I'm sorry I don't remember all the names of them, but my aunt was really into it. We loved going out, and we could literally walk down the road and alongside the road and see twenty or thirty different kinds."

The ranch activities were endlessly fascinating to him as a child, says Tedesco, and remained so as he entered his teens. "We liked to come up here because there was a lot of activity," he says. "They actually picked the grapes, they brought them here, they crushed them here, the fermentation tanks were here. One of the jobs that we could do when we were younger was to hand-pump the wine from the fermentation tanks into the holding tanks." Tedesco says a rite of passage was learning from his grandfather John how to siphon wine. "He'd show us how to siphon from the large tanks into the smaller, fifty-gallon tanks where they were going to age the wine. The way we did it was to put a rubber tube into the barrel, suck on it, and then put it into the [tank]. Well, we were 12 or 13, and we'd get a pretty good buzz on. My grandfather would get a kick out of us walking back down to the house, falling down because we were drunk. And my grandmother would yell at him for letting us do that."

The seasonal pond near the Picchetti ranch complex and the hill above it beckoned Tedesco and his cousins. "We called it the lake, but it's probably by today's standards just a pond," he says. "There were some great places to go up behind the pond, and you could look down over the valley. You really felt like you were hundreds of miles away from civilization, yet when you just walked over this little ridge where the pond is, you'd see the valley, and you could see the entire valley from the South Bay all the way down into Morgan Hill and Gilroy."

The Picchetti orchards were picked by migrant workers, many of whom lived in tents on the property during the harvest. Tedesco says the newer prune trees did not yield enough fruit for the workers to pick, so that task was left to the youngsters. "We'd get all the kids and we'd go out and have our experience picking prunes. And my uncle who ran the ranch, he'd pay us whatever the going rate was, I don't know, a quarter a box. So if we did a box he'd give us a quarter. And then my grandmother would come along and give us five bucks!"

Today, Tedesco is struck by how little things have changed at Picchetti Ranch since he was a child. The winery is in business again, and the weekends bring visitors who come to stroll on the preserve's trails and picnic on the winery grounds. He says this would have pleased his grandmother Josephine, who wanted to sell the ranch to the District so that it would be preserved for the public to enjoy. Also being preserved is the Picchetti family history, which pleases Tedesco. "My great-grandfather and my grandfather were a big part of the history of this mountain," he says. "So it's really special to still be up on this hill and know that our family was an early part of it."

Patriarch of Picchetti Ranch/Vineyard, Vincenso and family.
Left to right, front row: Theresa, Vincenso, Hector, Louisa Cicoletti;
back row: John, Antone, Attilo

View of majestic oak tree at Pulgas Ridge Open Space Preserve

PULGA) RIDGE
OPEN)PACE PRE)ERVE

~

Within minutes of the City of San Carlos and busy I-280 and Highway 101 are 366 acres of meadows, woodlands, and chaparral available for your enjoyment. As you wander this preserve's three miles or so of trails, you may find it hard to imagine that for many years a large treatment center for tuberculosis patients stood atop Pulgas Ridge. Opened in 1926 by the City and County of San Francisco, the Hassler Health Home operated until 1972, when the property and its seventeen buildings were declared "surplus." Various proposals were made for the use of the property, including a park and a prison, but none was successful. The District acquired the property in 1983, and the buildings were demolished in 1985.

One of the District's most important and extensive restoration projects is being conducted here. District staff and volunteers are removing invasive non-native species such as acacia, broom, and eucalyptus, and replanting with sticky monkeyflower, California sage, yerba buena, coyote brush, purple needlegrass, slender needlegrass, and blue wild rye. This allows the many native species of trees, shrubs, flowers, and ferns found here to flourish. The preserve is known among Bay Area wildflower enthusiasts as a great place to see such early bloom-ing species as hound's tongue, milkmaids, fetid adder's-tongue, giant trillium, and mission bells. A favorite is the mile-long Polly Geraci Trail, which wanders through a creekside forest, and then zigzags uphill amid chaparral to open grasslands with great views of the surrounding area.

The District became involved with the Hassler Health Home in 1977, when it made an offer to help the City of San Carlos buy the site. When the city declined to participate, the District applied for a federal grant and also asked San Mateo County to consider joint purchase of the property. The District received the federal grant but was turned down by the county. In

View of the Blue Oak Trail at Pulgas Ridge Open Space Preserve

1979, more than five hundred residents in the neighborhood adjacent to the Hassler Health Home formed a special assessment district and raised more than $300,000 in taxes to aid the District in buying the site. That year, the District began formal negotiations with San Francisco for purchase at an appraised price of around $2.5 million.

The federal grant awarded to the District stated that the Hassler buildings, which had been neglected and vandalized since the treatment center closed, had to be either demolished or used for public outdoor recreational purposes. The District solicited proposals for use of the buildings, but received none that both qualified and was cost effective. In January 1982, the San Francisco Board of Supervisors voted to place Hassler on the auction block, and the District board voted immediately to begin an eminent domain action to acquire the property. That summer, Hassler was sold by San Francisco to the Hyundai Corporation for $3.5 million, subject to conditions. The parties seemed headed for the courtroom.

In a deal struck on the courthouse steps, the District acquired the property in May, 1983, from San Francisco for $3.5 million. Plans were made to demolish all seventeen buildings and begin intensive restoration of the site. But the District's hassles over Hassler were not yet ended. The San Mateo County Arts Council asked the District to preserve the Hassler buildings for use as art studios and rehearsal spaces. After a public hearing in July, the District board voted five to two to proceed with demolition, with the majority citing the restrictive terms of the federal grant, the high cost of renovation which the Arts Council would have to pay, and the commitment to the Hassler neighbors who voted to raise taxes to purchase open space, not an arts center.

With the demolition contract already let, the San Mateo County Board of Supervisors voted to support the Arts Council, and said they would delay the District's demolition permit. The Hassler neighbors threatened to sue the District and/or San Mateo County, as did the City and County of San Francisco, for violating the condition of the sale, which was to preserve open space. As a compromise, the District offered to share the cost of buying the property with San Mateo County. The County would hold title to the property and assume responsibility for the Arts Council proposal. The District would have a conservation easement over all the land except the twenty-acre building site. The County proposed instead that the District be a full partner with the Arts Council, but declined to help the District financially.

Unable to reach a compromise, the District board voted in December to go ahead with the demolition. Just as the bulldozers started rolling, a group called "The Coalition to Save Hassler" got a temporary restraining order, which halted everything. Court battles ensued, but the District ultimately prevailed. Herb Grench was District general manager at the time. He describes the Hassler acquisition as "a bloody struggle," but says ultimately it was worth the effort. "You often hear 'when something is developed, it's gone,'" he says. "It's not long going to be natural. Well, I think this is a case where you can show it is possible to turn the clock back, to take a developed area and restore it to a more natural condition."

The Hetch Hetchy aqueduct runs under Pulgas Ridge Preserve, bringing water from the Sierra Nevada to Crystal Springs Reservoir. The 0.5-mile Cordilleras Trail, which parallels a meadow and then enters a wooded area next to seasonal Cordilleras Creek, is designated an "Easy Access Trail." The trail is designed to accommodate wheelchairs, strollers, or visitors desiring a less-strenuous open space experience. This preserve contains the District's only off-leash dog area. While in this area with your dog, you must have a leash in your possession and keep your animal under voice control. Dogs must not be allowed to interfere with or harass park users, other dogs, or wildlife. You must clean up after your pet. For a copy of the District's "Dog Access Guidelines" pamphlet, please call the District office: (650) 691-1200.

"There are several things I really like about Pulgas," said District board member Ken Nitz. "The impressive 100-foot oak trees at the beginning of the Blue Oak Trail are amazing. The fact it's a near-urban preserve that the District is working to restore to its previous natural habitat is great. Soon, the preserve will have a new staging area, several new trails, and an expanded off-leash dog area. It demonstrates the District understands its governing principles to acquire, protect, and restore and to provide environmentally friendly recreation."

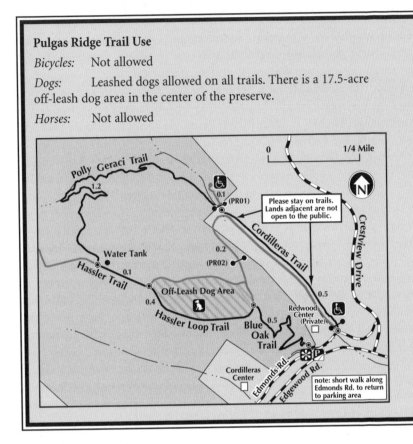

Pulgas Ridge Trail Use

Bicycles: Not allowed

Dogs: Leashed dogs allowed on all trails. There is a 17.5-acre off-leash dog area in the center of the preserve.

Horses: Not allowed

Trip 17. Hassler Loop

Two District information boards with a map holder greet you at the trailhead, where you pass through a gap in a wood fence. Your route is the Blue Oak Trail, which enters dense woodland that shelters a creek on your left. Using switchbacks to gain elevation, you stroll amid shady stands of coast live oak, madrone, California buckeye, and California bay. Where the forest gives way to open slopes, look for sun-loving shrubs such as manzanita, chamise, and sticky monkeyflower. Wildflowers in this part of the preserve include blue-eyed grass, bluedicks, hound's tongue, soap plant, and California buttercup.

Meandering uphill on a gentle grade, you pass a rest bench on your right. Now you begin to see the trail's namesake tree, blue oak, which is uncommon on District lands, but is being replanted as part of a District resource management plan. You can identify blue oak by its small, blue-green leaves, and its gray

PULGAS RIDGE OPEN SPACE PRESERVE

Trip 17. Hassler Loop

Length: 2.4 miles

Time: 1 to 2 hours

Rating: Moderate

Highlights: This rewarding route uses the Blue Oak, Hassler, Polly Geraci, and Cordilleras Trails to circle the site of the former Hassler Health Home, a tuberculosis sanitarium. An extensive habitat-restoration program underway here has removed most traces of the area's former existence, and has allowed the preserve's many native species of trees, shrubs, ferns, and flowers to thrive, truly a victory for open space! A 17.5-acre off-leash area allows dogs to run free, but you must have a leash in your possession and keep your dog under voice control at all times.

Directions: From I-280 west of Redwood City, take the Edgewood Road exit, go northeast 0.8 mile to Crestview Drive and turn left. Go 0.1 mile to Edmonds Road, turn left, and go 0.2 mile to a roadside parking area on the left.

Facilities: None

Trailhead: On the northwest side of Edmonds Road, across from the parking area

bark cut in vertical strips. Also here are some invasive nonnatives such as French, Scotch, and Spanish brooms. Soon you reach a clearing, where you join the Hassler Trail, a paved road, by turning left. After 100 feet or so, you pass a trail, right, that enters the off-leash dog area. Just ahead is a fence across the road with a car-sized gap, marking the main entrance to the off-leash dog area.

Now in the open, you enjoy a view southeast across Edgewood Road to Edgewood Park and Preserve, famous for its fine display of spring wildflowers. Climbing steadily, you are rewarded with a scenic vista stretching northeast across San Francisco Bay to the East Bay hills. Coastal fog often pours over Kings Mountain, which dominates the southwestern skyline. A line of eucalyptus trees to your right is a reminder that this preserve had several previous incarnations, including nearly fifty years as a tuberculosis hospital. Other nonnative or planted trees here include several species of cedar and pine.

At a junction with the Hassler Loop Trail, a paved road joining from the right, continue straight. A fence here marks the boundary of the off-leash dog area, and just beyond it another paved road veers right to a viewpoint overlooking the headwaters of Cordilleras Creek. Staying on the Hassler Trail, you pass a large water tank on the right and then reach a junction with the Polly Geraci Trail, at about the 1-mile point. Here turn right and begin to descend on a single-track trail, traversing a hillside that falls away to your right. Sticky monkeyflower, blue witch, and several species of ceanothus join with manzanita and chamise to form a corridor of chaparral. Western scrub-jays and wrentits favor this type of terrain, and they may be seen and heard here.

A sweeping bend to the right and then a switchback left bring you down into a canyon treasured by wildflower enthusiasts, especially for its early blooming species. Here you may find fat Solomon, fetid adder's-tongue, woodland star, mission bells, and giant trillium. More switchbacks drop you farther into a shadowy realm, where the trees grow spindly as they strain upward for light. A lush understory of gooseberry, snowberry, and ferns lends a rain forest feel. Now curve left to cross a bridge over seasonal Cordilleras Creek. Just ahead is a T-junction with the Cordilleras Trail, a dirt road that is designated an "Easy Access Trail." Here turn right and after about 50 feet come to a fence and a gate with a gap between them.

Go through the gap and stay on the Cordilleras Trail by veering left. To your right is a paved road, and your trail runs parallel to it. Flowering lupine and mule ears decorate the hillsides to your left, which are also graced by oaks interspersed with nonnative conifers. The Hetch Hetchy aqueduct runs under Pulgas Ridge Preserve, and the San Francisco Water Department owns the land

Dog off-leash area at Pulgas Ridge Open Space Preserve

View facing southwest from the top of Pulgas Ridge Open Space Preserve

and the buildings on the other side of the road. Soon you reach Edmonds Road, where there are two District information boards with a map holder. Immediately to your right is the paved road, which also serves as the entrance to the Redwood Center, a private facility. Bear right and follow Edmonds Road several hundred feet to the parking area.

Daniel Bernstein is a cofounder of Peninsula Access for Dogs (PADS): "For many of us who love the outdoors and have dogs, enjoying the great open spaces on the San Francisco peninsula with a dog can be quite a challenge, since so many parks and open space preserves are off-limits to hikers with dogs. It's really great to have some open space areas to explore and enjoy with a dog, and the District offers some of those places. The two areas I think are especially noteworthy are Pulgas Ridge, because it has a very nice off-leash area, which is much appreciated, and the [Hamms Gulch–Spring Ridge Trails] loop at Windy Hill. The Windy Hill loop is great because it's long enough to be interesting, with great views and shade for dogs in the summer time."

View of the redwoods and understory at
Purisima Creek Redwoods Open Space Preserve

PURISIMA CREEK REDWOODS OPEN SPACE PRESERVE

~

With more than three thousand acres and around twenty-one miles of trails and historic logging roads to traverse, this beautiful and historic preserve is one that you will want to visit many times. Steep ridges and forested gulches sweep skyward more than a thousand feet from redwood-lined Purisima Canyon to a zone of Douglas-fir, madrone, tanbark oak, and coastal scrub. Here visitors can enjoy wandering along the banks of Purisima Creek, passing the stumps of giant redwoods felled by loggers, and the clearings used for their mill sites in the nineteenth and early twentieth centuries. Native plant enthusiasts will revel in the preserve's botanical diversity, and birders will want to carry binoculars and hone their "birding-by-ear" skills to identify the forest flyers that call this preserve home. Views of the San Mateo coast and the Pacific Ocean from the upper parts of the Harkins Ridge and Soda Gulch Trails are superb. The Whittemore Gulch Trail, which drops steeply from its junction with the North Ridge Trail to Purisima Creek, is a favorite among mountain bicyclists in summer and fall when the trail is dry.

No one tells the history of Purisima Canyon, or "The Purisima," better than Ken Fisher, a longtime area resident. He says that Purisima Canyon had a logging history that lasted nearly seventy years, and included some of the earliest mills in the area—and also some of the last coast redwoods to be cut. Beginning in the 1850s, logging came to Kings Mountain, as the two thousand-foot-high ridge running northwest from Bear Gulch Road is called. In the next fifty years, says Fisher, "every tree that was not too inaccessible or too tiny or too twisted to justify the trouble was cut." Kings Mountain was denuded, a fact that is hard to imagine today, given the mountain's beautifully forested hillsides and densely wooded gulches. Today, a handful of old-growth redwoods remain hidden in "The Purisima's" steep terrain.

The coast redwoods that filled "The Purisima" were huge, ten- to twenty-foot-diameter trees that were up to a thousand years old. After they were felled by ax and saw, they were blasted with dynamite into pieces small enough to be milled. Teams of oxen dragged logs over "skid roads" to the sawmills. In the 1880s, steam-powered donkey engines replaced oxen for log hauling. There was plenty of water in the 4-mile-long canyon, which holds year-round Purisima Creek, to drive the steam engines used to power the saws and run the donkeys. Although the terrain made it easy to skid or haul the logs down the hillsides to the mills in the canyon, it was expensive to then get the lumber up and over Kings Mountain to Redwood City, the port used to ship wood to San Francisco.

Purisima Creek Redwoods Trail Use

Bicycles: Allowed on all trails except the Bald Knob, Irish Ridge, Lobitos Creek, Redwood, and Soda Gulch Trails, and the 0.5-mile segment of the North Ridge Trail from the parking area to its junction with the Harkins Ridge Trail

Dogs: Not allowed

Horses: Allowed on all trails except the Bald Knob, Irish Ridge, Lobitos Creek, Redwood, and Soda Gulch Trails, and the 0.5-mile segment of the North Ridge Trail from the parking area to its junction with the Harkins Ridge Trail

PURISIMA CREEK REDWOODS OPEN SPACE PRESERVE

Trip 18. Harkins Ridge

Length: 7 miles

Time: 3 to 5 hours

Rating: Difficult

Highlights: Using the Harkins Ridge Trail, this invigorating loop starts by climbing more than 1,000 feet from the shady confines of redwood-lined Purisima Creek to a ridge with superb views of Half Moon Bay and the surrounding hills. The relaxing return is via the delightful Soda Gulch and Purisima Creek Trails, giving you an opportunity to learn about and enjoy the second- and third-growth redwood forest community that thrives here despite extensive logging in the nineteenth and early twentieth centuries.

Sending wood to Half Moon Bay was easier, but the demand there was less than in booming San Francisco.

The name Purisima is Spanish for "most pure," and comes from the original land grant for the area, *Cañada Verde y Arroyo de La Purísima,* or "green forest and creek of the most pure," certainly an apt description. But the American pioneers who settled here paid little heed to spelling, especially of foreign words. So you find "Purissima" and "Purrisima" scattered liberally throughout the nearby landscape. Even the late Frank Stanger, head of the San Mateo County Historical Association and author of *Sawmills in the Redwoods,* perpetuates the error. On USGS maps, however, the name of

Directions: From the junction of Highway 1 and Higgins Purisima Road south of Half Moon Bay, take Higgins Purisima Road east 4.5 miles to a parking area on the left.

Facilities: None at the trailhead, but there is a vault toilet about 100 yards east on the Purisima Creek Trail.

Trailhead: Gate PC05, at the east side of the parking area

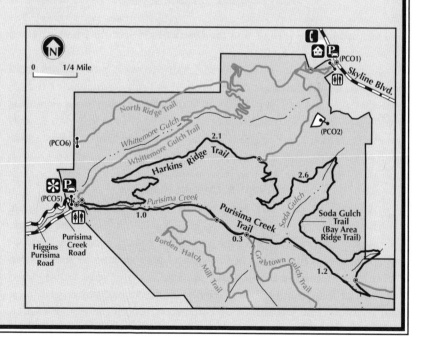

Early photo of Purisima Mill, Site 2

the creek is properly spelled, and the District followed suit when it named the preserve.

The Redwood Trail, which has wheelchair-accessible picnic tables and a vault toilet, is designated an "Easy Access Trail" and is suitable for visitors of all physical abilities. The trail was built with a grant from Peninsula Open Space Trust. The preserve was established with the help of a $2 million gift from Save-the-Redwoods League, and was the District's first acquisition of a significant redwood forest.

Trip 18. Harkins Ridge

A gated dirt road runs east from the parking area and the trailhead. Between the gate and a fence to its left is a gap for hikers to pass through. A wider gap to the right of the gate accommodates equestrians, but logs partially buried in the ground across this gap prevent entry by motorcycles. The dirt road leads you into a dense, secluded forest of coast redwood, red alder, bigleaf maple, and tanbark oak. The understory of this coastal forest includes such common shrubs as coffeeberry, thimbleberry, gooseberry, oceanspray, and elk clover. Look beside the road for shade-loving wildflowers such as miner's lettuce, hedge nettle, forget-me-not, and two species of fairy bells, Hooker's and Smith's.

After several hundred feet you come to a junction marked by two District information boards and a map holder. Here the Purisima Creek Trail, which you will use later on the return part of this loop, goes straight, and a short connector to the Harkins Ridge and Whittemore Gulch Trails goes left. You turn left, crossing lovely Purisima Creek on a wood bridge, and then come to a T-junction. A right turn puts you on the gently rolling Harkins Ridge Trail, a dirt road that, for a while, runs parallel to the redwood-bordered creek. Various wildflowers associated with redwood forests grow nearby, including redwood sorrel, which has clover-like leaves and pink flowers; crimson columbine, told by its beautiful orange-and-yellow blossoms; Pacific starflower, each with a delicate flower held aloft on a thread-like stem; and red clintonia, a member of the lily family that produces clusters of pink blooms in early summer and blue berries later in the year.

The grade steepens, and soon you begin a series of sweeping switchbacks that bring you to a brighter, more open realm, home to venerable coast live oaks. Taking advantage of the terrain are shrubs such as blue blossom, sticky monkeyflower, and red elderberry. The tangle of vegetation bordering the road also includes California sagebrush, cow parsnip, mugwort, stinging nettle, golden yarrow, and French broom (an invasive nonnative species). Coveys of California quail, the state bird, may be hiding in the underbrush. The view to

Soda Gulch bridge in Purisima Creek Redwoods Open Space Preserve

your right takes in the canyon holding Purisima Creek and the ridge rising just south of the creek to Bald Knob, more than 2,000 feet above sea level.

At one of the road's right-hand switchbacks, you have a fine vantage point that looks west toward Half Moon Bay and the Pacific Ocean. Finally gaining a ridge top, you follow it uphill over rough ground, past stands of Douglas-fir, madrone, and acacia. Many of the tree limbs here are draped with lace lichen, which resembles the Spanish moss of the Southern United States. Evergreen huckleberry, golden chinquapin, toyon, and blue witch line the route. In places,

Purisima Creek Redwoods Trail Use

Bicycles: Allowed on all trails except the Bald Knob, Irish Ridge, Lobitos Creek, Redwood, and Soda Gulch Trails, and the 0.5-mile segment of the North Ridge Trail from the parking area to its junction with the Harkins Ridge Trail

Dogs: Not allowed

Horses: Allowed on all trails except the Bald Knob, Irish Ridge, Lobitos Creek, Redwood, and Soda Gulch Trails, and the 0.5-mile segment of the North Ridge Trail from the parking area to its junction with the Harkins Ridge Trail

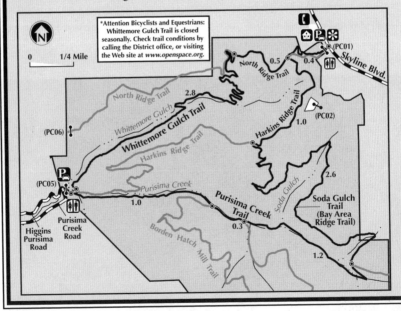

the grade is very steep, stretching calf muscles to their limit. Otherwise it is a long, steady climb on a moderate grade, decorated in spring by flowering currant, Douglas iris, and yellow bush lupine. Around the two-mile point, you reach a junction with the Soda Gulch Trail, which is part of the Bay Area Ridge Trail. Here you turn right and follow the route description for "Purisima Creek" on pages 192–93. When you reach the short connector to the Harkins Ridge and Whittemore Gulch Trails where you began this loop, continue straight to the parking area.

PURISIMA CREEK REDWOODS OPEN SPACE PRESERVE

Trip 19. Purisima Creek

Length: 10.1 miles

Time: 4 to 6 hours

Rating: Difficult

Highlights: One of the premier routes on District lands, this challenging loop uses the North Ridge, Harkins Ridge, Soda Gulch, Purisima Creek, and Whittemore Gulch Trails to explore the northern half of this expansive preserve. Dropping more than 1,500 feet to Purisima Creek, you pass the giant stumps of old-growth redwoods, and can imagine yourself going back in time to an era when the canyons here echoed with the sounds of people and machinery hard at work, harvesting a seemingly endless resource. Completing the loop via a vigorous climb, you pass through a Douglas-fir forest and then a zone of coastal scrub, making this one of the most botanically diverse routes in this book.

Directions: From the junction of Skyline Boulevard and Highway 92, take Skyline Boulevard southeast 4.5 miles to a parking area on the right.

Facilities: Vault toilet; telephone is just northwest of the parking area in front of the former store.

Trailhead: At the southwest corner of the parking area

Trip 19. Purisima Creek

From the trailhead, go through a gap in a wood fence, passing two District information boards and a map holder on your right. From here, a dirt road descends on a gentle grade, and after 100 feet or so you reach a junction with a hiking-only trail on the right. This single-track trail, signed NORTH RIDGE TRAIL, is part of the Bay Area Ridge Trail. Here you bear right. Tanbark oak, Douglas-fir, madrone, and bigleaf maple (which turns yellow and orange in fall) grow beside the trail. Poison oak and thimbleberry, both also colorful in autumn, are nearby, along with coffeeberry, oceanspray, evergreen huckleberry, ferns, and berry vines.

On your switchbacking descent, Steller's jays may investigate and then complain noisily about your passage through their forest domain. After about 0.5 mile, you reach a four-way junction. Going left is the dirt road you abandoned just past the trailhead. The North Ridge Trail turns right, but you go straight, now on the Harkins Ridge Trail, also part of the Bay Area Ridge Trail. This trail, a wide dirt path, is open to horses and bikes. Now on a level course, with the upper reaches of Whittemore Gulch on your right, you pass a stand of coast redwood, the first of many on this route. Accompanying the redwoods are fragrant California bay trees.

Soon the trail crosses a culvert draining the seasonal creek that flows through Whittemore Gulch. This is one of the many tributaries of Purisima Creek, which eventually deposits its gathered waters into the Pacific, south of Half Moon Bay. Willows, blue blossom, and western creek dogwood inhabit the possibly wet areas beside the trail. After following the trail through several bends, you reach open ground on a scrubby hillside that drops to the right. Sticky monkeyflower, goldenrod, and coffeeberry line the route. The Pacific coastline and Half Moon Bay, visible on a clear day, are in the distance to your right. Just past the 1-mile point, you reach a T-junction with a closed road on

The Marbled Murrelet

A small, secretive seabird called the marbled murrelet has been spotted in the preserve's mature redwoods and Douglas-firs. Unlike other seabirds, which nest along the coast or on offshore islands, marbled murrelets prefer inland sites in undisturbed forests. They fly back and forth to the ocean, where they dive from the surface to feed on fish. The marbled murrelet is federally listed as a threatened species.

the left. Here you turn right and descend on a dirt road bordered by coyote brush, yerba santa, lupine, and California poppies. After a steep, eroded pitch, the road curves right, levels, and leads to a junction.

Turn left on the Soda Gulch Trail, also part of the Bay Area Ridge Trail. The single-track trail, closed to bikes and horses, crosses an open slope of coastal scrub containing shrubs such as blue blossom, blue elderberry, and sticky monkeyflower. This is perfect habitat for a secretive bird called a wrentit, more often heard than seen. Listen for a stuttering song that sounds like someone trying to start a reluctant car. This small songster is brown with a buffy breast, and has a long tail often held nearly vertical. This trail is great for viewing spring wildflowers, and growing beside it you may find blue-eyed grass, paintbrush, soap plant, scarlet pimpernel, and Douglas iris. A weedy herb called cow parsnip, which produces large umbels of white flowers, lines your route in places. Now descending via switchbacks, you pass a beautiful stand of coast live oaks, their twisted, gnarled limbs draped with lace lichen. Gooseberry and golden yarrow, both of which produce colorful blossoms, grow beside the trail.

A sudden transition brings you into the realm of the redwoods. A rest bench, left, invites you to spend a few minutes contemplating these towering giants in cool and shady surroundings. Some of the trees are fire-scarred, and some grow in so-called family circles, also referred to as fairy rings, around a fallen ancestor. A redwood forest fosters a community of plants that thrive in its moist, shady environment. A thick layer of redwood duff—twigs and needles on the forest floor—inhibits the growth of some species but favors others, including sword fern, trillium, fairy bells, Pacific star flower, and redwood sorrel. As you continue to lose elevation on a gentle grade, you pass a second rest bench and several seasonal creeks. Soda Gulch, another tributary of Purisima Creek, is downhill and to the right.

When you reach Soda Gulch, turn sharply right and cross a wood bridge that spans a creek bed of rocks and fallen logs. Early bloomers such as hound's tongue, milkmaids, and miner's lettuce grow beside the trail. Later in spring look nearby for the orange-and-yellow flowers of crimson columbine. A small bridge takes you across a seasonal creek, and soon the route emerges briefly onto an open hillside before ducking back into the redwoods. An unnamed tributary of Purisima Creek is at the bottom of a steep-walled canyon to your right. You descend to the tributary and cross it on a wood bridge. Now zigzag uphill to a junction with the Purisima Creek Trail, a dirt road.

Here at about the four-mile point, join the Purisima Creek Trail by bearing right. Then follow the road as it curves left and descends to Purisima

Creek, which flows under the road through a culvert. Now the road bends right, and you have a lovely view of the creek flowing from pool to pool over rocks and logs. Just ahead, a seasonal creek joins from the left through a culvert. You enjoy a level walk through a riparian corridor lush with red alder, hazelnut, elk clover, and red elderberry. Soon a bridge takes you across Purisima Creek, which is now on your left. The creek from Soda Gulch joins from the right, and you cross it on the next bridge. Look here for tiger lilies in late spring.

Wintering ladybugs sometimes gather here by the thousands, and you may see them massed on the leaves and branches of trailside plants. Descend on a moderate grade to the creek and cross it on a bridge, soon passing a junction with the Borden Hatch Mill Trail, left. One of Purisima's many lumber mills stood in a clearing near this now junglelike area of ferns, thimbleberry, and hazelnut, all presided over by lofty redwoods. A fence on your right signals the approach to a junction with a short connector to the Whittemore Gulch and Harkins Ridge Trails. A vault toilet is left, and the Higgins Purisima parking area is about 100 yards ahead.

Lady bugs at Purisima Creek Redwoods Open Space Preserve

Turn right at the junction and cross lovely Purisima Creek on a wood bridge. About fifty feet ahead is a T-junction. Here the Harkins Ridge Trail goes right, but instead follow the Whittemore Gulch Trail, a rocky dirt road, to the left. Soon you pass a fence with a gate that prevents access by bikes and horses during wet weather. (When the gate is closed, hikers can pass through a narrow gap in the fence.) Asters, one of California's late blooming wildflowers, decorate the roadside, as does trillium, an early bloomer. Soon the road curves right, narrows to a single track, and begins to climb. Whittemore Gulch, holding a tributary of Purisima Creek within its steep and narrow walls, is left. It was in Whittemore Gulch, according to local historian Ken Fisher, that San

Mateo's last grizzly bear was killed in 1879, with a piece of poisoned beefsteak.

The grade alternates between moderate and steep as you pass impressive rock cliffs on the right. The layers of marine sediments in these cliffs have been tilted almost vertically by geological forces almost too great to imagine. Keep a sharp eye out for descending bicyclists. Now on a rolling course, you stroll through stands of redwoods

Crimson columbine adds a delightful dollop of color to the dark redwood forest.

and a forest of red alder. This area has a dark, rainforest feel. A small bridge takes you across the creek in Whittemore Gulch, and then you climb into a brighter zone of Douglas-fir and coastal scrub. An old-growth redwood grove stands on the opposite side of Whittemore Gulch.

Aided by switchbacks, you continue to gain elevation, passing a junction, left, with a short connector to the North Ridge Trail. After more twists and turns, you come to another seasonal-closure gate and then a T-junction with the North Ridge Trail. Now bear right on a dirt road and enjoy a mostly level walk through a Douglas-fir forest. At the four-way junction where you started this loop, turn left onto the hiking-only trail and retrace your route uphill to the parking area.

COAST REDWOODS

Coast redwoods *(Sequoia sempervirens)* are the world's tallest trees and among the longest lived. One specimen in northern California stands more than 350 feet high. The oldest known redwood was more than 2,000 years old when it was cut, and mature redwoods may regularly live 400 to 500 years. Redwoods have been on Earth for millions of years. Fossil redwoods have been found that date back to the Cretaceous period, the time of the dinosaurs. Redwoods inhabit a narrow coastal band extending from central California to southern Oregon. These stately conifers are always found near the Pacific Ocean, but rarely on the immediate coastline, because redwoods rely on fog for moisture but are unable to tolerate salt air. Seasonal rains and annual flooding deposit nutrients along the banks of coastal creeks and rivers, providing a perfect environment for redwoods. Despite their size, redwoods lack a main taproot. Instead, each tree sends out a wide network of shallow roots about ten to twelve feet underground. The tree gains stability by interlocking its roots with those from neighboring trees. These roots draw moisture from the soil, which is watered in winter by rain, and in summer by fog condensing on the forest crown and then dripping to the ground, a process called fog drip.

A redwood forest is a special place—cool and shady, and with a thick carpet of duff made from fallen twigs and needles. Only certain other plants can thrive in this environment. Tanbark oak, California bay, hazelnut, thimbleberry, evergreen huckleberry, redwood sorrel, trillium, and western sword fern are some common redwood companions. A redwood has two methods of reproduction. The most common is from dormant buds in the tree's trunks and roots. Damage or stress to the tree stimulates the growth of these buds, which eventually form burls. Burls can sprout into new limbs or entire new trees, a form of cloning. An extreme example of this is found in logged redwood forests. Circles of second-growth trees frequently form around the stump of a fallen ancestor. These family circles (or fairy rings, as they are sometimes called) are evidence of sprouting from burls. Redwoods also produce small cones that contain seeds, but these have a hard time penetrating the dense redwood duff on the forest floor. When fire burns away the duff, however, redwood seeds have a chance to sprout.

Wildfires are often beneficial to coast redwoods. They rejuvenate the forest by reducing the build-up of duff and converting plant material to nutrients. Coast redwoods have evolved three defenses to withstand fire: thick, insulating bark; fire-resistant sap containing tannic acid; and a high crown that is beyond the reach of most flames. A fire-carved cavity in a redwood trunk is called a goosepen, because early settlers used the cavities, often with a gate across them, to shelter geese and other livestock. Even redwoods completely hollowed by fire may survive. But the ancient trees could do little to protect themselves against the logger's ax and saw. Before the arrival of Europeans, redwoods were plentiful, but logging in the nineteenth and twentieth centuries reduced the vast old-growth forest to a few enclaves in federal, state, and private hands. In the building boom that followed California's Gold Rush and statehood, many of the Bay Area's redwood forests were logged, including those in the Santa Cruz Mountains. By the early 1900s, the only trees left standing were ones that were too hard to reach or too deformed to cut.

According to local historian Ken Fisher, California's most spectacular redwood groves are in Humboldt County, site of Humboldt Redwoods State Park, Headwaters Grove, and other significant redwood preserves. Despite this, early logging in the Santa Cruz Mountains proceeded at a faster pace than in Humboldt County because of local demand from developing Bay Area cities. When the dust settled in the early twentieth century, the only significant ancient redwoods in the Santa Cruz Mountains that could be saved by the nascent forest preservation movement were in the southern area, in what later became Big Basin Redwoods State Park. Sempervirens Fund and Save-the-Redwoods League played an important role in the early years of the twentieth century in the establishment of redwood parks in Santa Cruz, Humboldt, and Del Norte counties.

Redwood forests harbor a wide array of birds and mammals. Spotted owls, marbled murrelets, pileated woodpeckers, and Vaux's swifts depend on old-growth forests for their survival. Steller's jays and varied thrushes are common in redwood forests, along with woodpeckers, flycatchers, and chestnut-backed chickadees. Black bears, deer, elk, porcupines, and an assortment of smaller mammals thrive in the shade of towering redwoods. There is a handful of old-growth redwoods, along with plentiful stands of second-growth redwoods, on District lands, primarily in Purisima Creek Redwoods and El Corte de Madera Creek Preserves.

Coast redwoods line the Harkins Ridge Trail near Purisima Creek.

Scenic vista view from Rancho San Antonio Open Space Preserve

RANCHO SAN ANTONIO OPEN SPACE PRESERVE

~

This 3,800-acre preserve bears the name of a large Mexican land grant given by Governor Alvarado to Juan Prado Mesa in 1839. Mesa was the grandson of a soldier who had come to Alta California with the Anza Expedition. Mesa named his rancho, which consisted of more than 4,000 acres of former Mission Santa Clara land between Adobe and Stevens Creeks, for St. Anthony of Padua, a Franciscan saint. Mesa died in 1845, heavily in debt. After California became a state in 1848, many of the Mexican land grants were challenged in court, and the large ranchos were often broken up and sold to pay expenses.

In 1853, San Francisco merchants William and Henry Dana, along with several others, filed claims on Rancho San Antonio. Four years later, they received title to about 3,500 acres. Mesa's heirs got about 900 acres bordering Adobe Creek. In the years that followed, the land was divided and changed hands. Two brothers from Boston, Theodore and George Grant, obtained 360 acres in 1860. They raised wheat, horses, and cows, operated a dairy, and may even have tried to start a silver mine. A one-room cabin dating from the 1850s was on the property when the Grants arrived. A second room was added sometime later, and the ranch foreman lived there. The cabin was built without vertical framing, and its walls and roof were supported only by the siding. You can see this cabin, which has been reframed, restored, furnished with artifacts by the District, and is maintained by dedicated volunteers, if you visit Deer Hollow Farm.

The Grants built a Victorian house and farm buildings, including a carriage shed and an apple shed, which are still standing. Two barns were built near the house; the ones in Deer Hollow Farm have been rebuilt on the original sites. In the 1870s, the Grants built a forty-foot-wide road, bordered by a redwood picket fence, that eventually extended from their ranch to Mountain View. This was the beginning of Grant Road. (In the late 1940s, the part of Grant Road nearest their ranch site was renamed St. Joseph Avenue after the nearby seminary.) The Grants and their neighbors also started San Antonio School for the education of their children. Theodore was one of the first people in the Santa Clara Valley to own an Edison phonograph, and it attracted many visitors. With his audience seated outdoors and the machine's speaker protruding from a window, Theodore would demand absolute silence. It is said that he would turn off the music and dismiss his guests at the slightest interruption.

The Grants sold their ranch in 1937 to the Perham family, who raised cattle and ran a construction business. The District became interested in the property after being approached by an attorney representing the Perhams. Located close to Los Altos, Mountain View, Sunnyvale, and Cupertino, and certain to be developed if not protected, the Perham property was an ideal candidate for open space acquisition for the new District. In 1974, the District bought nearly 400 acres from the Perhams after a sometimes difficult period of negotiation. Mrs. Perham received a life estate in the property and remained there until her death.

In 1977, Frank and Josephine Duveneck, the owners of Hidden Villa Ranch, an environmental education center that adjoins Rancho San Antonio Preserve, gave the District a 430-acre parcel called the Windmill Pasture Area, located a few miles north of Black Mountain. The District later purchased open space easements over much of Hidden Villa Ranch, ensuring that it would never be developed. The monies that were paid for the easements helped to fund Hidden Villa's programs, which are complementary to the District's. The remaining Rancho San Antonio Preserve acreage comprises multiple acquisitions from businesses and private landowners.

Elizabeth Dana, one of the Duveneck's daughters, grew up at Hidden Villa and remembers the beauty of the Windmill Pasture Area and the need the family felt to see it preserved. "Everybody in the family thought that it would be too bad to develop Hidden Villa's land," she says. "I think my parents both felt that they'd like to preserve the Windmill Pasture Area because it was on a ridge, and it would be very visible if you built houses up there."

Dana recalls riding horses up to the ridge above Hidden Villa and watering them at the windmill. "We used to ride up there all the time," she says. "The windmill was there because we used to pass through on our horses. And they used to have to come all the way down to Adobe Creek to get water. So my father and whoever the foreman was then decided to put a windmill up there to pump water for the horses. Well, it's beautiful to go up there. The views up toward the mountain and down toward the valley—you can see the whole valley from up there if you go to the right spot. It connects with the trails to Hidden Villa, and you can also take a trail from there and go all the way up to the top of Black Mountain."

Asked what would have happened if the land had not been protected, Dana considers the question carefully. "This land up here would have sold for a million dollars an acre," she says. "That's what buildable lots are going for in Los Altos Hills now, which is shocking. Well, you'd see huge houses up there because it's beautiful land with views down the valley, it would be incredible." Instead, thanks to the foresight and generosity of the Duveneck family, the public gets to enjoy a stunning swath of open space that is still home to the bobcats, foxes, coyotes, deer, and mountain lions Dana remembers from her childhood.

"Rancho," as it is affectionately called, is one of the District's most popular and busiest preserves, with about 23 miles of trails. It is also, paradoxically, one of the best preserves to see wildlife. Lorraine Alleman, a District Volunteer Trail Patrol member, recalls an encounter with a bobcat. "I was hiking by myself and I was going up the High Meadow Trail," she says "and the bobcat was at the top of the hill coming down. Usually, if they see you, they just run, but it kept coming right down the middle of the trail and I kept going up the trail. So I finally decided I maybe just better stop, and I did stop just at the side of the trail. And it came down the trail and looked at me all the way. Got very close to me, stuck its nose in the air, and went by. I could have reached out and touched it, but I wasn't about to. It was interesting because the animals are really pretty tame. But some people are quite frightened of them."

The District's Foothills office is located at Rancho San Antonio. Paul McKowan, the District's volunteer programs coordinator, worked at the Foothills office in the early 1990s. He describes a more intense encounter with an animal rarely seen by visitors to District preserves. "I came across a mountain lion during my morning run at Rancho," he says. "I was just down from the knoll, and it came out onto the trail and luckily turned away from me and the direction I was running. It was approximately twenty-five yards away, and it walked down the trail for about twenty yards. I kept my distance, and it turned off the trail. I gave it a minute or two to clear and continued my run. About a quarter-mile down the trail, I met another runner coming the opposite way and told him about my encounter as we passed. A couple of minutes later, I heard the runner coming up behind me. He had decided he would just head back this way with me today."

Wild turkeys are common at Rancho and can be aggressive, especially during mating season. As a member of the District's Volunteer Trail Patrol, Rodger Alleman has offered many visitors various forms of assistance over the years, but one incident sticks in his mind. "We met turkeys that were massed at a gate," he says. "There were probably ten or twelve of them, and mothers with strollers and babies were on both sides of the gate, which was open. But the turkeys were there and they didn't want people to come through. So the mothers were kind of concerned about it, and I figured as a Volunteer Trail Patrol member, I ought to be responsible for getting them through. So I spread my 'wings' or arms and started flapping at them and going toward them, and they didn't give an inch. In fact, they had me backing up a little bit. But at any rate, we dispersed them and made loud noises and the mothers got through and everybody was happy."

Alleman tells of watching an encounter between wild turkeys and a great blue heron that took place in an open field near the county park's tennis courts. "So this morning we looked down and there were a bunch of turkeys and a great blue heron," he says. "The turkeys were moving slowly toward the heron because they apparently didn't like the idea that the blue heron was there. The heron was aware of them, but the closer they got, the faster they went, and pretty soon they got really close and they all lowered their heads and started picking up speed and ran at him. There were probably twenty or thirty turkeys at the same time, so the heron waited till they got fairly close and then merely flew away and went down about a hundred feet and it started all over again." Alleman says this jousting was repeated about a dozen times before the heron flew away.

Wild turkeys at Rancho San Antonio Open Space Preserve

Bobcat at Rancho San Antonio Open Space Preserve

Marc Auerbach is a former District volunteer with the Preserve Partners program and an avid jogger. "I see fewer bobcats than I did ten years ago. Especially at the higher up trails, but I'm seeing a lot more coyotes. I've seen several coyotes very close. In fact, one day I was running down the Rogue Valley Trail, and it was already quite dark, and I see a coyote right off the trail foraging around under a tree. It's not more than thirty feet from me, and as I run by, it doesn't even take any notice of me, so I run by and I stop, and there's another man up there, and we just watch it for awhile and it's totally unperturbed by us."

Auerbach says he wasn't surprised by the encounter, given the lateness of the hour and the secluded area of the preserve he was in. "But just a few days later," he says, "I was running back at three o'clock in the afternoon on the same trail, and I look up, and trotting up the trail right toward me is a coyote. I see it coming, so I step off the trail just two feet, it steps off the trail two feet, doesn't even really look at me, doesn't stop, never breaks its stride. Trots right past me, just ten feet away, doesn't look at me while passing, goes down about another twenty feet, gets back on the trail and trots off just as nice as could be. A gorgeous-looking coyote, obviously well-fed, beautiful bushy squirrel-like tail and really in great shape. That was interesting to be that close for a moment."

Rancho's terrain is varied and diverse. Beside a tributary of Permanente Creek, visitors can amble through a riparian corridor lush with beautiful groves of fragrant bay trees, tall bigleaf maples, and willows. Along the Chamise Trail

Rancho San Antonio Trail Use

Bicycles: Allowed only on designated trails from the county park entrance to Deer Hollow Farm; not allowed west of Deer Hollow Farm

Dogs: Not allowed in the county park or at this preserve

Horses: From the county park's equestrian staging area to the preserve, allowed only on the Coyote Trail; not allowed on the Farm Bypass Trail and the hiking-only segments of the Lower Meadow and Wildcat Canyon Trails

RANCHO SAN ANTONIO OPEN SPACE PRESERVE

Trip 20. Wildcat Canyon and Deer Hollow Farm

Length: 4.8 miles

Time: 2 to 3 hours

Rating: Moderate

Highlights: This aerobic semi-loop uses the Rancho San Antonio, Permanente Creek, Lower Meadow, Farm Bypass, Rogue Valley,

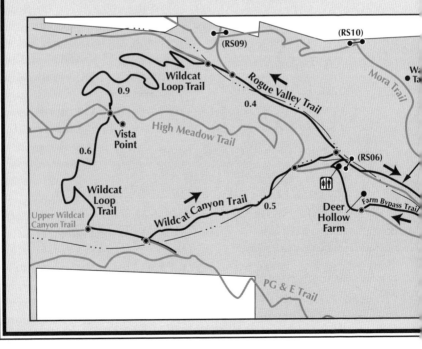

Wildcat Loop, and Wildcat Canyon Trails to explore the east half of one of the District's few urban preserves, located near the heart of Silicon Valley. The rustic buildings at Deer Hollow Farm harken back to an earlier era, and the riparian corridor along a tributary of Permanente Creek is lush with beautiful groves of fragrant bay trees, tall bigleaf maples, willows, oceanspray, and coffeeberry. This route is popular with runners, so be alert. Rancho San Antonio is the District's busiest preserve and parking may be unavailable. Please have an alternate destination to visit if the parking areas are full.

Directions: From I-280 at the Cupertino–Los Altos border, take the Foothill Expressway/Grant Road exit and go south on Foothill Boulevard 0.1 mile to Cristo Rey Drive. Turn right, go 0.8 mile to a traffic circle, and continue on Cristo Rey Drive by going halfway around the circle. At 1 mile, turn left into Rancho San Antonio County Park. Now bear right and go 0.3 mile to two parking areas, one on each side of the road.

Facilities: Restrooms, telephone, water

Trailhead: At the northwest corner of the northwest parking area

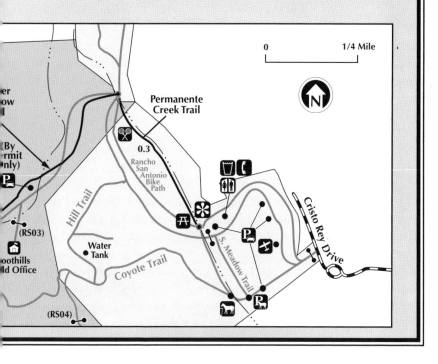

Trail descends through stands of chaparral shrubs at Rancho San Antonio Open Space Preserve.

to the Duveneck Windmill Pasture Area, in the preserve's backcountry, are acres of chaparral-clad hills with vantage points that afford great views of the Santa Clara Valley and the South Bay.

The main access to the preserve is through Rancho San Antonio County Park, which the District operates under a management agreement with the Santa Clara County Parks and Recreation Department. On many days, and especially on weekends, the county park's parking areas are filled, often by mid-morning. In late afternoon, the preserve is also busy. Please have an alternate destination to visit if the parking areas are full.

Trip 20. Wildcat Canyon and Deer Hollow Farm

From the trailhead, take the county park's Rancho San Antonio Trail, a paved hiking and bicycling path, and bear left. Almost immediately you cross a bridge over Permanente Creek and then come to a four-way junction. Here turn right onto the Permanente Creek Trail, a dirt path signed FOOT PATH, DEER HOLLOW, ST. JOSEPH AVENUE. Willows, alder, and black cotton-wood grow beside the creek, which is to your left. Passing an open area with picnic tables and barbecues, you come to a large California bay tree on the left followed by a set of tennis courts, also on the left. Just past the courts is a fork where you turn left. After a few feet you come to a three-way intersection. Continue straight (using the crosswalk) to the start of the Lower Meadow Trail. Three District information boards and a map holder are on the left. Follow the

hiking-only Lower Meadow Trail, a dirt track, past stands of coast live oak, California bay, and California buckeye (a paved road parallels your route to the right). Acorn woodpeckers and Steller's jays are among the most active and noisy birds found in this preserve; look for them high in the treetops or flying across open fields. Soon you merge briefly with the paved road you've been walking beside, and then veer right into a dirt, permit-only parking area. The Lower Meadow Trail continues from the northwest corner of the parking area, just to the right of a wood fence.

A tributary of Permanente Creek is downhill and right, and your trail soon turns right, descends slightly, and crosses the creek on a wooden bridge. This wooded, riparian area is a good place to look for birds that travel in flocks, including dark-eyed juncos and golden-crowned sparrows. This area is full of blue elderberry, which sports decorative cream-colored flowers in late spring. The paved road you have been following is now on your left, and soon the Mora Trail, a dirt road, is beside you on your right. At about 0.8 mile from the trailhead, a potentially confusing junction requires some attention. Your trail meets the paved road just where the road begins to bend to the right. The Mora Trail joins the paved road immediately to your right. Also to your right is the continuation of the Lower Meadow Trail. And across the junction to your left is a single track, signed FARM BYPASS TRAIL.

Bear left across the paved road and get on the Farm Bypass Trail. After about 30 feet, cross a bridge over a tributary of Permanente Creek and then follow the trail as it turns right. Coast redwoods grow beside the tributary, as do blue elderberry, hazelnut, poison oak, and tangles of berry vines. This preserve is home to large flocks of California quail, the state bird. You may hear them rustling in the underbrush, clucking furtively to each other, or giving their unmistakable "Chi-ca-go" calls. Climbing on a gentle grade, and shaded by valley oaks, you begin to notice the buildings of Deer Hollow Farm, downhill and right.

At about the 1-mile point, you meet the Coyote Trail joining on the left. Stay on the Farm Bypass Trail by angling right. After several hundred feet, the trail turns right, crosses a culvert, and then bends sharply right, following a mostly level course. Now descend gently to a junction where you leave the Farm Bypass Trail and angle sharply right. Still descending, you reach a T-junction in about 100 yards. There are vault toilets on the right and a covered picnic area ahead. The Wildcat Canyon Trail is left, but instead turn right toward Deer Hollow Farm, which you will visit later.

After several hundred feet, you come to another T-junction, where you turn left onto the Rogue Valley Trail. Passing three District information boards, head northwest on the Rogue Valley Trail, following a line of willows that hides the tributary of Permanente Creek you followed earlier. Your route is a dirt road bordered by coyote brush, coffeeberry, and olive trees. Look here for the California thrasher, a plain, gray-brown bird with a long, decurved bill. About the size of a Steller's jay, thrashers may be found scratching among dry leaves for food or perching atop chaparral shrubs. Passing a junction with the Ravensbury Trail, right, go several hundred feet to a junction with the Wildcat Loop Trail, where you turn left.

Now on a single-track trail, climb through a corridor of coyote brush, coffee-berry, oceanspray, and spiny redberry into a forest of bay and coast live oak. A series of switchbacks and rising traverses helps you ascend a northeast-facing hillside on a steady, gentle grade. In places, openings in the dense foliage give you an opportunity to admire the surrounding scenery. At one vantage point, you are rewarded with terrific views of familiar Bay Area summits—Mt. Tamalpais, Mt. Diablo, and Mission Peak. On a clear day, you can also pick out San Francisco, Oakland, Palo Alto, and the bridges that cross San Francisco Bay. But not all the vistas are unmarred. Just north of the preserve in Los Altos Hills, housing developments crowding up to the preserve boundary offer strong testimony in favor of preserving open space.

At a T-junction with the High Meadow Trail, turn left and walk about 50 feet to a four-way junction. Here the High Meadow Trail veers left, and a short trail going straight climbs a grassy hill, where more great views await. Your route, signed WILDCAT LOOP TRAIL, turns right. The trail, a single track, descends on a gentle, winding course through a lovely forest and stands of chaparral shrubs, including toyon, buckbrush, chamise, California sagebrush, and sticky monkey-flower. A row of power line towers marches uphill toward Black Mountain, which is to the southwest atop Monte Bello Ridge. Just past the three-mile point, you meet the Upper Wildcat Canyon Trail, which goes right. Here you turn

---

Deer Hollow Farm

Deer Hollow Farm, which is a delightful place to bring children, is just an easy stroll from the Rancho San Antonio parking areas. The farm includes a hay barn, a garden, an orchard, animal pens, a duck pond, a blacksmith shed, and the restored Grant Cabin. Some of these are remnants of the historic Grant Ranch. Deer Hollow Farm is funded through a cooperative agreement between the City of Mountain View, Santa Clara County, and the District, with support from the Friends of Deer Hollow Farm. The farm is closed on Mondays. The farm's animals may include sheep, goats, pigs, rabbits, ducks, chickens, geese, and a cow. This is a working farm, not a petting zoo; the main purpose of the farm is education. Volunteer docents and a naturalist conduct environmental education programs and summer day-camps at the farm. For more information, call Deer Hollow Farm: (650) 903-6430.

---

sharply left to stay on the Wildcat Loop Trail, which follows a tributary of Permanente Creek downstream to Deer Hollow Farm.

About 100 feet past the junction, cross the tributary on a wooden bridge. Now in the bottom of a cool, shady canyon, you enjoy a level walk through beautiful groves of fragrant bay trees and tall bigleaf maples. The trail here is lined with willows, oceanspray, coffeeberry, and ninebark. Where a trail signed COUNTY PARK departs to the right, continue straight, passing through a gap in a fence (horses prohibited). Now the tributary flows under the trail through two large culverts and reappears on your right. Blue elderberry and dense thickets of thimbleberry grow along the stream bank. Three more bridges help you across the tributary at various points ahead. Then the canyon widens, and soon you reach another fence with a gap, and then a junction.

To your left is the High Meadow Trail, but instead continue straight on the Wildcat Canyon Trail. Follow it to the T-junction with the Rogue Valley Trail mentioned above. Here turn right onto the Lower Meadow Trail and enter Deer Hollow Farm, managed as an old-fashioned homestead and funded by the City of Mountain View, the District, and Santa Clara County, with support from Friends of Deer Hollow Farm. A large covered barn with picnic tables is on your right, as is a garden of herbs, vegetables, and flowers. Ahead there are more farm buildings and livestock, including sheep, goats, pigs, rabbits, ducks, chickens, geese, and a cow. Drinking water is on your left. The farm's animal and garden products are used to support daily farm activities. The oldest remaining building on the farm

Rancho San Antonio Trail Use

Bicycles: Allowed only on designated trails from the county park entrance to Deer Hollow Farm; not allowed west of Deer Hollow Farm

Dogs: Not allowed in the county park or at this preserve

Horses: From the county park's equestrian staging area to the preserve, allowed only on the Coyote Trail; not allowed on the Farm Bypass Trail and the hiking-only segments of the Lower Meadow and Wildcat Canyon Trails

RANCHO SAN ANTONIO OPEN SPACE PRESERVE

Trip 21. Duveneck Windmill Pasture

Length: 9.2 miles

Time: 4 to 6 hours

Rating: Difficult

Highlights: From the hustle and bustle of the county park and the area around Deer Hollow Farm, escape to the Duveneck Windmill Pasture Area, a lovely wilderness saved from development by a generous gift from Frank and Josephine Duveneck, ardent conservationists and pioneers in outdoor education. This out-and-back route uses the Rancho San Antonio, Permanente Creek, Lower Meadow, Farm Bypass, Rogue Valley, and Chamise Trails to wander far into the western half of one of the District's few urban preserves, located near the heart of Silicon Valley. Great views and the chance to study native chaparral shrubs add to your enjoyment.

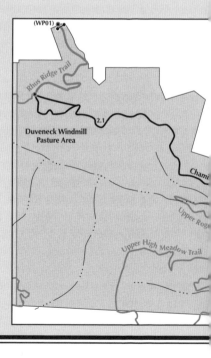

Directions: Same as for "Wildcat Canyon and Deer Hollow Farm" on pages 206–7

Facilities: Restrooms, telephone, water

Trailhead: Same as for "Wildcat Canyon and Deer Hollow Farm" on pages 206–7

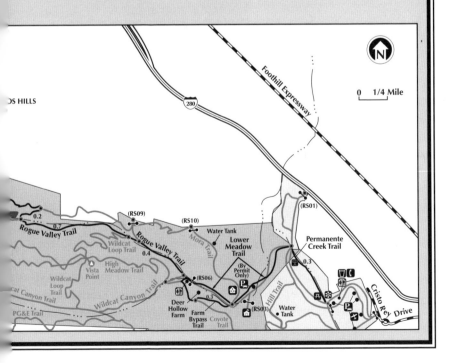

*Windmill Pasture Area of
Rancho San Antonio
Open Space Preserve*

is the two-room Grant Cabin, originally a single room, built in the 1850s. In 1996, the interior of the cabin was restored and furnished with artifacts by the District.

After crossing a tributary of Permanente Creek on a bridge, you reach a junction. A paved road continues straight, but instead angle left onto the hiking-only Lower Meadow Trail. In late spring, you may notice the sweet aroma of black locust trees in bloom. These East Coast natives are in the pea family and produce dangling clusters of fragrant white flowers. Traveling parallel to the paved road, you soon return to the potentially confusing junction about 0.8 mile from the trailhead. Here you cross the Mora Trail, then veer left onto the continuation of the Lower Meadow Trail and retrace your route to the parking area.

Trip 21. Duveneck Windmill Pasture

Follow the route description for "Wildcat Canyon and Deer Hollow Farm" on pages 206–7 to the junction of the Rogue Valley and Wildcat Loop Trails. Here you continue straight on the Rogue Valley Trail, entering a tranquil forest of coast live oak and California bay. A tributary of Permanente Creek is to your right. At a junction with the Chamise Trail, turn right and cross an earthen dam. The dam creates a seasonal pond, which is on the left. Once across the dam, turn right again and begin a moderate climb, now on a dirt road. Soon the grade eases, and where the road makes a sharp left-hand bend, you pass a trail leading to gate RS09 and Ravensbury Avenue.

You are traveling through a fascinating world of chaparral shrubs—hardy plants adapted to fire, drought, and poor soil conditions. Chamise is the most common chaparral shrub, but also here are mountain mahogany, hollyleaf cherry, scrub oak, spiny redberry, toyon, and silk tassel. An unsigned road joins sharply from the right; ignore it. As you continue to climb, take time to stop, turn around, and admire the view. San Jose and its surrounding communities form the foreground to a dramatic view of Mt. Hamilton, rising in the distance. From here, it's easy to marvel at how lucky we are to be able to enjoy this vista from an open space preserve trail, instead of from a subdivision! You may be observed from above by a flock of ravens, those larger cousins of crows, made famous by Edgar Allen Poe. You can distinguish a raven from a crow by noting its larger size, generally deeper voice, and wedge-shaped tail.

At about the three-mile point, you meet another unsigned road but continue straight. Monte Bello Ridge, crowned by Black Mountain, looms high on the southwest skyline. Two oaks usually found on dry slopes—blue and scrub—grow beside the road. Blue oak has light gray bark cut in vertical strips, and blue-green leaves with shallow lobes. Scrub oak has similar bark, and green leaves that often have spine-tipped teeth. Blue oak leaves average from one to three inches, whereas scrub oak has leaves of 1 inch or less. Now atop a ridge, the road curves right and climbs to a T-junction not shown on the District map. Private property is to your right, so turn left, still on the Chamise Trail. Climbing moderately, you pass a fork, where you stay to the right.

As you gain more elevation, you begin to get fine views, through gaps in the foliage, northwest toward San Francisco and Mt. Tamalpais, and northeast across San Francisco Bay to the East Bay hills and Mt. Diablo. Descending briefly to a saddle, you now follow a rolling course, finding welcome shade in groves of coast live oak and madrone. Where the road begins to curve left, you pass a trail on the right that you will use later. Just ahead is a sign marking the Duveneck Windmill Pasture Area, some 430 acres given to the District in 1977 by Frank and Josephine Duveneck. The Duvenecks owned Hidden Villa, adjacent to the preserve, and ran it as an environmental education center for children. Now the nonprofit Trust for Hidden Villa continues to operate the center, with eco-friendly buildings and organic produce. A windmill once stood here, drawing water for horses from a well.

From here the trail winds uphill to a five-way junction at about the 5-mile point. The Black Mountain Trail is left, the Rhus Ridge Trail is straight ahead, and two single-track trails go to the right. The farthest right of these, your route, angles more gently across a hillside and soon rejoins the Chamise Trail. Now retrace your route to the start of the Rogue Valley Trail just west of Deer Hollow Farm. From here follow the route description for "Wildcat Canyon and Deer Hollow Farm" on pages 206–7 from the farm back to the parking area.

REMEMBERING THE DUVENECKS

If you care to travel beyond the crowds at Rancho San Antonio Preserve, follow the Rogue Valley and Chamise Trails a couple of miles past Deer Hollow Farm. You will eventually find yourself on a gorgeous piece of land called the Duveneck Windmill Pasture. The Duvenecks figure large in the history of land stewardship and progressive causes on the Peninsula. Elizabeth Dana is the daughter of Frank and Josephine Duveneck, who in 1977 gave the District this 430-acre parcel that once was part of their Hidden Villa Ranch.

"I grew up here," Dana says. "We originally lived in Palo Alto, and my parents used to drive around in the hills. They saw a gate on Moody Road that said 1,000 ACRES, CHEAP. So they went in and looked at it. They'd seen it from above the road and they thought, what a neat place. So when they found out where it was, they decided they'd buy it. Dad was very concerned with the watershed there, so we traded some land so that he could have the complete watershed of Adobe Creek."

This was in 1923. From then on, the family spent weekends and summers at Hidden Villa Ranch, as the property was called, staying in a house that was constructed in the late 1800s. Dana says her parents built a new house, which the family occupied on Thanksgiving Day, 1930. The Sierra Club's Loma Prieta Chapter was founded in the Duveneck's living room a few years later, and chapter meetings were held there for more than ten years. "Politically, they were very liberal," Dana says. "Dad got involved with the Sierra Club—I guess it was because they lived out there and they just loved the land." During World War II, Frank and Josephine started a youth hostel and an interracial summer camp for children, a novelty at the time. The Duvenecks had also been instrumental in founding the Peninsula School for Creative Education, now called Peninsula School, a progressive elementary school in Menlo Park. "Mother had all these great schemes for saving the world," Dana says. "Dad was much more cautious, shall we say. So I often think that it was a good thing that they were so opposite, because oth-

Frank and Josephine Duveneck

erwise mother would have gone sky-high with her projects, and dad would have been kind of stuffy."

Frank Duveneck and Josephine Whitney were married in Boston in 1913, having met at her debutante ball. Frank's mother came from a wealthy New England family, and his father was a respected artist. Frank was trained as a mechanical engineer. The newlyweds spent the next year circling the globe, passing through San Francisco on their way to China and Japan. After their honeymoon, they returned to Boston, where their first two children, Elizabeth

and Francis, were born. Dana says her parents grew weary of the cold winter weather and moved to Carmel, California. Frank left for the war shortly afterward, having just become a father for the third time. The Duvenecks named their new daughter Hope. During the war, Josephine moved the family to Palo Alto. After Frank returned from Europe, a fourth child, Bernard, was born. For a time, Frank worked at the Stanley Steamer Agency in San Francisco. He also taught math and shop at Peninsula School, and worked at Stanford in the physics department.

Hidden Villa Ranch became a center of social activism in the years following the second world war, welcoming those involved in the struggle for racial justice, nuclear disarmament, and human rights. In 1960, the Duvenecks incorporated Hidden Villa as a nonprofit organization, now the Trust for Hidden Villa. Dana says her parents were concerned over the urbanization of what was formerly an agricultural area. In 1970, the Duvenecks started an environmental education program at Hidden Villa. Its purpose was to give local children the experience of a working farm, complete with farm animals. "So we had cows, sheep, pigs, goats, chickens, ducks," Dana says. "But Hidden Villa was never a money-making proposition. My father used to say that his most important crop was children." Josephine's autobiography is called *Life on Two Levels,* and Dana says her father always threatened to write one called *Life on a Low Level.* Josephine died in 1978, and Frank died in 1985, at age 98.

Today, the programs continue and have expanded in scope. The public is welcome on Hidden Villa's trails, Dana says, as they were when her parents lived there. "Mother had a little book out there near the house where people would sign in, and then they could go and use the trails. That's been a tradition in our family. If you were lucky enough to have all that beautiful property, you should share it with somebody. So I think that was sort of the beginning, and Hidden Villa still does this to this day. Anybody can come and walk there." In addition to donating the Windmill Pasture, the Duvenecks sold the development rights of the property to the District to preserve Hidden Villa's 2,000 acres for future generations. For more information about Hidden Villa Ranch, call (650) 949-8650.

Ravenswood Preserve Trail, part of the Bay Trail,
explores a restored salt marsh on San Francisco Bay.

RAVENSWOOD OPEN SPACE PRESERVE

~

This preserve takes its name from a town that once thrived on the shore of San Francisco Bay, near present-day East Palo Alto. In 1848, a 1,500-foot wharf was built here to access relatively deep water. A few years later, a town was laid out with the hope that it would become a shipping port for redwood lumber cut and milled in the nearby hills. The name Ravenswood may have been bestowed on the town by Isaiah C. Woods, a local landowner and member of Adams and Company, a San Francisco banking and express firm. The firm financed a sixty-ton side-wheeler called the *Jenny Lind*, which made a regular run between Ravenswood, Alviso, and San Francisco. In 1853, the steam-powered vessel exploded, with much loss of life, and two years later Adams and Company failed. Woods absconded with much of the firm's gold and fled, disguised as a woman, aboard a ship bound for Australia.

Hopes that the Central Pacific Railroad would choose Ravenswood as a terminus for its line from Sacramento convinced Lester P. Cooley to buy a parcel of land that included the shipping wharf. Cooley's Landing, as it was then called, handled lumber, grain, and hay for a long while. The railroad ultimately went to San Jose instead, and Ravenswood also lost out to Redwood City, which became San Mateo County's most important port. Attempts to revive the town's flagging fortunes with a brickworks and then a chicken farm failed. The wharf fell into disrepair, and the area was later used as a dump site for San Mateo County. The Cooley Landing property is currently owned by Peninsula Open Space Trust, which purchased the property with a promised grant from the Packard Foundation. This property will eventually become a part of the publicly owned bay-front heritage preserved for future generations in East Palo Alto.

A levee built in the 1950s isolated the 150-acre salt marsh just north of Cooley Landing so that it could be used for salt production. The District acquired the salt pond and adjacent land from Leslie Salt in 1981. In 2000, Aventis CropScience USA Inc. (formerly Rhone-Poulenc Inc.) began a remediation project that drained the pond and strategically cut the levee to restore both tidal action and the former salt marsh. It will take from three to five years for the salt marsh vegetation to flourish, and the site will be monitored for at least twenty years.

This 373-acre preserve, one of the District's two holdings on San Francisco Bay,

---

Ravenswood Trail Use

Bicycles: Allowed on all trails

Dogs: Not allowed

Horses: Not allowed

RAVENSWOOD OPEN SPACE PRESERVE

Trip 22. Ravenswood Preserve Trail

Length: 2.4 miles

Time: 1 to 2 hours

Rating: Easy

Highlights: This out-and-back route will appeal to birders, especially during spring and fall migration, when San Francisco Bay plays host to incredible numbers of shorebirds, waterfowl, and waders. The trail skirts a restored salt marsh, a testament to the ability of previously altered landscapes to heal themselves with a little help from their friends. The Ravenswood Preserve Trail is designated an "Easy Access Trail." The trail and observation decks are accessible to visitors with wheelchairs or strollers.

Directions: From Highway 101 northbound in East Palo Alto, take the University Avenue exit, which puts you on Donohoe Street. Turn left, go one block to University Avenue, and turn right. After 0.6 mile, turn right at the traffic signal onto Bay Road. After 0.4 mile, Bay Road narrows at the intersection with Pulgas Avenue. At 0.7 mile, Bay Road turns to dirt, and at 0.8 mile you come to gate RW01. Continue another 0.1 mile to a parking area on your left.

is divided into two parts. The north part is adjacent to the Dumbarton Bridge and is not suitable for hiking or bicycling; a very rough levee extends south beside a salt evaporation pond for about 0.5 mile. The south part of the preserve has a 1.2-mile trail beside the former salt evaporation pond. Public access here has been improved, and now includes two observation decks and a twelve-car parking area. The trail and observation decks are accessible to visitors with wheelchairs or strollers. These improvements were funded by the Coastal Conservancy, and represented a joint effort by San Mateo County and the District.

From Highway 101 southbound in East Palo Alto, take the University Avenue exit, go north on University Avenue, and follow the directions above.

Facilities: None
Trailhead: Just west of the parking area

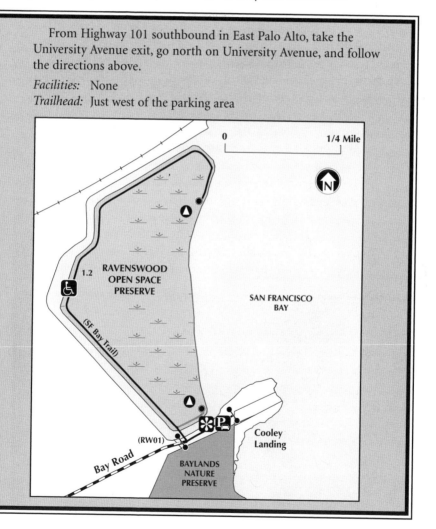

Trip 22. Ravenswood Preserve Trail

The trailhead has two District information boards and a map holder. Take a paved path heading west and parallel to the preserve's entrance road. After about 0.1 mile, turn right to cross a bridge over a tidal channel. Signs here inform you that this route, the Ravenswood Preserve Trail, is part of the San Francisco Bay Trail. The Bay Trail, like the Bay Area Ridge Trail, is a system of trails, existing and proposed, that is intended to encircle San Francisco Bay. Just across the bridge is a T-junction. The right-hand trail goes to an observation deck, and the left-hand trail begins a northward journey along the eastern edge of the Cooley Landing salt pond, which is now a restored salt marsh.

Salt marshes, also called tidal wetlands, are among the world's most productive ecosystems, providing habitat and nourishment for a variety of plants and animals. Researchers estimate that about 80 percent of the wetland habitats along the San Francisco Bay shoreline have been destroyed in the past two hundred years. Much of this destruction was done in the name of progress—to provide more acreage for agriculture, housing, industry, and transportation. Salt production was also a factor, especially in the South Bay. Today, thanks to innovative programs, some of this lost habitat is being reclaimed. The marsh you are exploring today is one such example. By breaching levees and restoring tidal action, former salt ponds can slowly be transformed into healthy salt marshes.

Turning left at the T-junction, follow a level path that is designated an "Easy Access Trail" and is designed to accommodate visitors with wheelchairs

---

San Francisco Bay Trail

More than 80 percent of San Francisco Bay's original wetland habitats have been lost because of levee construction for salt production, and filling for industrial and residential development and for roadways and airports. In the 1970s, only about four miles of Bay shoreline were open to the public. The passage of Senate Bill 100 in 1987 created the "Ring Around the Bay" concept, and the San Francisco Bay Trail was born. Today, about half of the proposed four hundred-mile trail system is in place. The District has actively supported and participated in the creation of this trail, which one day will link parks and preserves around San Francisco and San Pablo bays. The Ravenswood Preserve Trail is part of the San Francisco Bay Trail.

Clapper rail, a specialized salt marsh dweller listed on the
federal endangered species list

and strollers. As you proceed, be sure to scan the marsh frequently. San Francisco Bay is one of the world's greatest birding locations, thanks to its strategic position on the Pacific Flyway, a major bird migration route. Each year, the Bay hosts thousands of migratory waterbirds and up to one million shorebirds. Year-round residents include gulls, rails, herons, and egrets. Both common species of egret—great and snowy—are found in this preserve. Great egrets are large wading birds with a thick, yellow bill and black legs. Snowy egrets are smaller, with a slim, black bill, black legs, and yellow feet. Both species feed mostly on fish. Great egrets tend to stalk their prey by standing still, whereas snowy egrets often move quickly through shallow water, stirring up the muddy bottom with their feet.

Among the common shorebirds that visit here, usually from fall through spring, are willets, long-billed curlews, marbled godwits, dowitchers, and small sandpipers. Because they breed elsewhere, these and many other species of shorebirds are absent from San Francisco Bay during the summer. American avocets and black-necked stilts, on the other hand, breed locally and may be seen year-round. In addition to time of year, the tide influences the presence of shorebirds in marshes and on mudflats around

Restored salt marsh at
Ravenswood Open Space Preserve

the Bay. Low tide finds shorebirds widely dispersed and hunting for food, which generally consists of worms, small mollusks, and other invertebrates. As the tide rises, the birds are pushed closer to shore and within range of binoculars or a spotting scope. At high tide, you may see large numbers of shorebirds congregating on any remaining dry ground near the water's edge, including pickleweed-covered islands in salt marshes. Such high-tide roosting areas, like other marshlands around the Bay, are critical to the survival of shorebirds.

Salt marsh plants can tolerate levels of salinity that would kill other types of vegetation. Salt marshes are subject to tidal flooding twice each day. The height of the highest tide varies during the month, depending on the phase of the moon. Thus, some areas of a salt marsh may be under water for several hours each day, whereas other areas get soaked only a few times each month. Salt marsh plants arrange themselves in the marsh by elevation, which controls how much saltwater reaches their roots. For example, saltwater cord grass is found in the lowest zone of a salt marsh, pickleweed in the middle zone, and gumplant in the upper zone.

Some animals are specialized salt marsh dwellers. Two of these, the California clapper rail and the salt marsh harvest mouse, are on the federal endangered species list. Clapper rails are large but secretive marsh dwellers

most often seen around high tide, when they are forced out of their homes in the cord grass and may have to swim across open water. Salt marsh harvest mice, a species found only in the salt marshes of the San Francisco Bay Area, spend most of their lives hidden in pickleweed and are rarely seen.

Your route follows a levee around the west side of the marsh, affording views of the East Bay hills, crowned by Mt. Diablo and Mt. Hamilton, and the Santa Cruz Mountains from Black Mountain to Mt. Umunhum. The trail eventually curves right and then reaches an observation platform, where you can rest, enjoy the view, and scan the marsh and Bay for birds. Be sure to check the power line towers and sky for common raptors such as red-tailed hawks, northern harriers, and white-tailed kites. When large numbers of ducks and shorebirds are present, look for merlins and even peregrine falcons, fearsome aerial hunters who can strike fear into feeding or resting flocks.

Power lines overhead, the air traffic from the nearby Palo Alto airport, and a railroad trestle and bridge jutting out into San Francisco Bay—these signs of civilization mark this as anything but a wilderness area. Still, Ravenswood Preserve is one of the few remaining places in Silicon Valley where you can actually walk to the water's edge. When you have finished enjoying this unusual setting, retrace your steps to the parking area.

Field of wildflowers at Russian Ridge Open Space Preserve, one of the best places in the Bay Area to view wildflowers

RUSSIAN RIDGE
OPEN SPACE PRESERVE

~

This 1,827-acre preserve is frequently named as one of the best places in the Bay Area to view wildflowers. Reports from docent-led activities in spring sometimes include spotting more than fifty species within a few hours. Lupine, clarkia, checker mallow, red maids, California buttercup, fiddleneck, purple owl's-clover, Johnny jump-ups, mule ears, tidy-tips, and California poppies are among the most common grassland species found here. In the preserve's cool, forested canyons, you may find shade-loving plants like trillium, fairy bells, mission bells, and hound's tongue. About eight miles of trails await visitors on foot, on bicycle, and on horseback. Located on a steep, southwest-facing ridge, the preserve encompasses the headwaters of Alpine and Mindego Creeks, which are part of the San Gregorio Creek watershed.

Deane Little is a member of the District board of directors. He says that Russian Ridge Preserve represents the pinnacle of the Open Space District. "It's not the highest point within the District, but I think it's the most spectacular place in the District," he says. "I've hiked that preserve a lot over the years. And it's pretty much central to the District's properties. It has the most stunning views from anywhere in the Santa Cruz Mountains. From the top of Borel Hill, you can see the Marin Headlands, Mt. Tamalpais, the San Francisco skyscrapers. You can see the whole sweep of the Bay on a clear day. All of the bridges. Mt. Diablo, Mt. Hamilton. And to the south, the Monterey Peninsula and Monterey Bay. So you'll often see layers and layers of ridges, outlined against one another in the haze. And then beyond that, the Pacific Ocean. So it's a pretty spectacular place. And it's one that's very special, I think, for people who have visited it."

Russian Ridge was named for Mr. Paskey, a Russian immigrant who grazed cattle and ran a dairy here from about 1920 to 1950. Paskey originally leased his

Bicyclists heading northwest on the Ridge Trail near Borel Hill

land from James "Sunny Jim" Rolph, Jr., then mayor of San Francisco, and later California's governor. Rolph owned more than 3,000 acres of land in this area. (For more on the career of this colorful and influential man, see "Skyline Ridge" on pages 268–272.)

Native Americans are thought to have used the area for gathering seeds, and may have burned some of the grasslands to encourage a bountiful crop the following year, and also perhaps to reduce the buildup of fuel for wildfires. Alpine Road, at the preserve's south end, follows a historic route across a low point in the Sierra Morena (as this part of the Santa Cruz Mountains is known). It provided a relatively easy connection between San Francisco Bay and the Pacific Ocean.

The preserve's highest point is Borel Hill, named for Antoine Borel, a Swiss banker who lived here from 1885 to 1910. Borel was involved with the Spring Valley Water Company, which later created Crystal Springs Reservoir. Much of Russian Ridge's crest is open, affording expansive views of the San Mateo coast, the Santa Cruz Mountains, and the San Francisco Bay Area. At an elevation above 2,000 feet, the ridge top is often blanketed in fog, buffeted by wind, and sometimes dusted with snow. Especially during spring and fall migration, Russian Ridge Preserve attracts birders looking for raptors. Red-tailed hawks, Cooper's hawks, sharp-shinned hawks, falcons, and golden eagles have been spotted here. Coyotes, foxes, deer, and mountain lions call this area home, although the latter are rarely seen. Mountain bicyclists love this preserve for its challenging trails, scenic vistas, and open terrain.

To control the growth and spread of yellow star thistle and other invasive nonnative plants, the District sometimes conducts prescribed burns on parts of Russian Ridge Preserve as part of its Grassland Management Study. Burning is one method to control invasive species and allow native plants to flourish. Burning is done in the summer, and by the next spring, the renewed grasslands may be bursting with colorful wildflowers. (See the section "Resource Management" on pages 353–57 for more information on the District's open space management policies and practices and the Russian Ridge Grasslands program.)

The District began acquiring the preserve in 1978 (through a complex series of transactions) from its owners, who were planning to subdivide and build houses. The Bay Area Ridge Trail—actually a network of existing and yet-to-be-built trails that is intended to ring the ridges around San Francisco and San Pablo Bays—passes through the preserve on its way from Skyline Ridge Preserve to Rapley Ranch Road. From the parking area on Alpine Road just west of Skyline Boulevard, you can go through a tunnel under Alpine Road to enter Skyline Ridge Preserve. There is additional parking at the Caltrans Vista Point, on the east side of Highway 35, 1.1 miles northwest of the Alpine Road parking area.

The map for Russian Ridge Preserve is part of the District's South Skyline Region map.

Fog and conifers form a photogenic scene as viewed from the Ridge Trail.

Russian Ridge Trail Use

Bicycles: Allowed on all trails

Dogs: Not allowed

Horses: Allowed on all trails

RUSSIAN RIDGE OPEN SPACE PRESERVE

Trip 23. Ancient Oaks

Length: 2 miles

Time: 1 to 2 hours

Rating: Moderate

Highlights: Justly famous for its wildflowers, this preserve also offers visitors stunning scenic vistas that take in much of the Bay Area and the often fog-shrouded San Mateo coast. This short loop, using the Ridge, Ancient Oaks, and Mindego Trails, merely whets your appetite for further adventures in what many enthusiasts claim is the jewel in the District's crown of open space lands. From wind-swept grasslands to shady forest canyons, there is something for everyone on this enchanting route.

Directions: From the junction of Skyline Boulevard and Page Mill Road/Alpine Road south of Palo Alto, take Skyline Boulevard northwest 1.1 miles to the Caltrans Vista Point parking area on your right.

From the junction of Skyline Boulevard and Highway 84 in Sky Londa, take Skyline Boulevard southeast 6.2 miles to the Caltrans Vista Point parking area on your left.

Facilities: None

Trailhead: On the southwest side of Skyline Boulevard, across from the parking area

Trip 23. Ancient Oaks

A gate marked RR01 is where you start this scenic loop. Passing through a gap in a wood fence to the right of the gate, follow a dirt road a few feet to two District information boards and a map holder. Just beyond the information boards is the first of several junctions. There are two Ridge Trails

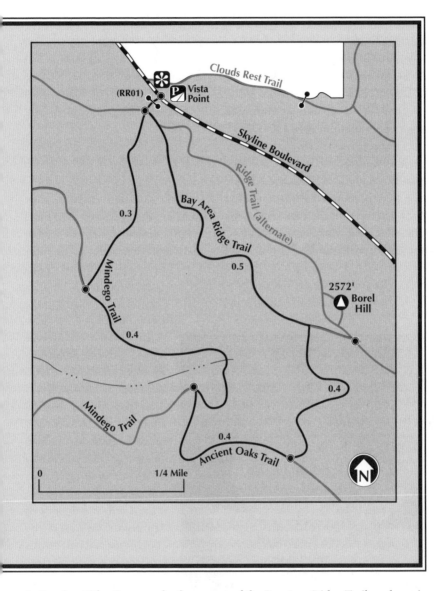

in Russian Ridge Preserve: both are part of the Bay Area Ridge Trail, and one is a 0.5-mile segment of dirt road that traverses Borel Hill, which is designated in this book as Ridge Trail (alternate).

You angle left at the first junction and get onto the Ridge Trail, a wide single track. After about 100 feet, you cross a dirt road heading up Borel Hill, the

Ridge Trail (alternate). Stay on the single-track trail, climbing on a moderate grade, and enjoy the expansive views west across rolling hills and wooded ravines toward the Pacific Ocean. The trail winds its way uphill, staying just below the ridge top, which is to your left. Famous for their wildflowers, the open grasslands of Russian Ridge are home to lupine, clarkia, checker mallow, red maids, California buttercup, fiddleneck, purple owl's-clover, Johnny jump-ups, mule ears, tidy-tips, and California poppies.

Soon you reach a junction with a 0.4-mile connector to the Ancient Oaks Trail. If you wish to ascend Borel Hill, the highest named peak in San Mateo County, continue straight on the Ridge Trail for several hundred feet to a junction with the Ridge Trail (alternate). Turn sharply left, go about 100 feet, and then turn right on a single-track trail. A short, moderate climb puts you atop Borel Hill, where 360° views await. From more than 2,500 feet above sea level, most of the Bay Area is revealed for your viewing enjoyment. (Interestingly, the authoritative *California Place Names* has no listing for Borel Hill, but attributes the name Borel Creek to a San Mateo County landowner named Antoine Borel. The location of Borel Creek, however, is a mystery.)

Tidytips and purple owl's-clover splash color on the hillsides at Russian Ridge Open Space Preserve.

If you choose not to climb Borel Hill, veer right on the connector trail, a single track that cuts across a hillside sloping downhill and right. A ravine, right, holds a tributary of Mindego Creek, and the cool, moist habitat here is perfect for California bay, coast live oak, bigleaf maple, blue elderberry, and willows. A sharp right-hand bend in the trail reveals beautiful stands of canyon oak, tanbark oak, and Douglas-fir. Shrubs such as hazelnut, gooseberry, and wood rose make up the understory of this enchanting woodland. Look here for shade-loving plants like trillium, fairy bells, mission bells, and hound's tongue.

A gentle climb brings you to a T-junction with the Ancient Oaks Trail. Here you turn right on a wide single track and follow a ridge top downhill. The steep hillside on your left falls to a canyon that is frequently filled with fog. Russian Ridge catches the fog pouring over the coastal hills from the Pacific, and moisture dripping from trees may cause the ground underfoot to be wet and slippery. Check the meadows beside the trail for spring bloomers such as miniature lupine, popcorn flower, and winecup clarkia. Common birds in this area include Steller's jay—a raucous denizen of the forest—and red-tailed hawk—an aerial hunter that preys mostly on rodents.

Oak limbs arching over the trail form a welcoming canopy, and soon the trail curves right and enters a dense forest. Many of the oaks and buckeyes here are cloaked with a thick layer of moss. Oceanspray, a common shrub with fragrant leaves and springtime spikes of white flowers, lines your route. A fine assortment of ferns decorates the forest floor, along with low-growing herbs such as slim Solomon. Losing elevation on a gentle grade, you soon merge with the Mindego Trail, a dirt road. This junction, which is near a tributary of Mindego Creek, is a good place to look for California newts during the rainy season.

Go straight on the Mindego Trail, walking through a corridor of thimbleberry, gooseberry, and pinkflower currant. Where the road bends left to cross two culverts, you find stinging nettle, a tall, weedy plant with large, toothed leaves and dangling strands of tiny green flowers. As its name implies, you should avoid touching any part of this plant. Transitioning from forest to open grassland, you pass a hillside, right, that may have rivulets of water running down it. Large monkeyflower, sporting yellow flowers with orange dots, grows in this wet area, as does water cress, a nonnative from Eurasia.

The road meanders on a level course to a junction with the Alder Spring Trail, left. Follow the Mindego Trail as it bends right and climbs slightly east of north toward a notch in the hills. The grade varies between gentle and moderate, and you are out in the open. This is a good place to look for hawks and falcons, such as American kestrel and northern harrier. At a four-way junction with a dirt road, go straight. Just ahead is the junction with the Ridge Trail, right, where you began this loop. From here continue straight to gate RR01, Skyline Boulevard, and the Caltrans Vista Point parking area.

Russian Ridge Trail Use

Bicycles: Allowed on all trails

Dogs: Not allowed

Horses: Allowed on all trails

RUSSIAN RIDGE OPEN SPACE PRESERVE

Trip 24. Borel Hill

Length: 7.3 miles

Time: 3 to 4 hours

Rating: Difficult

Highlights: This remarkable ramble through what many consider the District's most scenic preserve uses the Ridge, Ancient Oaks, Mindego, Alder Spring, and Hawk Trails to sample a wide variety of habitats, from the riparian corridor along Mindego Creek to the dazzling wildflower meadows atop Borel Hill, whose displays intensify week by week during spring. Birders will want to have binoculars handy to pick out soaring hawks and falcons. Part of this semi-loop route follows the Bay Area Ridge Trail, which runs along the spine of Russian Ridge, parallel to Skyline Boulevard.

Directions: From the junction of Skyline Boulevard and Page Mill Road/Alpine Road south of Palo Alto, take Alpine Road west about 100 yards to a parking area on the right. (This parking area serves both Russian Ridge and Skyline Ridge Preserves. On busy days parking may

Trip 24. Borel Hill

Your route, the single-track Ridge Trail, heads northwest from the trailhead, past two District information boards and a map holder. The Ridge Trail is part of the Bay Area Ridge Trail. In Russian Ridge Preserve, the Ridge Trail runs along the spine of Russian Ridge parallel to Skyline Boulevard. In this preserve, there is also a 0.5-mile segment of dirt road called the Ridge Trail that climbs up and over Borel Hill. This book, designates this as the Ridge Trail (alternate). Russian Ridge Preserve is famous for its springtime displays of wildflowers, and within a few steps of the parking area you may be greeted by colorful California poppies, mule ears, and purple owl's-clover.

be unavailable. Additional parking with access to the preserve's trails is available at the Caltrans Vista Point parking area, 1.1 miles northwest on Skyline Boulevard.)

Facilities: Vault toilet

Trailhead: At the west side of the parking area

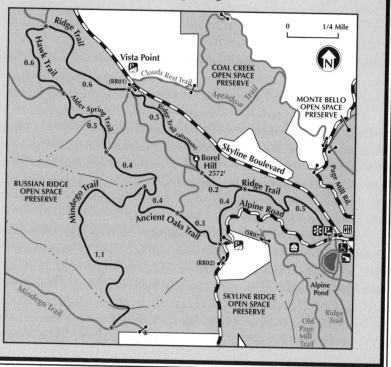

California buckeye trees add to the collage when their candlelike spikes of white flowers erupt in late spring and early summer.

Aided by several switchbacks, you steadily gain elevation and are rewarded by ever-improving views east across the San Andreas fault to Monte Bello Ridge and Black Mountain, and southeast to Mt. Umunhum and Loma Prieta, sites of the District's southernmost holdings. You pass under a set of power lines, and then the rocky and eroded track, now a dirt road, steepens. In spring, the surrounding grasslands are decorated with California poppies, lupine, purple owl's-clover, tidy-tips, and Johnny jump-ups.

After about 0.5 mile, you turn left at a junction with a connector to the Ancient

---

Poison Oak — "Leaflets of Three, Let It Be"

Poison oak comes in three forms—herb, vine, and shrub—and can be recognized by the three glossy, coarsely scalloped or lobed leaflets on each stem. Poison oak belongs to the cashew or sumac family, and is a close relative of poison ivy. The leaves, stems, and roots of the plant carry an oil called *urushiol*, a severe, itch-provoking skin irritant to most people. Even a bare, leafless stem is full of urushiol, so remember that no matter which form it takes, the same rule applies: "leaves of three, let it be."

Oaks Trail. Now you follow a dirt road that is curving left past a wooded ravine, home to California bay, canyon oak, buckeye, and blue elderberry. Expansive views to the left lead your eye southward to Butano Ridge, a long ridge on the horizon. Descending on a gentle grade, you pass under the outstretched limbs of a large coast live oak. With Alpine Road immediately left, you go through a grove of oaks and young Douglas-firs to a junction with the Ancient Oaks Trail. Turning right on a single track, you enjoy a splendid view of the Pacific Ocean as you make a rising traverse across a grassy hillside dotted with California poppies and vetch. This is surely one of the most picturesque scenes on District lands.

The trail curves left, levels briefly, and then starts to descend to an oak woodland. Just past the 1-mile point, a connector to the Ridge Trail joins on the right, but you continue straight. Following a ridge top downhill, you skirt a steep hillside, left, that drops into a canyon often hidden by fog. Westerly winds from the Pacific push fog inland to Russian Ridge, where it helps provide water for plants during the dry season. Moisture dripping from trees may cause the ground underfoot to be wet and slippery. Meadows beside the trail hold spring flowers such as miniature lupine, popcorn flower, and winecup clarkia.

Soon the trail curves right and enters a dense forest, where many of the oaks and buckeyes are wrapped with a thick layer of moss. Hazelnut, with velvety leaves, and oceanspray, with springtime spikes of white flowers, line the route. Losing elevation on a gentle grade, you soon reach a junction with the Mindego Trail, a dirt road. This junction, which is near a tributary of Mindego Creek, is a good place to look for California newts during the rainy season. Now you turn sharply left and begin a winding descent through a possibly wet and muddy area. Stinging nettle, a plant to be avoided, grows beside the road. It is tall and weedy, with large, toothed leaves and hanging strands of tiny green flowers.

Tanbark oaks and tall Douglas-firs thrive in the moist, shady environment. Woodland star and Pacific starflower are at home here, as are several species of

View of the Bay from Borel Hill

fern. Emerging from the forest, you have a great view ahead of Mindego Hill, which is on private property just west of the preserve boundary. (Both the hill and the creek are named for Juan Mendico, a Basque who settled nearby in 1859 and grazed livestock here.) A winding descent over eroded ground eventually brings you to another tributary of Mindego Creek, which flows under the road through a culvert. Now in a forest dominated by grand Douglas-firs, you begin a moderate climb that soon changes to steep. A lovely violet of mixed evergreen forests and western heart's-ease grows beside the road. It has white flowers marked with purple blotches.

After leveling briefly, the rough track descends and curves left. Now bending sharply right, the road crosses a culvert holding Mindego Creek. From here to the next junction at gate RR03, the route is a steep, overgrown path. When you reach the gate, you pass through a gap between it and a wood fence. Here at about the 3-mile point, you have a T-junction with a dirt road. Respect the private property on your left. The continuation of the Mindego Trail, which you may wish to explore, is to the right. The views from here toward the coast are superb, and the road continues for about 1 mile to the preserve's western boundary. When you are finished enjoying this delightful spot, retrace your route to the junction of the Mindego and Ancient Oaks Trails.

From the junction, continue straight on the Mindego Trail, walking through a corridor of thimbleberry, gooseberry, and pinkflower currant. The road bends left to cross two culverts and then brings you from forest into open grassland. A wet hillside, right, has displays of large monkeyflower, whose yellow flowers have orange dots, and water cress, a white-flowered alien from Eurasia. The road wanders over level ground to a junction with the Alder Spring Trail. Now turn left and follow a dirt road through open grassland enlivened by blue-eyed grass, California buttercup, fiddleneck, and California poppies. Soon the road descends to cross a culvert holding a tributary of Mindego Creek.

You enjoy a level walk with views of Mindego Hill and, on a clear day, the Pacific Ocean. Descending on a moderate grade, the road alternates between wooded and open areas. A lone alder to the right of the road hints perhaps at the origin of this trail's name. Again on a level course, you come to a junction with the Hawk Trail around the 5-mile point. Join the Hawk Trail by bearing right. The single-track trail makes a rising traverse across a steep, open hillside. Where the trail bends to the right, you have another vantage point with fine views. The top-of-the-world feeling is enhanced as the trail rises toward a gap in the crest of Russian Ridge. As you walk, listen for the liquid call of the western meadowlark, a grassland bird often found in large flocks.

At a four-way junction with the Ridge Trail, a dirt road, turn right. From atop Russian Ridge, the unrivaled vista extends northeast across San Francisco Bay to the East Bay hills, east to Mt. Hamilton, and west to the Pacific. Lupine, poppies, mule ears, buttercups, blue-eyed grass, and checker mallow form a flowering foreground no matter which way you look. Ahead about 1 mile is Borel Hill, the geographic high point of this route. When you reach a four-way junction with the Mindego Trail, continue straight and begin a moderate climb. After about 75 feet, a single-track segment of the Ridge Trail veers right, but instead stay on the Ridge Trail (alternate), which soon starts to snake its way uphill.

Near the summit of Borel Hill is truly a sea of wildflowers, a carpet of color. At a four-way junction, a trail goes right to a vantage point, but instead turn left for the final push to the summit, where a sign shows you are 2,572 feet above sea level. From this dramatic perch, most of the San Francisco Bay Area is revealed. When you are ready to leave, put the elevation sign at your back and follow the trail in front of you. It soon joins the Ridge Trail (alternate) at a T-junction. Turn left and, after about 100 feet, merge with the Ridge Trail. Now you follow a mostly level route that goes uphill and right. The next junction, just shy of the 7-mile point, is with the connector to the Ancient Oaks Trail you used near the start of this trip. From here retrace your route to the parking area by continuing straight.

SEARCH AND RESCUE

District rangers patrol the preserves, enforce District regulations, perform basic trail maintenance, answer questions, and generally help visitors have an enjoyable outdoor experience. Sometimes they do a lot more, says David

Sanguinetti, superintendent of the District's Skyline office. "We got a report that a woman who was distraught had left her house," he says, "and she had taken drugs and alcohol to do herself in. We found her car parked in the Caltrans pullout [at Russian Ridge], and there was a huge search-and-rescue effort—it started at about four or five in the evening and it went until midnight." Sanguinetti says San Mateo County Search and Rescue called off the search at midnight, which puzzled some of the searchers. "We all thought it was kind of strange because they hadn't found her, they found the car, there was information that she liked the preserve, so the feeling was that she was probably there." The County team packed up and left, says Sanguinetti, hoping to resume their efforts at first light. He and fellow ranger Patrick Congdon had no choice but to leave the scene as well.

Early the next morning, Sanguinetti's phone rang. "Patrick called me in the morning and said, 'You know, I just don't feel right.' And I was lying there looking at the ceiling—it's like five in the morning—and I said, 'You know, Pat, I don't feel right either. I'm going to come up. Why don't you and I start a search?' So we met at about six, and Patrick happened to go left on the Ancient Oaks Trail, and I continued down the Mindego Trail. There was an old path that a lot of people liked to use before we put in the formal trail system." Sanguinetti says he was inexplicably drawn to the path, which is not a designated trail. "So I hiked out there, and I came to the grove of oaks," he says. "I'm looking around underneath the oaks, and first I found a purse, an I.D., and then all these drug bottles lying around. And a bottle of booze that was three-quarters gone. I got on the radio and gave the license number, and they confirmed, 'That's the person.'"

Nestled in leaf litter, the woman they had been searching for was all but invisible. "All of a sudden I saw this movement," says Sanguinetti. "It startled me, and I looked, and it was a person. It looked like she was part of the ground. I went over to her, and she was still alive. She was barely breathing and had no pulse. I couldn't get a pulse at all because she was so cold, she had been out there all night. She was delirious. At first she started to fight me, and then she just got up close to me like she wanted help. I covered her with a blanket—for some reason she had brought a blanket there and I covered her with that." Sanguinetti was joined shortly at the scene by his search partner Congdon, and then by a helicopter with paramedics on board. The woman was transported to a hospital and ultimately survived her ordeal. "One of the highlights of my career," Sanguinetti says, "to find somebody like that and save them. That was pretty great. I still think about it. I always wonder how she's doing now and if she's okay."

The Saratoga Gap Trail offers easy connections to nearby parks and preserves.

SARATOGA GAP
OPEN SPACE PRESERVE

~

The steep hillsides plunging northeast from the Saratoga Gap Trail to Stevens Creek hold oak and mixed-evergreen forests that once yielded bark for tannin as well as wood for charcoal, both important commodities for early settlers. Families homesteaded the area in the nineteenth century. Native Americans traveled through the Santa Cruz Mountains, according to former District ranger Patrick Congdon, and used sites that today are within the preserve. "The Santa Cruz Mountains are very interesting," he says, "in that we know something about what Native Americans did in the area, who they were, where they traveled, and travel routes. But we don't know as much as we do about, say, tribes or groups from the Southwest. The weather was probably harsh, there was some food, but there was probably a lot of movement from the coast to the Bay. So most use was probably during spring and summer, and then they would move down into the lowlands."

Congdon says that there are a number of archeological and cultural sites associated with Native Americans in the Santa Cruz Mountains, but almost all that is left in terms of artifacts are bedrock mortars used for grinding acorns and other seeds, some of which are on District lands. "Now that the Silicon Valley has changed and is more of a high-tech valley, people have gotten away from farming and their agricultural roots, we've also forgotten about those people that lived here from thousands of years ago until just 150 years ago. And if you allow yourself, you can just kind of put yourself in the position of a Native American and imagine what they were actually doing at the site, and how difficult it was to go out and gather seeds and nuts, look for bulbs, and just survive in the area. And Saratoga Gap affords that." The rugged hillsides and forested canyons that make up this part of the Santa

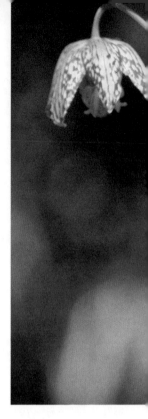

Members of the lily family,
mission bells bloom
from February through June.

Cruz Mountains provide visitors the opportunity to let their imaginations transport them back in time, as Congdon suggests.

In 1959, a small fighter plane based at Moffett Field crashed into a gully above Stevens Creek. The pilot was killed, and the evacuation of his body involved the Santa Clara County Sheriff's Department and a volunteer fire company from Saratoga. The crash site, which was described in several books, is now on District land, and Congdon remembers getting a call from a gentleman from Arizona who wanted to pay a visit. "There are actually groups of people out there who travel around the country looking for aircraft crash sites," he says. "Well, what was interesting was that he asked me how long I thought it would take, and I think if I remember right he was coming from Kingman, Arizona, because he said all he wanted to do was come out and see that site. So he was driving from Kingman, Arizona to Saratoga Gap to go to this crash site, and then turning around and driving back home. The site is in a very rugged area of the preserve. There are no trails. He was able to go down, and in a letter written back to me a couple of months later, he said that it was well worth the trip."

The preserve's main entrance is located near the junction of Skyline Boulevard and Highway 9. The 2-mile Saratoga Gap Trail runs between the

preserve's main entrance and a trailhead just across Skyline Boulevard from Long Ridge Preserve and the trailhead for the Hickory Oaks Trail. The Saratoga Gap Trail is an important link in the Bay Area Ridge Trail and other trail networks, allowing long-distance travelers access to Sanborn Skyline County Park, Castle Rock State Park, Big Basin Redwoods State Park, Upper Stevens Creek County Park, Long Ridge Preserve, Skyline Ridge Preserve, and Monte Bello Preserve. The narrow trail is very popular with mountain bicyclists making connections to other parks and preserves. As another option, the new 1.7-mile Achistaca Trail is open to hiking and equestrian use. This alternate to the Bay Area Ridge Trail is located across Skyline Boulevard (Highway 35) in Long Ridge Preserve, and provides a key connection between Long Ridge Preserve and California State Parks' Skyline-to-the-Sea Trail. The District acquired the first parcel of the preserve in 1974 from Paul and Nessie Cheseborough, supporters of open space, who made a gift of about 165 acres to the District. Today, the preserve spans more than 1,200 acres. Sempervirens Fund, a local, nonprofit land trust, provided critical support for acquisition of parts of this preserve.

The map for Saratoga Gap Preserve is part of the District's South Skyline Region map.

Saratoga Gap Trail Use

Bicycles: Allowed on all trails; uphill travel only on Charcoal Road in Upper Stevens Creek County Park

Dogs: Not allowed

Horses: Allowed on all trails

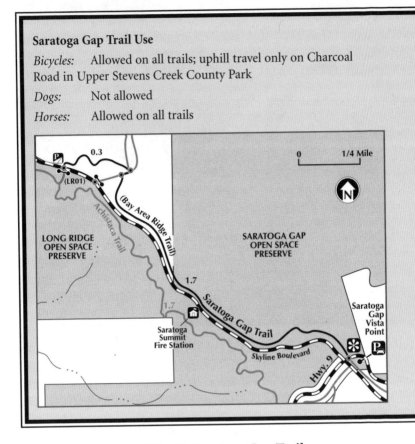

Trip 25. Saratoga Gap Trail

A wood fence at the trailhead has two gaps, a narrow one for hikers and a wider one to accommodate bicycles. The bicycle entrance has a low barricade of logs designed to block motorcycles. There are two District information boards and a map holder just beyond the fence. Your route, the single-track Saratoga Gap Trail, is part of the Bay Area Ridge Trail, and also connects District lands with nearby state and county parks in Santa Cruz and Santa Clara counties. Climbing on a gentle grade, you walk under the outstretched limbs of a large canyon oak and then switchback up a grassy slope dotted in spring with flowering lupine. This trail is heavily used by bicycles, so be alert.

Now the trail curves right and climbs an open hillside brightly colored by California poppies and lupine. Skyline Boulevard is downhill and left, but soon

SARATOGA GAP OPEN SPACE PRESERVE

Trip 25. Saratoga Gap Trail

Length: 4 miles

Time: 2 to 3 hours

Rating: Moderate

Highlights: This out-and-back route, heavily used by bicyclists, will also delight hikers, provided they keep a sharp eye and ear out for two-wheeled traffic! Although never far from busy Skyline Boulevard, you get a remarkable feeling of seclusion as the route drops into a mixed evergreen forest with massive Douglas-firs and a few California nutmeg trees, an evergreen that is uncommon on District lands. (This tree resembles a young coast redwood, but has spine-tipped needles.) The trail enters Upper Stevens Creek County Park and crosses Charcoal Road before rising to a trailhead beside Skyline Boulevard, just across from gate LR01 and the Hickory Oaks Trail in Long Ridge Preserve.

Directions: A paved roadside parking area is located on the north side of Highway 9, a few hundred feet east of its junction with Skyline Boulevard.

Facilities: None

Trailhead: Gate SG01, at the north side of the parking area

you descend into a dense forest and lose sight of the busy roadway. As you enter the trees, look to your left. Here a hefty madrone has intertwined its roots with a venerable canyon oak, and these two trees are now joined for life. In ancient times this unusual coupling might have inspired a local legend, perhaps of giants locked in mortal combat, or star-crossed lovers finally bound in ever-lasting bliss.

The rocky trail descends past stands of tanbark oak and California bay. Dropping into a deep, wooded canyon, you now follow a rolling course below and just northeast of Skyline Boulevard. Thimbleberry, snowberry, hazelnut, oceanspray, poison oak, ferns, and berry vines form the forest understory. Milkmaids, fairy bells, mission bells, hound's tongue, and western heart's-ease are some of the shade-loving wildflowers that grow beside the trail. A towering rock formation just uphill and left of the trail is an example of what

---

The Pileated Woodpecker

The first reported sighting of a pileated woodpecker on the east side of the Santa Cruz Mountains was made at Saratoga Gap in 1990, according to former District ranger Patrick Congdon. He says pileated woodpeckers are known to breed in the Table Mountain area of Upper Stevens Creek County Park. Slightly smaller than crows, pileated woodpeckers give a call in flight that one field guide describes as "a loud wuck." The only larger North American woodpecker is the ivory-billed, and it is almost certainly extinct.

---

geologists call *tafoni*. *Tafoni* is formed by acidic rain eating away at exposed outcrops of sandstone. This sometimes results in caves, pockmarks, and decorative etchings in the rock. *Tafoni* is fragile, so please do not climb on it. (A more extensive *tafoni* formation is located in El Corte de Madera Creek Preserve, described on pages 64, 65, 72–75.)

California nutmeg, a tree found on only a few District preserves, grows nearby. An evergreen, it can be identified by its dark green, spine-tipped needles. Also here is bigleaf maple, one of the few trees in the Bay Area to produce fall colors. Passing a short connector that leads left and uphill to Skyline Boulevard, work your way over a rocky stretch of trail and then through stands of massive Douglas-firs, some of which reach neck-craning heights. Climbing on a gentle grade, you come to a boundary with Upper Stevens Creek County Park, at about the 1-mile point.

The amount of sunlight an area receives is one of the factors that determine its vegetation. As you enter the county park, you pass through a small clearing with many sun-loving shrubs, including buckbrush, coffeeberry, toyon, and yerba santa. Also nearby are California buckeye and blue elderberry. How different from the mixed-evergreen forest of just a few minutes ago! Now back in forest, your mostly level ramble changes to a moderate climb, and then you descend on a gentle grade to a four-way junction with Charcoal Road, a dirt road. Stay on the Saratoga Gap Trail by continuing straight.

Slim Solomon and fat Solomon are two related members of the lily-of-the-valley family found in mixed-evergreen and redwood forests, and they are present along the Saratoga Gap Trail. Both are low-growing plants with alternate, oval leaves that are pointed at their tips. They produce white flowers in spring, which ripen into berries in summer. As their names imply, you can tell them apart by the shape of their leaves—elongated (slim) versus oval (fat)—and also by their flowers. Slim Solomon produces tiny flowers, each on its own stalk. Its cousin has flowers in a brushy cluster at the end of the plant's main stem. The unusual common names refer to Solomon's seal, an East Coast plant similar in appearance, but botanically unrelated, which has flowers said to resemble a mystic double-triangle associated with the Biblical wise man.

The trail curves left and then begins to snake its way uphill on a gentle grade. Three partially buried logs laid across the trail, intended as a motorcycle barricade, signal your approach to Skyline Boulevard, which is just about 100 feet ahead. There is roadside parking along the highway shoulder. Gate LR01 for the Long Ridge Open Space Preserve is across the pavement on the south side of Skyline Boulevard. From here you can retrace your route to the parking area at Saratoga Gap.

For a longer hike that includes incredible vistas of Butano Ridge, Ben Lomond Mountain, and the Pescadero Creek watershed, enter Long Ridge Preserve on the Hickory Oaks Trail. After crossing through the gate, travel approximately 100 yards to a fork. The single-track Achistaca Trail is left. You will follow the dirt road to the right. After 0.2 mile, you will reach a single-track trail to the left, which leads up to a vista point with spectacular views. After enjoying the views, retrace your steps back to gate LR01.

Jacques Ridge, view south from the upper serpentine meadow

SIERRA AZUL
OPEN SPACE PRESERVE

∾

This preserve takes it name from the rugged and remote "blue" mountains that rise near Highway 17 and extend southeast to Loma Prieta. With more than 17,000 acres, Sierra Azul is the District's largest preserve and also its southernmost. The riparian forests, serpentine grasslands, and chaparral-clad hillsides that give this preserve its special character are home to an exceptional variety of plants and animals, some of them rare, unusual, or endangered. Among these are the California red-legged frog, Santa Clara red ribbon clarkia, and Metcalf Canyon jewelflower. Deer, bobcats, and coyotes are common. Mountain lion tracks and kills are found here. Aerial hunters such as hawks, falcons, and even golden eagles soar overhead. Winter and early spring are great times to visit the preserve. The scorching heat of summer and fall is long past, and some of the chaparral shrubs anticipate the new year by blooming as early as December. Storms on Mt. Umunhum are legendary. Rangers and open space technicians describe winds so fierce that they could barely stand or hold onto a shovel. The 3,486-foot summit is high enough to receive occasional dustings of snow. The mountain's unusual name may come from a Native American word meaning hummingbird, or resting place of hummingbirds.

Sierra Azul is divided into four distinct areas—Kennedy–Limekiln, Rancho de Guadalupe, Cathedral Oaks, and Mt. Umunhum. The Kennedy–Limekiln Area, nearly 3,000 acres, features some fifteen miles of excellent trails that are open to hikers (including those with leashed dogs), bicyclists, and equestrians. Several trips of varying length are possible here, including the popular Limekiln–Priest Rock Loop, and a double loop using the Limekiln, Priest Rock, and Kennedy Trails. There is no public access to the Rancho de Guadalupe Area and the 2,340-acre Cathedral Oaks Area, as the area is surrounded mostly by

Mount Umunhum

The former Almaden Air Force Station that sits atop Mt. Umunhum was divided into two sections. There were barracks for enlisted personnel and housing for about a dozen officers, including a three-bedroom house for the base commander. Families lived on the base as well. There was an officers club called the Top of the Rock, a two-lane bowling alley, and a swimming pool, which Dave Knapp, who is currently Cupertino's city manager, says was justified "on the basis that it was an emergency water supply." At the height of the Cold War, about seventy-five people lived on the base, which generated its own electricity and had its own water and sewer system. A security gate and a guard station protected the radar installation. The radar dome was a sphere about three times the diameter of its six-story concrete base, which is still standing, although it was damaged in the 1989 Loma Prieta earthquake. This six-story structure, which is visible from many South Bay vantage points and helps locals identify Mt. Umunhum, is often referred to as "the monolith."

private property and there are no established trails. As the District continues to acquire property in this area, a trail system will be developed to accommodate safe, secure public use. A master planning process is currently scheduled for this entire preserve as well as for neighboring Bear Creek Redwoods Preserve. Preserve access and use will be addressed in this process.

The Mt. Umunhum Area contains nearly 12,000 acres and includes the former Almaden Air Force Station, whose radar scanned the skies for Soviet bombers during the Cold War. Dave Knapp, who is currently Cupertino's city manager, was in the Air Force in the 1960s, and he became very familiar with Mt. Umunhum, visiting the station three or four times each year to certify it as combat-ready. Knapp says that there were three radars atop Mt. Umunhum that could pinpoint the location of any aircraft within about a 220-mile radius of the station. The radar antenna emitted a tremendous amount of power. "If you stood in front of the antenna, it would fry you from the inside out like a microwave oven," Knapp says. Almaden Air Force Station was one of fifteen or so radar sites on the West Coast of the United States and Canada, all part of the North American Air Defense Command (NORAD). Signals from these radars were fed via phone lines into a computer at Adair Air Force Station near Corvallis, Oregon.

Knapp tells what would happen if the computer was unable to identify an aircraft based on known flight plans and identification signals. "We had various fighter bases around," he says. "The computer would identify the

View of the summit of Mt. Umunhum at Sierra Azul Open Space Preserve

target. If we didn't have a good identification on it, we'd scramble fighters, and vector them up to it. And so the fighter would look it over and either identify it or not. Or identify it as a friend or not, and of course we had the capacity to shoot it down if we had to. We never had to shoot any down, fortunately." Knapp says visual identification was required about once a day, usually because a commercial airliner was off course, or the pilot of a small plane had neglected to file a flight plan. But a couple of times each month, a Soviet aircraft called an electronic intelligence collector would purposefully penetrate the U.S. air-defense zone to learn what frequencies the NORAD radars were using. In the 1970s, radar sites such as the one at Almaden Air Force Station became

---

Hard Chaparral Versus Soft Chaparral Plants

Botanists often draw a distinction between hard chaparral and soft chaparral (which is also called coastal scrub). This distinction is based on stem and leaf characteristics. Hard chaparral plants, including chamise, manzanita, buckbrush, and mountain mahogany, have woody stems and stiff, leathery leaves. The leaves retain moisture under hot, dry conditions, and allow the plants to survive on sunny, well-drained slopes. Soft chaparral plants, such as California sagebrush, coyote brush, and sticky monkeyflower, have flexible stems and soft leaves. These plants do well close to the coast where fog is prevalent, and they also grow inland in many locations. Some shrubs, notably toyon and yerba santa, may be classified in either group, depending on which plant guide you use. All may be found along the trail to Bald Mountain.

obsolete, because the Soviets (and the United States) put many of their nuclear missiles aboard submarines.

Knapp describes the drive up to the radar station, and how the landscape has changed. "After just leaving San Jose, at about Hamilton Avenue, we would drive a little two-lane road through the blossoms of the prune and plum trees and vineyards," he says. "It was very, very agricultural, and it was way out in the country. If you drive it today, it's busy Silicon Valley and a major housing supply for all of south San Jose. Of course I did it for a few years, but then I was gone for several years. When I came back, it had changed so dramatically, and it took a long time for it to dawn on me that this was the same location. In fact, I'd lived here for quite a while before I recognized that old tower. The radar dome was gone, but I kept seeing that blockhouse up there, and it took me a couple of years before I remembered that's the old Almaden site."

Access to the Mt. Umunhum Area is currently limited, and there is no public access to the mountaintop because of the potentially toxic materials and unsafe structures left behind by the Air Force. The District is working toward a cleanup of the site, and intends eventually to restore the area to a more natural condition suitable for public access and use. There are several multiuse trails in the Mt. Umunhum Area open to the public at this time. A short trail to the summit of Bald Mountain, which is about 1.5 miles due east of Mt. Umunhum, rewards visitors with sweeping views of the South Bay and the Almaden and Santa Clara valleys. The 6.2-mile Woods Trail, which is part of the Bay Area Ridge Trail, winds around the north side of Mt. Umunhum and then climbs to near the summit of Mt. El Sombroso, which is just shy of 3,000 feet, before meeting the Kennedy and Limekiln Trails. Dogs are not allowed in the Mt. Umunhum Area.

District staff and consultants have mapped and evaluated a portion of the preserve's natural and cultural resources. The findings so far include five earthquake faults, 472 landslides, and 63 plant communities. A number of endangered or special-status plant and wildlife species have also been identified on the preserve, including red ribbon clarkia, most beautiful jewelflower, wicker buckwheat, the California red-legged frog, and the southwestern pond turtle. Sierra Azul also has significant hydrological resources. Much of the area is in the headwaters of Guadalupe and Los Gatos Creeks, which play an important role in the water supply for the Santa Clara Valley.

"It's a first for the District, studying the whole Sierra Azul area before we do anything with it," says Pete Siemens, a member of the District board of directors. "We're putting a lot of money and time into research. Before putting in much in the way of new trails, we're designing a whole plan. We work with consultants

Sierra Azul Trail Use

Bicycles: Allowed on all trails

Dogs: Leashed dogs allowed only on trails in the Kennedy-Limekiln Area

Horses: Allowed on all trails

SIERRA AZUL OPEN SPACE PRESERVE

Trip 26. Bald Mountain

Length: 1.4 miles

Time: 1 hour or less

Rating: Easy

Highlights: This short out-and-back route leads to a magnificent vantage point overlooking San Jose and the Santa Clara Valley. Mt. Umunhum, with its concrete monolith left over from the Cold War, and Loma Prieta, both usually glimpsed in the distance from other District lands, are here close at hand. A fine array of chaparral shrubs along the trail, including Fremont's silk tassel, mountain mahogany, and leather oak, will delight native plant enthusiasts. This trip makes a pleasing complement to "Woods Trail," described on pages 262–63.

Directions: Follow the directions for "Woods Trail" on pages 262–63. From the junction of Hicks Road and Mt. Umunhum Road, take Mt. Umunhum Road southwest 1.7 miles to a roadside parking area, with room for two to three cars, on the right, just before locked gate SA08.

Facilities: None

Trailhead: Gate SA07, on the southeast side of Mt. Umunhum Road

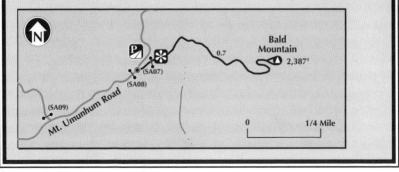

to prepare a detailed study of the preserve. We're going to be really careful before we start putting in trails. Where are the endangered species, where are the endangered plants? We don't want a trail to go right through a creek area that is a known frog habitat. We want to be really careful. The idea is to try to set a pattern for how we might plan other preserves in the future. So Sierra Azul is going to be well planned and be the template for the future."

Trip 26. Bald Mountain

A dirt fire road heads eastward from the trailhead through mostly open country toward Bald Mountain, the aptly named hill directly ahead. Mt. Umunhum, topped by its concrete radar tower left over from the Cold War, is behind you to the west. Mt. El Sombroso is to the northwest, and Loma Prieta, bristling with communication towers, is to the southeast, beyond a deep valley. Although the trail to Bald Mountain is short—only about 0.7 mile—the roadside is teeming with native plants, most of them members of the chaparral community.

The botanic richness of this area is amazing. An uncommon chaparral plant, Fremont's silk tassel, grows beside the road—look for a large woody shrub with shiny green, oval leaves. Two oaks, leather and scrub, also members of the chaparral community, thrive here. Both have small, stiff leaves; leather oak's leaves are cupped, whereas those of scrub oak are flat. Also here are two

Red ribbons clarkia

View of Bald Mountain at Sierra Azul Open Space Preserve

plants most often found in coastal forests, blue elderberry and coffeeberry. The road rises gently and approaches a ravine crowded with California bay trees, indicating the presence of water below the seasonally parched topsoil. Beyond the ravine, you stay on the Bald Mountain Trail as it curves right, now crossing a grassy hillside dotted with only a few clumps of poison oak and spiny redberry.

As you near the top of Bald Mountain, the road forks and makes a loop around its summit. The name Bald is attached to more than 100 summits in California, making it, along with Black and Red, one of the most popular appellations. From the top of this Bald Mountain, about 2,300 feet above sea level, you have 360° views of the South Bay, including San Jose and the Almaden and Santa Clara valleys, as well as other summits, such as Mission Peak, Monument Peak, and Mt. Hamilton. The terrain to the south and west of Bald Mountain is extremely rugged, and it is remarkable to have this much wilderness so close to one of California's largest cities. The open grasslands on the flanks of Bald Mountain are ideal hunting grounds for birds of prey, including hawks and falcons. When you have finished enjoying this superb vantage point, retrace your route to the parking area.

Sierra Azul Trail Use

Bicycles: Allowed on all trails

Dogs: Leashed dogs allowed only on trails in the Kennedy-Limekiln Area

Horses: Allowed on all trails

SIERRA AZUL OPEN SPACE PRESERVE

Trip 27. Limekiln–Priest Rock Loop

Length: 5.2 miles

Time: 2 to 3 hours

Rating: Moderate

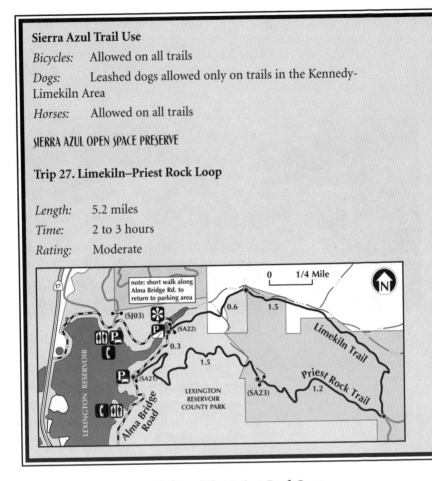

Trip 27. Limekiln–Priest Rock Loop

From the trailhead, you begin climbing northeast on the Limekiln Trail, a formerly paved road that is part of Lexington Reservoir County Park's trail system. Almost immediately, you come to a fence and a gate marked FIRE LANE. Passing through a gap in the fence, you climb the rough and rocky road on a moderate grade past stands of coast live oak, California bay, bigleaf maple, and madrone. Chaparral shrubs such as scrub oak, mountain mahogany, toyon, and silk tassel line your route. A creek flows through Limekiln Canyon, which is downhill and left. Still climbing, now on a gentle grade, you follow a winding course up a hillside that drops steeply left.

Highlights: This loop, which starts and ends in Lexington Reservoir County Park, uses the Limekiln and Priest Rock Trails, and a short stretch of Alma Bridge Road, to visit the northwest corner of the District's largest, most remote preserve. Much of the journey is over serpentine soil, which gives rise to a fascinating community of shrubs and wild-flowers. Early blooming shrubs, such as manzanita and currant, may add splashes of unexpected color as early as December, and the bright red toyon berries attract numerous species of hungry songbirds. Often blazingly hot in summer, this route is perfect for a winter ramble, although the trails may be wet and muddy after storms.

Directions: From Highway 17 northbound, exit at Alma Bridge Road south of Los Gatos. At 0.7 mile, you pass a parking area, right, for Lexington Reservoir. (There is a fee for parking in the county park parking area.) At 1.2 miles, stay right at a fork with the entrance road to Lexington Quarry. Roadside parking is just ahead on the right side of Alma Bridge Road.

From Highway 17 southbound, take the Bear Creek Road exit south of Los Gatos. After 0.1 mile, you come to a stop sign at a four-way junction. Turn right, cross over Highway 17, and turn left to get on Highway 17 northbound. Go 0.4 mile to Alma Bridge Road, turn right and follow the directions above.

Facilities: None

Trailhead: Gate SA22, on the southeast side of Alma Bridge Road, across from the parking area

Steller's jays, dark-eyed juncos, hummingbirds, northern flickers, and California towhees are among the common birds found in this preserve. Late fall through early spring is a good time to go birding, because much of the foliage that often hides the birds from view is gone. Also, birds are attracted to shrubs such as toyon, which are usually loaded with berries during this time. The Sierra Azul (or "Blue Mountains" in Spanish) boasts a rich array of native plants, and you may find chamise, hollyleaf cherry, spiny redberry, and sticky monkeyflower growing in the preserve. Now the road turns left and crosses a creek that drains into Limekiln Canyon, named for furnaces used to reduce limestone to lime—a handful of these operated in the canyon from the late nineteenth century until the 1930s. The road here may be very wet and muddy.

This is a landslide-prone area, and there are young manzanita bushes growing atop piles of dirt, helping to stabilize the soil.

After climbing out of the slide area, the road swings right. Clumps of leather oak, a low shrub with curved and prickly leaves, indicate the presence of serpentine in the soil. Many plants cannot tolerate the chemicals in this type of soil, but a specialized group of species thrives in it. Now you descend into a cool and shady forest of mostly bay, bigleaf maple, and alder. Soon you reach the preserve boundary and begin a moderate-to-steep climb over very rocky ground. Through openings in the trees, left, you can see the Lexington Quarry, a massive rock quarry. Coffeeberry, gooseberry, bush lupine, and wood rose provide an attractive understory. A stand of oracle oak, a hybrid of black and interior live oak, may provide colorful foliage in fall. Also here is California nutmeg, an evergreen with spine-tipped needles found in only a few District preserves. Chaparral pea, growing in thickets beside the road, also sports spines, and in summer erupts with gorgeous magenta flowers.

The plant world sometimes seems out of synch with the calendar, especially in the Bay Area, with its mild climate. For example, some early flowering shrubs, such as manzanita and chaparral currant, are true harbingers of spring, blooming in December. Herbs like black sage may sprout new leaves around Christmas. This phenomenon is one of the joys of winter hiking in the Bay Area. With the deep valley and chaparral-clad hills of Limekiln Canyon to your left, continue your uphill trek. At about the 2.5-mile point, you reach a fence with a gate. Just beyond the fence is a junction. Here the Limekiln Trail continues straight, and the Priest Rock Trail, a dirt road, goes left and right.

If you turn left, the rugged road climbs nearly 1,000 feet

California has nearly sixty species of manzanita, a shrub found in chaparral.

in 1.5 miles to a junction with the Kennedy Trail. From there you can make a 4.6-mile loop back to the Limekiln–Priest Rock junction by turning right onto the Kennedy Trail and right again onto the Limekiln Trail. You can also just climb part or all of the way up the Priest Rock Trail for more great views—Mt. Tamalpais and Mt. Diablo are visible on a clear day—and further study of chaparral plants, such as chamise, manzanita, buckbrush, bush poppy, yerba santa, and Fremont's silk tassel.

Whatever you choose, begin the return part of your route by heading northwest from the Limekiln–Priest Rock junction on the Priest Rock

Coyote brush, a soft chaparral plant

Trail. A gentle ascent ends with a short, steep pitch, and now you are on level ground, passing stands of interior live oak, madrone, and young eucalyptus trees. An unsigned dirt road, not shown on the District map, joins sharply from the left, and then a short trail to a viewpoint departs right. This window on the world below offers a fine view that stretches north from San Jose to the East Bay hills and Mt. Diablo. Crossing under a set of power lines and a tower, the road bends sharply left. A fence is just to the right of the road, and Priest Rock, a modest formation, rises behind it, half hidden in the chaparral.

Now the road begins to snake its way downhill, and you have a fine view ahead of St. Joseph's Hill Preserve, described elsewhere in this book. At about the 3.5-mile point, you reach gate SA23 and the preserve boundary. The road continues into Lexington Reservoir County Park, descending on a grade that alternates between gentle, moderate, and steep. To the right is a ravine holding a seasonal creek that empties into Limekiln Canyon. Leveling briefly, the road then climbs gently through a possibly wet area filled with willows and tall eucalyptus trees, whose bark strips may cover the road. Passing a dirt road, left, you continue winding downhill to the bottom of the Priest Rock Trail. Here at gate SA21, turn sharply right to meet paved Alma Bridge Road. Cross it carefully, turn right, and walk northeast along the road shoulder about 0.4 mile to the parking area.

Sierra Azul Trail Use

Bicycles: Allowed on all trails

Dogs: Leashed dogs allowed only on trails in the Kennedy-Limekiln Area

Horses: Allowed on all trails

SIERRA AZUL OPEN SPACE PRESERVE

Trip 28. Woods Trail

Length: 5.4 miles

Time: 2 to 3 hours

Rating: Moderate

Highlights: This out-and-back stroll along the Woods Trail to its junction with Barlow Road lets you sample some of what the District's largest and most remote preserve has to offer. From the forested canyon holding Guadalupe Creek to chaparral-clad slopes of serpentine soil in the shadow of Mt. Umunhum, this botanically rich route will delight native-plant enthusiasts. Occasional glimpses of San Jose and the Santa Clara Valley belie the wilderness feeling that this preserve inspires. A connection with

Trip 28. Woods Trail

The Woods Trail is a dirt road that heads westward from the trailhead, descends to cross Guadalupe Creek, and then contours across the north slope of Mt. Umunhum, meeting Barlow Road along the way. After crossing Rincon Creek, the road turns north to ascend Mt. El Sombroso, then veers northwest just below that mountain's 2,999-foot summit. After another 0.5 mile or so, the Woods Trail meets the Kennedy and Limekiln Trails, offering great opportunities for long-distance hiking, trail running, cycling, and horseback riding.

The Woods Trail is fenced and gated at the trailhead, but there is a gap in the fence to provide access for hikers, bicyclists, and equestrians. A low barricade of logs just beyond the fence is designed to block motorcycles. Mt. Umunhum, topped by its tell-tale "monolith," rises directly ahead to a height of 3,486 feet above sea level, making it the highest point on District lands. The rolling hills to other Sierra Azul trails offers opportunities for long-distance travel. This trip makes a pleasing complement to "Bald Mountain," described on p 255.

Directions: From Highway 85 in San Jose, take the Camden Avenue exit and go south on Camden Avenue. At 1.7 miles turn right on Hicks Road. Go 6.4 miles to Mt. Umunhum Road and turn right. There is a parking lot immediately on your right with space for fourteen cars.

Facilities: Vault toilet

Trailhead: Gate SA06, at the west side of the parking area

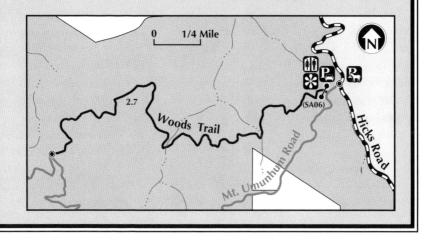

the right of the road drop steeply to the canyon holding Guadalupe Creek. The creek, which starts high on Mt. Umunhum, eventually flows through San Jose on its way to San Francisco Bay.

Hugging the 1,400-foot contour line, the road curves back and forth to follow the terrain. Coast live oak, interior live oak, scrub oak, California bay, madrone, and bigleaf maple grow beside the road. Occasional breaks in the foliage reveal views north toward San Jose and the East Bay hills, including Mission and Monument peaks. Common shrubs here include coyote brush, California sagebrush, and spiny redberry. Berry vines, honeysuckle, and ferns add to the understory. Where the road passes under power lines, look for manzanita and leather oak, the latter indicating the presence of serpentine soil. Because it is toxic to many plants, serpentine soil gives rise to a specialized community of trees, shrubs, and wildflowers of interest to botanists and native-plant lovers.

Soon the road reaches the head of a ravine holding a seasonal tributary of Guadalupe Creek, and then bends to the right. The power lines you just passed under span the canyon to your right and march single file up Mt. El Sombroso. Guadalupe Reservoir is just visible downhill and right. Now losing elevation on a gentle grade, you pass stands of California buckeye, canyon oak, and Douglas-fir. The road, which follows a curvy course, is bordered in places by steep, rocky cliffs decorated with green moss and Pacific stonecrop, a member of the sedum family that has fleshy gray-green leaves arranged in a circle. Mt. Hamilton, topped by white observatory domes, rises in the distance above the often haze-filled Santa Clara Valley.

You descend toward Guadalupe Creek, which may be forming delightful little waterfalls as it splashes from pool to pool. California nutmeg, easily mistaken for a young fir or redwood until you touch its spine-tipped needles, grows in this canyon. The leafy forest floor provides food and cover for a number of birds, including the spotted towhee. This sparrow relative, slightly smaller than a robin, used to share the name "rufous-sided" with a similar bird found east of the Rocky Mountains, but ornithologists have determined that they are, in fact, two different species. This is also good habitat for the hermit thrush—listen for what one field guide describes as "a low, soft, dry *chup*" coming from the underbrush.

The road drops to a saddle where Guadalupe Creek flows through a large culvert. Beyond the creek, the road swings sharply right and climbs on a moderate, then gentle, grade. The road here may be covered with leaves and strips of bark from a nearby stand of eucalyptus trees. A tall cypress and a big Douglas-fir grow beside the road as well. Soon the terrain opens, and you pass under the power lines again. Chaparral shrubs such as chamise, chaparral pea, manzanita, and mountain mahogany thrive here on the sunny slopes. Joining them is oracle oak, a hybrid of black oak and interior live oak. You can identify oracle oak by its oval leaves that are fringed by bristle-tipped teeth. In autumn, oracle oak's leaves turn yellow, making this hybrid easier to spot.

Sierra Azul is a botanically rich preserve, and as you re-enter the dense oak-and-bay forest, look for tanbark oak—not a true oak, but prized nevertheless by Native Americans and early settlers for its large acorns and tannin-rich bark. Emerging onto a chaparral-clad hillside, you may find jimbrush, chaparral currant, poison oak, yerba santa, black sage, and wartleaf ceanothus. The steep and rugged north face of Mt. Umunhum, topped by a concrete radar tower left over from the Cold War, is just ahead. The mountain may take

Buckbrush, a hard chaparral plant

its name from the Ohlone word for hummingbird (or resting place of hummingbirds) and these fascinating fliers are one of this preserve's many attractions. Now back in the shade, you enjoy a level walk that soon brings you to a junction with Barlow Road. From here retrace your route to the parking area.

MOUNTAIN LIONS

Mountain lions *(Felis concolor)*—also called cougars, pumas, and panthers—are large cats found mostly west of the Rockies. They inhabit rugged terrain such as chaparral, and prey on deer and other mammals. Secretive, wide-ranging, and generally nocturnal, a mountain lion is a rare sight in the Bay Area, but an unmistakable one: no other feline has a tail almost 3 feet long. "My first, my only, experience with seeing a mountain lion was in 1986," says Tom Lausten, a Foothills office supervising ranger. "I had only been working for the District for about two or three months. I was working late; it was close to midnight. I was by myself and I was in Rancho San Antonio. I was driving down a road from a well-known area where there sometimes were late-night activities that were prohibited, and I saw this giant cat cross the road. All I saw was basically from its mid-quarters back. And then I saw this long tail. By the time I got the spotlight flipped around and turned on, the cat was gone." Lausten says he was not thinking about mountain lions in those days, especially not close to an urban area. "I thought, wow, you know, I'm working by Los Altos Hills, somebody must have had a circus cat that got loose. And then it dawned on me, you know, that was a mountain lion!"

David Topley is the District's support services supervisor. In 1992, he was a ranger working at Monte Bello Preserve with former ranger Joan Young on trail maintenance. "Joan was a person who was into dreams and dream analysis," he says. "She would wake up in the middle of the night, and she would remember her dream and write it down. And the next day at work she would always be talking about the dream and analyzing what it meant in her life. To me it was entertaining." Topley says Young had several dreams about seeing a mountain lion, and that she was jealous when she heard other people say they had caught a glimpse of one of these elusive cats. Turning off their chainsaws for a moment's rest, Topley says he and Young happened to look up at a nearby knoll. "There was a full-grown mountain lion just standing on the knoll looking at us," he says. "And it wasn't running away. It was just an eye-to-eye contact with this beautiful animal. It seemed like it stood there a long time, a couple of minutes. It might have only been 30 seconds. We knew we weren't dreaming. Neither of us will ever forget that. It's one of the special days for the rest of our lives. And neither of us has seen a mountain lion since then."

David Sanguinetti, superintendent of the District's Skyline office, recounts: "I've seen two mountain lions in my career. One of them was at Windmill Pasture. As I was walking up the trail at Rhus Ridge Road that goes up to Windmill Pasture, I came around a corner and surprised a mountain lion. I was probably five feet from it. At first, I thought it was a greyhound off leash until it turned around and looked back at me, and I realized it was a mountain lion. I was so close that it was like, oh my God, I'm too close here. But it just took off away from me, and it was so graceful in how it ran. It just ran up the trail, and then it just started running along the side of the contour and disappeared into the trees. The second time was two years ago, as I was going home. One crossed the road at Long Ridge from the eastern side of the road, just past the Jikoji Buddhist organization driveway."

Janet Schwind, a longtime resident of the South Skyline area, was walking alone near her house in broad daylight. She says an animal came "bounding" down from a neighbor's house and ran into a brushy area. "My first impression was a bobcat," she says. "So I headed towards that brush. I was talking to the bobcat, and I'm walking around this circular area of brush talking to the bobcat. All of a sudden something in my brain thought, You know what? That's not a bobcat. It had a long tail, and so I got out of there. But fortunately the mountain lions that traverse the Skyline area are still very wild and very scared. And that's the way it should stay."

SKYLINE RIDGE
OPEN SPACE PRESERVE

~

With more than 2,100 acres draped on steep terrain southwest of Skyline Boulevard, this preserve offers visitors about ten miles of superb trails for hiking, bicycling, and horseback riding. Two artificial ponds, which have been maintained by the District, attract water birds, and the preserve's forested enclaves, grassy slopes, and chaparral-covered hillsides are home to coyotes, bobcats, deer, rabbits, and even mountain lions. Although the large cats are rarely seen, Stan Hooper, a lead open space technician at the Skyline office, did manage to see and later photograph one here. Dennis Danielson, a supervising ranger also at the Skyline office, lives nearby. He says Skyline Ridge Preserve is a good area for seeing and hearing wildlife. "At night, living there, I hear coyotes howling. Not every night, but certainly at the times of year when they are active. And in large family groups. I've gone out with a flashlight and had seven or eight pairs of eyes looking at me. Also quite large groups of deer; I just had a group of nine pass through my backyard. And I'll be lying on the couch and see bobcats walk by the back window."

Much of the land that became Skyline Ridge Preserve (and also Russian Ridge Preserve) was at one time owned by James Rolph, Jr., or "Sunny Jim," as he was known to his constituents. Rolph was one of California's most colorful politicians, serving as mayor of San Francisco from 1912 until January 1931, when he resigned to become the state's newly elected governor, a post he held until his death in 1934. Born in San Francisco in 1869, Rolph went to school in the Mission District and worked his way up from office boy to bank president and head of a ship-building company. He was a hearty optimist with a big smile—hence his nickname—and he could relate to the common folk, despite the fact that he was a successful businessman and a millionaire.

Adda Quinn is the Trails Chair of the San Mateo County Horsemen's Association (SMCHA), and founder of the nonprofit organization EnviroHorse: "The large acreage and contiguous preserves of the District are a perfect place to take your horse for a ride. Horsemen need longer trails than most trail users in order to keep our animals in good shape. Also important is simply having a place to enjoy nature with your horse without urban distractions. The interaction of man with an animal, such as a horse, promotes a non-anthropocentric worldview that facilitates a unique appreciation of the environment."

Coming on the heels of San Francisco's graft and corruption scandals of the early 1900s, Rolph was considered a breath of fresh air. He is credited with many civic achievements, including construction of the Civic Center, complete with a new city hall; the Hetch Hetchy aqueduct; and the Panama Pacific International Exposition. As California's governor, Sunny Jim did not fare so well. The state was beginning to feel the effects of the Depression, and Rolph had to confront a banking crisis and the threat of a recall petition. In November, 1933, two men who were awaiting trial for kidnapping the son of a San Jose businessman were yanked from jail and lynched in a nearby park. Rolph spoke out in favor of the vigilante action and was immediately dubbed "Governor Lynch." While trying to weather the storm of bad publicity, Rolph fell victim to a heart attack and died on June 2, 1934. He was 64 years old. (An excellent account of Rolph's career can be found in *Historic San Francisco*, by Rand Richards.)

Rolph was an outdoorsman who loved to hunt, fish, and ride horses. He had a ranch called Pony Tracks that he would use as a summer home, and during his days as governor, a barn there supposedly sported a gold papier-mâché dome, mimicking the one atop the statehouse in Sacramento. A house and barns that once stood where the District now has its Skyline field office may have been used by Rolph's ranch foreman. Some say Rolph built a large redwood dance floor for parties, located where a dam later created Alpine Pond.

After Rolph, the northern part of what became Skyline Ridge Preserve was owned by Mr. John Rickey of Rickey's Hyatt House in Palo Alto, who used it for a thousand-head hog ranch. The hogs were fed with food scraps from restaurants owned by Mr. Rickey, and from day-old bread collected from bakeries. Alpine Pond and Horseshoe Lake were constructed in the 1950s to provide water for the ranching and agriculture operations. Alpine Pond had a boathouse and a dock, and was also used for swimming, boating, and fishing.

Later the property passed to the Wasserman family, who used it to raise cattle and graze horses. It was the Wassermans who established the Christmas-tree farm that still exists on the preserve today. The District purchased the land in 1982, with the Wasserman family keeping a parcel of land containing several houses on a life-estate basis.

There is archeological evidence, including a bedrock mortar near Alpine Pond, that this area may have been used by Native Americans as a seasonal food-processing camp. Ohlone women used the bedrock mortar, which is soft sandstone, to grind hulled acorns into flour. The flour, which had to be leached in water to remove the bitter tannin, could then be used to make mush or bread.

Skyline Ridge Trail Use

Bicycles: Allowed on all trails except the hiking-only segments of the Bay Area Ridge, Pond Loop, and Horseshoe Loop Trails

Dogs: Not allowed

Horses: Allowed on all trails except the hiking-only segments of the Bay Area Ridge, Pond Loop, and Horseshoe Loop Trails

SKYLINE RIDGE OPEN SPACE PRESERVE

Trip 29. Alpine Pond

Length: 0.5 mile

Time: 1 hour or less

Rating: Easy

Highlights: This short and easy Pond Loop Trail is fun for people of all ages and abilities, but children will especially enjoy the chance to peer into the pond's shallow water in search of tadpoles, frogs, and other aquatic and amphibious creatures. Bring binoculars to scan the cattail-fringed pond for ducks, coots, cormorants, and red-winged blackbirds. The David C. Daniels Nature Center at the pond is open to the public on weekend afternoons from April to mid-November, and to school groups, grades 3–6, by arrangement with the District. This route is designated an "Easy Access Trail," and is accessible to visitors with wheelchairs or strollers. This trip can be combined with an out-and-back jaunt along the Ridge Trail, described on pages 282–83, for a longer hike.

The southern part of Skyline Ridge Preserve had been settled in the 1850s by Lambert Dornberger, a German immigrant who operated a hay and dairy ranch. Apparently, Dornberger was known to many by just his first name. The Dornbergers lived in the Palo Alto area, and there is a Lambert Street there today. Lambert shale, a type of rock, and Lambert Creek also owe him their names. In more recent times, Italo and Mary Incerpi owned land that included a chestnut orchard with hundred-year-old trees that still produce chestnuts. This orchard drew many visitors in the fall, and was operated for a while as a "u-pick" chestnut farm.

A three-mile section of the Bay Area Ridge Trail passes through the preserve, as does the alignment of what some say could be Old Page Mill Road, which, in

Directions: From the junction of Skyline Boulevard and Page Mill Road/Alpine Road south of Palo Alto, take Alpine Road west about 100 yards to a parking area on the right. (This parking area serves both Skyline Ridge and Russian Ridge Preserves. On busy days parking may be unavailable. Additional parking with access to the preserve's trails is available at the parking area for Horseshoe Lake, 0.9 mile southeast on Skyline Boulevard.)

Facilities: Vault toilet; nature center at Alpine Pond

Trailhead: At the south side of the parking area

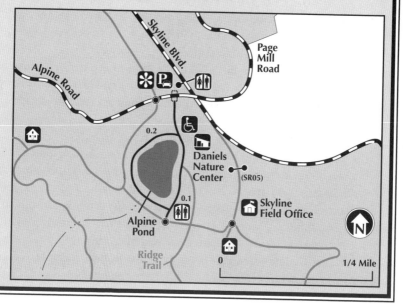

Dennis Danielson, a supervising ranger at the District's Skyline office, raves about the views encountered as you travel into the heart of the preserve. "On the Ridge Trail, you have tremendous views over the upper Lambert Creek and Peters Creek drainages, which are tributaries of Pescadero Creek," he says. "And you look across and see Butano Ridge, and you look down on Portola State Park. And there are spots where you can see the ocean and it's heavily forested. I love that Ridge Trail section. Particularly at sunset on that trail it is just incredible when the fog's rolling in in the summer and laying up in the canyons. Or if there's a winter sunset with the high clouds and lighting, it's just spectacular."

1868, served a redwood mill built by William Page in what is now Portola Redwoods State Park and allowed him to haul lumber to the waterfront in Palo Alto. There are two "Easy Access" trails at the preserve to accommodate visitors with wheelchairs or strollers: the Pond Loop Trail at Alpine Pond, and the Horseshoe Lake Trail at Horseshoe Lake. Development of the preserve was assisted by funding from the California Park and Recreation Facilities Act of 1984, and the federal Land and Water Conservation Fund.

Trip 29. Alpine Pond

A set of steps and also a wheelchair-accessible path lead down from the parking area to a District information board, that includes a sign indicating the hours of the David C. Daniels Nature Center at Alpine Pond. Just ahead, your route, the Ridge Trail, passes under Alpine Road through a tunnel. The Ridge Trail is part of the Bay Area Ridge Trail, and from here to the parking area serving Horseshoe Lake it is closed to bikes and horses. (Bicyclists and equestrians headed for Horseshoe Lake and beyond must use a trailhead just across Alpine Road and then follow an alternate trail.)

Lying slightly west of the Santa Cruz Mountains' crest, this preserve is subject to all of the meteorological vagaries of coastal weather, including fog and wind; because you are above 2,000 feet, cold may be a factor as well. Fortunately, you soon enter a sheltering forest of coast live oak, canyon oak, valley oak, madrone, and Monterey pine. After passing a gravel road that joins from the left, you soon arrive at Alpine Pond and the nature center. The Pond Loop Trail, a short route around the pond, joins sharply from the right. A deck partially rings the nature center, and a wildlife viewing platform juts out into the pond, which is fringed by cattails.

This lovely pond is an oasis of life, providing habitat for mammals, birds, fish, and amphibians—including red-winged blackbirds, coots, crayfish, bluegills, and western pond turtles. The nature center has attractive displays on the different habitats found in this preserve, including riparian, mixed evergreen, oak woodland, grassland, and chaparral, and the most common plants and animals that live in each.

Just past the nature center you come to a fork where you bear right. As you begin to circle the cattail-fringed pond on the Pond Loop Trail, you soon reach a junction. Here a trail goes left to a paved road and a vault toilet, but your route now turns right and runs atop the earthen dam that formed the pond. A viewing platform about halfway across the dam on the right gives you a vantage point amid the rushes and cattails. On the pond's opposite shore is the well-designed nature center, blending into the forest.

Hidden in trees downhill and left is a site where Ohlone Indians once gathered to grind acorns. A large, flat-topped boulder with well-worn holes—called a grinding rock—marks the site. Passing a rest bench, left, you come to a fence with a gap. Beyond it you merge with a dirt road. To visit the grinding rock, turn left and walk downhill for several hundred feet to a junction with a paved road. Just across the junction is a single-track trail leading a few feet to the rock. Please be respectful of the site. If you do not wish to visit the rock, veer right onto the dirt road mentioned above. Curving right, the road crosses a bridge and brings you to a fork. The alternate Ridge Trail, open to bikes and horses, is left, but you stay on the Pond Loop Trail by angling right.

After about 100 feet you come to another fence with a gap: past here bikes and horses are prohibited. Willows, coyote brush, and tangles of berry vines grow beside the trail. On your left is a rest bench, and on your right is a short path that leads toward the pond. Continuing straight, you soon cross two small bridges and then reach the wildlife viewing platform you passed earlier on the way to the nature center. Just ahead is the Ridge Trail. When you reach it, turn sharply left and retrace your route to the parking area.

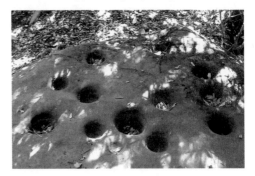

Ohlone Indian grinding stone near Alpine Pond at Skyline Ridge Open Space Preserve

Skyline Ridge Trail Use

Bicycles: Allowed on all trails except the hiking-only segments of the Bay Area Ridge, Pond Loop, and Horseshoe Loop Trails

Dogs: Not allowed

Horses: Allowed on all trails except the hiking-only segments of the Bay Area Ridge, Pond Loop, and Horseshoe Loop Trails

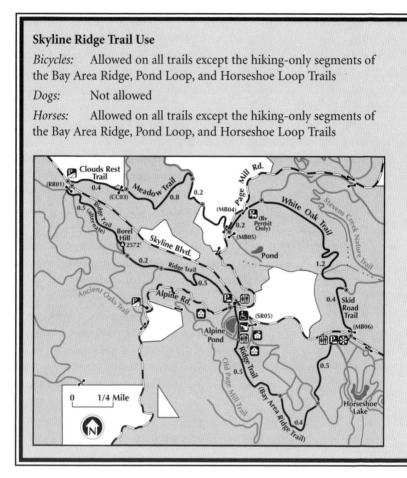

Trip 30. Grand Loop

The trailhead has a wood fence with two gaps, a narrow one for hikers, and a larger one designed to accommodate bicycles and horses, but with a low barricade of logs to block motorcycles. About thirty feet ahead is Skyline Boulevard, which you carefully cross. In front of you is another wood fence and a metal gate across a dirt road. This is gate MB06 for the Monte Bello Open Space Preserve. Next to the gate blocking the dirt road is a smaller gate that prevents access by bikes and horses during wet weather. (When the gate is closed, hikers can pass through a narrow gap in the fence.)

Just past the gates, turn left on the Skid Road Trail, a rough dirt road that descends gently through a brushy area decorated in spring with California

SKYLINE RIDGE OPEN SPACE PRESERVE

Trip 30. Grand Loop

Length: 6.5 miles

Time: 4 to 5 hours

Rating: Difficult

Highlights: This varied and vigorous loop visits four adjoining District preserves—Monte Bello, Coal Creek, Russian Ridge, and Skyline Ridge. Each preserve offers something different: shady oak woodlands, forested canyons, wildflower-strewn slopes, and grassy ridges. The route combines the Skid Road, White Oak, Meadow, Clouds Rest, and Ridge Trails with a short stretch of Alpine Road, to explore the heart of the South Skyline Region, where open space acquisitions have made it possible to wander over some of the Bay Area's most beautiful terrain.

Directions: From the junction of Skyline Boulevard and Page Mill Road/Alpine Road, take Skyline Boulevard southeast 0.9 mile to an entrance to Skyline Ridge Preserve on the right. Bear right and go 0.2 mile to a parking area.

Facilities: Vault toilet; nature center at Alpine Pond

Trailhead: About 200 feet east of the parking area, on the north side of the preserve entrance road

buttercup and blue-eyed grass. Stands of valley oak, canyon oak, and madrone frame your view of the Stevens Creek headwaters and Monte Bello Ridge, both right. Dropping into a dense forest, you soon reach a junction, left, with the White Oak Trail. Tall Douglas-firs and California bays compete for light, and tower over an understory of snowberry, gooseberry, oceanspray, poison oak, ferns, and berry vines. Some early blooming wildflowers grow here, including trillium, hound's tongue, and slim Solomon. You may also find western heart's-ease and Pacific starflower nearby.

The trail snakes its way down a canyon, where a wood bridge helps you across a creek. Pinkflower currant, wood rose, and coltsfoot are among the plants that thrive in this damp, rainforest-like area. After crossing the creek and wandering through a possibly muddy area, the trail makes a rising traverse across a grassy hillside, home to the trail's namesake Oregon oaks. With lobed leaves similar to valley oaks, these trees have chalky white bark and erect limbs that don't droop to the ground. Oregon oaks are found mostly from Northern California to Vancouver Island, British Columbia, but a few stands occur from Marin south to Santa Clara counties. Identification can be tricky, and it took the District several years to decide that these were in fact Oregon, and not valley, oaks.

Joining the oaks, some of which are dreamily draped with lace lichen, are grassland wildflowers such as Douglas iris, mule ears, lupine, and purple owl's-clover. This savanna-like terrain, with its combination of wooded groves and open meadows, is a great place to look for birds. Some common species seen here include spotted towhee, northern flicker, and Steller's jay. Climbing moderately via switchbacks, you gradually win back lost elevation, and this change in perspective provides dramatic views that extend east to Monte Bello Ridge and Black Mountain, and southeast to Mt. Umunhum and Loma Prieta. The San Andreas fault, mover and shaker of so much in California, runs parallel to Monte Bello Ridge through the canyon holding Stevens Creek.

Continuing to climb on a moderate grade, you pass briefly through a wooded area and then crest a hill that offers great views west to Russian Ridge Preserve, which you will visit later on this loop. Crowning Russian Ridge is Borel Hill, at 2,572 feet the highest named peak in San Mateo County. Soon you come to a wood fence and a green metal gate, just beyond which is a T-junction. Here the White Oak Trail heads right, but you turn left on a short connector, actually a dirt road, that leads to Page Mill and Alpine roads. After about 0.1 mile, you come to a paved driveway to a permit-only parking area. Gate MB04 and Page Mill Road are both to the right. You cross the driveway and then follow a single-track trail that parallels Page Mill Road.

At about the 2-mile point, you reach a junction and gate MB05. A short trail to a pond departs left, but instead turn right and pass through a gap in a wood fence to reach Page Mill Road. Here you cross carefully and get on Alpine Road, which heads generally northeast. The first fifty feet or so of Alpine Road are paved, but once you pass a driveway, left, and then a gate, it changes to dirt and gravel. This part of Alpine Road is closed to vehicles, but it gets a lot of bicycle traffic, so stay to the right. In addition, the first 0.3 mile of road passes through private property, so visitors should stay on the road. Starring in the woodland drama unfolding beside the road are Douglas-fir, Monterey pine, California buckeye, coast live oak, bay, willow,

---

The David C. Daniels Nature Center

The David C. Daniels Nature Center at Alpine Pond was funded in part by the Daniels family in memory of their son, and by Peninsula Open Space Trust. Featuring habitat exhibits, touchable displays, and a pond community mural, the center is open to the public on weekends from April through mid-November, and to school groups, grades 3 to 6, by arrangement with the District. For more information, call the District office: (650) 691-1200.

---

and madrone. Playing supporting roles are understory shrubs such as oceanspray, thimbleberry, gooseberry, and pinkflower currant. The villain on this stage is played by stinging nettle, a tall, weedy plant with hairy stems and large, serrated leaves.

At a junction marked with a District information board and a sign for the Meadow Trail, turn left and enter Coal Creek Preserve. From here follow the route description for "Hidden Meadow" on pages 52–53 to the junction of the Meadow and Clouds Rest Trails. When you reach that junction, you turn left on the Clouds Rest Trail and head toward Skyline Boulevard. Climbing through a weedy, brushy area on a gentle grade, you soon come to a lovely grove of canyon oaks. Just ahead is gate CC03, which has a gap to its right through which you can pass. The dirt road continues for another 50 feet or so and then becomes pavement. Continuing to climb, the paved road eventually bends right, levels briefly, and then makes a final uphill push to Skyline Boulevard.

When you reach Skyline Boulevard, turn left and walk uphill along the road's east shoulder, facing traffic—be very careful of oncoming vehicles! After about 100 yards, you reach the northwest end of the Caltrans Vista Point parking area. Here turn right and very carefully cross Skyline Boulevard to reach an entrance to Russian Ridge Preserve at gate RR01. Passing through a gap in a fence, you follow a dirt road a few feet to two District information boards and a map holder. Just beyond the information boards is the first of several junctions.

The dirt road you are on is Mindego Trail. There are two Ridge Trail alignments in Russian Ridge Preserve: both are part of the Bay Area Ridge Trail, and one is a 0.5-mile segment of dirt road that traverses Borel Hill, which is designated in this book as the Ridge Trail (alternate). You angle left at the first junction and get on the Ridge Trail, a wide single track. After about 100 feet, turn left on the Ridge Trail (alternate), a dirt road heading up Borel Hill. From here follow the route description for "Borel Hill" on pages 236–237. When you reach the connector to the Ancient Oaks Trail, right, continue straight on the Ridge Trail for 0.5 mile to the Russian Ridge/Skyline Ridge parking area at the corner of Skyline Boulevard and Alpine Road.

From the parking area's south side, you descend a set of wood steps to meet a wheelchair-accessible path also coming from the parking area. You are now on the Ridge Trail. From here southeast to the parking area for Horseshoe Lake, the Ridge Trail is closed to bikes and horses. (Bicyclists and equestrians headed for Horseshoe Lake and beyond must use a trailhead just across Alpine Road, and then follow an alternate trail.) Take the Ridge Trail through

Skyline Ridge Trail Use

Bicycles: Allowed on all trails except the hiking-only segments of the Bay Area Ridge, Pond Loop, and Horseshoe Loop Trails

Dogs: Not allowed

Horses: Allowed on all trails except the hiking-only segments of the Bay Area Ridge, Pond Loop, and Horseshoe Loop Trails

SKYLINE RIDGE OPEN SPACE PRESERVE

Trip 31. Horseshoe Lake

Length: 1.3 miles

Time: 1 hour or less

Rating: Easy

Highlights: This easy and enjoyable semi-loop uses the Ridge, Horseshoe Lake, and Horseshoe Loop Trails to circle Horseshoe Lake, an artificial impoundment at the head of Lambert Creek. Perfect for a picnic, the wooded groves around the lake offer fine vantage points to spy on waterfowl gliding along the lake surface. Nearby thickets may hold coveys of California quail, the state bird. The Horseshoe Lake Trail is designated an "Easy Access Trail," and accommodates visitors with wheelchairs or strollers.

Directions: Same as for "Grand Loop" on pages 274–75. For handicapped parking, turn left 0.1 mile after entering the preserve.

a tunnel under Alpine Road, and then through a forest of coast live oak, canyon oak, valley oak, madrone, and Monterey pine. Welcome to Skyline Ridge Open Space Preserve!

After passing a gravel road that joins from the left, you soon arrive at Alpine Pond and the David C. Daniels Nature Center. The Pond Loop Trail, a short route around the pond, joins sharply from the right. A deck partially rings the nature center, and a wildlife viewing platform juts out into the pond, which is fringed by cattails. Just past the nature center you come to a fork. Here bear left and follow the route description for "Ridge Trail" on pages 282–83 to the parking area where you began this truly grand loop.

Facilities: Vault toilet

Trailhead: At the south side of the parking area

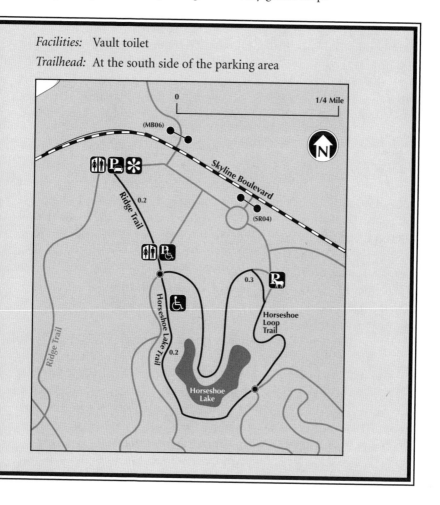

Trip 31. Horseshoe Lake

From the trailhead, take a dirt path about 30 feet to a small wood bridge, past which are two District information boards and a junction. Here veer left on the Ridge Trail, part of the Bay Area Ridge Trail, and pass through a field thick with willows, coyote brush, thistles, and teasels. California quail may be hidden in the underbrush. Listen for their worried murmuring and their plaintive "Chi-ca-go" calls. These birds sit tight until you are practically on top of them, and then take flight in low arcs on rapidly beating wings. Crossing a firebreak, you soon merge with a dirt-and-gravel road leading to a handicapped parking area, right.

Here you angle right, and then immediately veer left where the road forks. About 100 feet ahead on your left is the Horseshoe Lake Trail, also part of the Bay Area Ridge Trail. Descending a few steps, you are joined on the right by a gently sloping dirt path that starts at the south end of the handicapped parking area. The Horseshoe Lake Trail is designated an "Easy Access Trail," and is designed to accommodate visitors with wheelchairs or strollers. This trail is closed to bikes and horses. (An alternate Ridge Trail route to Horseshoe Lake, open to bikes and horses, starts at the south end of the handicapped parking area.)

Now pass through a hiking stile and then turn right, following a level course beside a seasonally wet area. Coffeeberry, yarrow, curly dock, and pennyroyal thrive nearby. The trail bends left and crosses a culvert. Soon you arrive at Horseshoe Lake, which is fringed with cattails and may be dotted with ducks and coots. The lake was formed by an earthen dam near the headwaters of Lambert Creek, which connects with the Pacific Ocean via Peters and Pescadero Creeks. Both Alpine and Horseshoe lakes were created in the 1950s by Mr. John Rickey, a hog farmer and restaurateur who once owned part of what became Skyline Ridge Preserve. At a T-junction, where the alternate Ridge Trail joins from the right, you turn left and cross a bridge over a spillway that drains the lake when it gets too full.

On your left is a rest bench, and from this vantage point you can see how the lake got its name. A curving arm of water extends northeast, mirroring the one you were traveling beside. Just south of the dam, the terrain falls steeply to form a deep, wooded canyon, the headwaters of Lambert Creek. Entering a forest of Douglas-fir, coast live oak, California bay, and bigleaf maple, you come to a junction. Here the Ridge Trail goes straight and climbs, but your route, signed HORSESHOE LOOP TRAIL, angles left. Both are multiuse trails.

Staying beside the lake, you pass several more rest benches ahead on your right. Soon you reach the end of this arm of the lake and cross a small wood bridge over a seasonally wet area. Hazelnut, oceanspray, thimbleberry, ferns, and berry vines grow beside the trail. Now in the open and gaining elevation on a gentle grade, you have a fine view of the lake on your left. Soon you come to a junction, left, with a trail signed NO BIKES, NO HORSES. Take this shortcut to avoid climbing to the equestrian parking area, which is uphill and right.

Veering left, you cross a brushy area and arrive at a T-junction with a trail descending from the equestrian parking area. You turn left, cross a culvert, and pass stands of canyon oak, madrone, young Douglas-fir, and pine. Again beside the lake, but this time about thirty or forty feet above it, you contour around the promontory that divides the lake's two arms. A picnic table is on your left, and soon the landscape on your left rises to meet the trail. Listen here for the characteristic descending, raspy call of a red-tailed hawk, given in one field guide as "keeeer" and in another as "cheeeeeeewv." When you reach the dirt-and-gravel road you crossed earlier, angle left, go about seventy-five feet, and turn right onto the Ridge Trail. From here retrace your route to the parking area.

Horseshoe Lake, artificial, gets its name from its distinctive U-shaped form.

Skyline Ridge Trail Use

Bicycles: Allowed on all trails except the hiking-only segments of the Bay Area Ridge, Pond Loop, and Horseshoe Loop Trails

Dogs: Not allowed

Horses: Allowed on all trails except the hiking-only segments of the Bay Area Ridge, Pond Loop, and Horseshoe Loop Trails

SKYLINE RIDGE OPEN SPACE PRESERVE

Trip 32. Ridge Trail

Length: 3.4 miles

Time: 2 to 3 hours

Rating: Moderate

Highlights: This out-and-back jaunt along the Ridge Trail rises from the forested environs of Alpine Pond to a breezy realm of grassland and chaparral, where views of Butano Ridge, Portola Redwoods State Park, and the Pacific coast await. The spring wildflowers here are superb, and it is easy to see why this stretch of trail, which is part of the Bay Area Ridge Trail, is a favorite among hikers, young and old alike. This trip can easily be combined with the circuit of Alpine Pond described on pages 270–71.

Trip 32. Ridge Trail

Follow the route description for "Alpine Pond" on pp 270–71 to the fork just past the David C. Daniels Nature Center. Here the Pond Loop Trail (signed as being wheelchair accessible) goes right, but instead follow the Ridge Trail, a single track, to the left. If the day is foggy, you may experience "fog drip," whereby trees and shrubs use their foliage to wring moisture from the air through condensation. The moisture then drips to the ground, helping to irrigate the plants.

On a damp day, the air may be fragrant with the scent of California bay. As you pass through the forest, you may hear the tapping of acorn woodpeckers. These gregarious birds are easily identified by their clownish face pattern, white rump, and white wing patches shown in flight. They store their namesake food by hammering acorns into holes drilled in tree trunks, and sometimes even in power poles.

And, at the halfway point, you can also add on the semi-loop trip to Horseshoe Lake described on pages 278–79.

Directions: Same as for "Alpine Pond" on pages 270–71

Facilities: Vault toilet; nature center at Alpine Pond

Trailhead: Same as for "Alpine Pond" on pages 270–71

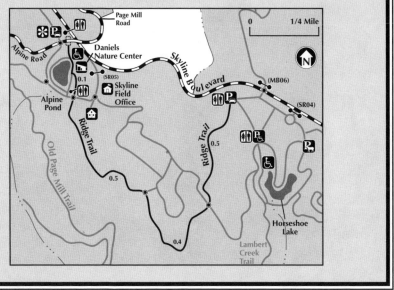

Now the trail crosses a culvert, angles right, and arrives at a four-way junction with a paved road. Continue straight, soon passing an unsigned trail and a fenced building, both uphill and left. Ahead, a massive canyon oak embraces a young Douglas-fir with outstretched, twisted limbs.

Emerging from the forest, make a rising traverse across an open hillside that drops to the right. California poppies, lupine, checker mallow, purple owl's-clover, red maids, and California fuchsia may add color beside the trail, depending on the time of year you visit. Now the trail makes a couple of bends, crosses a culvert, and then curves around the rock outcrop. A rest bench, one of the relatively few on District preserves, is left. Just beyond the bench, look to the right—you can see the Pacific coastline on a clear day.

From this vantage point, you climb steadily on a moderate grade into a zone of chaparral, consisting mostly of chamise, toyon, buckbrush, sticky monkey-flower, yerba santa, and hollyleaf cherry. Beyond an unsigned junction with a

Oaks and fog combine to create a picturesque scene along the Ridge Trail.

trail on the left, you round a rock outcrop that looms over a steep slope. Here the trail is buttressed by a concrete footing to hold it in place. There are more fine views from this spot, dubbed "Rattlesnake Point" by some District rangers, open space technicians, and contractor Gene Sheehan, who encountered the reptiles while building the trail.

A stretch of level trail leads you through trees and then through extensive groves of manzanita and stands of silk tassel. The trail here is merely a ledge carved from the slope. As the trail winds sharply left, you begin to get sweeping views that extend southeast toward Mt. Umunhum. Monte Bello Ridge, topped by Black Mountain, is northeast. The San Andreas fault and the canyon holding Stevens Creek run parallel to Monte Bello Ridge. The seemingly solid ground on which you stand is part of the Pacific plate, moving northwest about two to three inches per year, and slowly leaving most of North America behind.

Now you make a gently descending traverse across an open hillside that plunges about 600 feet to Lambert Creek. Bluedicks, blue-eyed grass, owl's-clover, and lupine may be dotting the grassland with color. At a four-way junction with the alternate trail for bicyclists and equestrians, continue straight and soon regain dense forest, decorated in spring with hound's tongue and milk-maids, and in fall with the yellow and orange leaves of bigleaf maple trees. Where the forest canopy opens and sunlight floods the hillsides, look for the yellow flowers of woodland madia, a member of the sunflower family.

Crossing a culvert, the route bends sharply right and then wanders downhill, eventually reaching a clearing, where you can see Skyline Boulevard to the right. Just ahead are two District information boards and a District parking area. (Past the information boards, the Ridge Trail bends sharply right and continues to Horseshoe Lake.) From here retrace your route back to the parking area.

View from "Rattlesnake Point" at Skyline Ridge Open Space Preserve

SOUTH SKYLINE AREA

Janet Schwind is a longtime resident of the South Skyline area and has become its historian. Like the rest of the Santa Cruz Mountains, the South Skyline area had its logging and sawmills, Schwind says. The early mills were located in redwood groves near Woodside and Searsville, and in the steep gullies on the east side of Windy Hill. Lumber was shipped to landings at Redwood City, Palo Alto, and other spots along San Francisco Bay. Much of the lumber was used to build San Francisco, which was growing rapidly after the Gold Rush. Later, she says, the loggers worked their way over the summit and down into the La Honda area. Mills were also located along what is now Highway 9 to Saratoga Gap, and then west of the gap along Oil Creek. Mills on the west side of the Santa Cruz Mountains sent most of their lumber to the San Mateo coast for shipping, Schwind says. By the turn of the last century, most of the mills had closed, although there was a brief revival after the 1906 earthquake, when lumber was needed to rebuild San Francisco.

Most of the early roads in the South Skyline area were logging roads that went down to either San Francisco Bay or the coast. The area's first cattle ranching settlements tended to cluster around these roads. Most of the vineyards and wineries that dotted Monte Bello Ridge were located well below its crest on the Santa Clara Valley side. There were isolated ranch roads along the crest of the Santa Cruz Mountains, but no public thoroughfare. The idea for Skyline Boulevard may have originated with James Welch, who was a California superior court judge from 1904 until his death in 1931. "Judge Welch convened a Skyline Conference," says Schwind, "where a lot of politicians in various counties got together in Redwood City and talked about building Skyline Boulevard. And they came up with a budget of $750,000. Each county was going to assess people to come up with a third of the cost. They were going to get a third of it from state highway funds, and they were going to get the final third from the federal government."

The appeal for federal dollars has a familiar ring to it. "Their argument to the federal government was going to be an issue of national defense," Schwind says. "You could see all the way to the coast. There would be no bridges to blow up. It would connect the presidios of San Francisco and Monterey, and this was going to be an important military route." The pitch for state funds relied on another modern concern, traffic. "They said it was going to relieve congestion on El Camino Real," she says. And last but not least, it was going to be a great scenic road. Construction of Skyline Boulevard began at Ocean Beach in San Francisco in 1922 and reached the South Skyline area around 1928, Schwind says. As it did in the Kings Mountain area to the northwest, the construction of Skyline Boulevard brought weekend tourists and people interested in building summer cabins to the South Skyline area. Because there were few, if any, existing public roads along the spine of the Santa Cruz Mountains to utilize, Skyline Boulevard was the first state highway designed and built from scratch, says Schwind.

Janet Schwind, her husband Dick, and several neighbors collectively helped form the South Skyline Association in the late 1960s to monitor development and maintain the area's rural beauty. "We lived south of Page Mill Road, and that area was very sparsely settled," she says. "There were some county parks up there, and then there were some large ranches." Schwind says there was a general worry at the time that economic pressures would force the ranchers to sell or subdivide their properties. Schwind says the price of land in the South Skyline area in the early 1960s was about $1,000 an acre. Although land was relatively cheap, there was no municipal water or sewer service. This lack of services was a barrier to residential development. "You couldn't put a subdivision in, because you couldn't meet the requirements for sanitation and water," she says.

The South Skyline Association was "very interested" in the formation of the Open Space District, Schwind says. "We had the Association going by that time. We were having regular meetings, and so we looked into it. We got hold of the state enabling legislation for the District. At that time it was the [Midpeninsula Regional] Park District. And we held a meeting down at what was called The Land at that time. There were buildings there, and they had a long 'house,' I think built by old Senator Louis Oneal, for meetings. And we invited the District promoters to our South Skyline Association meeting." Schwind says area residents were "mostly positive" about the District, viewing its formation as a way for larger landowners to preserve their holdings without having to break them up and sell off smaller parcels. One stumbling block, she says, was the District's power to use eminent domain to acquire land. "There was great hesitation about eminent domain. At that time we found out that it was unavoidable, because eminent domain was in the existing state legislation and there was nothing we could do about it."

Larry Hassett is a member of the District Board of Directors and another longtime resident of the South Skyline area. He also served as board president of the South Skyline Association, and was an active member for more than fifteen years. "I had purchased property prior to the District's formation, and I built a home up on Skyline," he says. "It didn't take long for us to be involved in the politics of the ridgeline, which were just starting to get a little bit steamy. There were very few homes up there then, relatively speaking, and there was a developer who had proposed a motorcycle park that included our acreage. And so the few people that did live up there at the time started to say that's not the kind of activity we want up here. So they formed a homeowners association that was called the South Skyline Association. And they went to battle with the motorcycle park. That was really the first issue that created the need for the South Skyline Association."

Hassett says there was great concern in the South Skyline area about the possible formation of a regional park district and its power of eminent domain. "There was an awful lot of pressure being created for preserving this area," he says. "Which meant that an open space district or park district was on everybody's mind. And once that happened, then people were very concerned about how long they would be able to live up there without being condemned by the state or by federal government or whatever." Once the District was approved by voters in Santa Clara County, Hassett says a few District board members met with a committee of the South Skyline Association to discuss the eminent domain issue and to reassure residents. "It was kind of like the smoking of the peace pipe between the residents and the Open Space District. And that seemed to soothe most people's apprehension about the District."

Still, Hassett says, keeping tabs on District activities was discussed at every South Skyline Association meeting. "Then it got real hot for us," he says, "because the [Midpeninsula Regional] Open Space District, relatively shortly

Pre-Skyline Boulevard

Early photo of Skyline Boulevard

after they added the San Mateo County area, purchased Long Ridge, and then went ahead and purchased Skyline Ranch (now Skyline Ridge Preserve) and started developing those preserves. I remember it was a real battle with the use and management of those preserves, and what was going to be allowed and what wasn't going to be allowed. For me, the real issue was with the development of Skyline Ranch. When it was purchased, I think it was considered the crown jewel of the open space purchased by the District. It was the hub. It was where the greatest potential for creating the centerpiece for the District was going to occur. So when the [District's] Use and Management Committee held their workshops, all the different interest groups were there. The bikers were there, the hikers were there, the equestrians were there, and the astronomers were there. And they were all fighting for their little piece of the pie and making sure they weren't excluded in the plans."

Hassett says that the way the District went about acquiring land in the South Skyline area and balancing the needs of various interest groups won it widespread support. Today, District preserves here include Coal Creek, Long Ridge, Los Trancos, Monte Bello, Russian Ridge, Saratoga Gap, and Skyline Ridge. "I think there was a genuine interest by some of the board members to have neighborhood input. South Skyline was the major area where the District was acquiring land. So the comfort level for people on the ridge now, you see almost total support for the District. The District has demonstrated so much good judgment that they're really happy with what the District has been able to preserve."

Trail through oak woodland at St. Joseph's Hill Open Space Preserve

ST. JOSEPH'S HILL
OPEN SPACE PRESERVE

~

In addition to the hikers, bicyclists, and equestrians who enjoy about four miles of trails located on the slopes of St. Joseph's Hill, Native Americans, Spanish missionaries, American explorers, mountain men and women, lumberjacks, Chinese railway workers, and Jesuit priests have all passed by here. The route across the Santa Cruz Mountains between the Pacific coast and the Santa Clara Valley had probably been used by Native Americans for many centuries before becoming the Santa Cruz branch of El Camino Real, the Spanish missionary road, in the 1790s. Captain John C. Frémont explored along Los Gatos Creek in February of 1846, on his expedition to the Monterey area. His diary describes a splendid forest of coast redwoods, tanbark oaks, and madrones.

Homesteading in the area began a few years later, and some of the colorful characters who arrived to seek their fortunes are remembered in John V. Young's history, *Ghost Towns of the Santa Cruz Mountains,* a compilation of his newspaper articles that appeared in 1934 in the Sunday *San Jose Mercury Herald.* Zachariah "Buffalo" Jones was a lumberman whose nickname apparently referred to his physical stature, his bellowing voice, and perhaps also his bodily odor. Jones Mill later became the town of Lexington, and Jones Road was the route across St. Joseph's Hill that linked Lexington and Los Gatos. "Mountain" Charley McKiernan built what may have been the first frame house in the Santa Cruz Mountains. Later he survived being mauled by a grizzly bear and lived out his days with a metal plate in his skull above his left eye. Another Charley, Charley Parkhurst, was a one-eyed, tobacco-chewing, foul-mouthed stage driver who began life as Charlotte but managed to conceal her female identity until the day of her funeral.

View of St. Joseph's Hill Open Space Preserve from Sierra Azul

John Alexander Forbes laid out a town and built a grist mill on Los Gatos Creek in the early 1850s. The mill eventually failed, but Forbes Mill became the Town of Los Gatos. In 1880, a narrow-gauge railway line built largely by Chinese laborers began service between San Jose and Santa Cruz, bringing tourists to the coast and to the redwood forest resorts that lined the route. The railway also helped put the stage line out of business, but stimulated the development of lumber mills, orchards, and vineyards. Eventually the railway in turn was displaced by cars and highways. In 1888, just as Los Gatos was being incorporated, Jesuit seminarians settled on St. Joseph's Hill and began planting vineyards and making wine. The Novitiate seminary lasted nearly eighty years, until declining enrollment forced its closure. One of the seminarians, Edmund "Jerry" Brown, Jr., went on to become California's governor and then mayor of Oakland. The vineyards were later abandoned and the winery closed its doors in 1985. Today, a number of local wineries occupy the former Novitiate winery. Lexington Reservoir, built in 1952, flooded the historic towns of Lexington and nearby Alma.

Although relatively small in size, St. Joseph's Hill Preserve is rich in plant life, and includes one of the most extensive manzanita forests on District land. Oak and California bay dominate the steep hillsides above Los Gatos Creek, but as you ascend St. Joseph's Hill, the wooded areas give way to chaparral and then to open, grassy slopes that once held vineyards used to make Novitiate wine. From atop the hill's 1,253-foot summit, you have 360° views that stretch from the rugged ridges of the Sierra Azul to the skyscrapers of San Francisco. St. Joseph's Hill Preserve provides the scenic backdrop for Los Gatos, and its trails link the town's Novitiate Park with Lexington Reservoir County Park. The preserve consists of 170 acres purchased jointly by the

District and the Town of Los Gatos in 1982. Current District board member Pete Siemens, who was on the Town Council at the time, helped initiate the first (and to date only) joint project between the Town of Los Gatos and the District to purchase St. Joseph's Hill. "This is an important preserve for the town and the District as it protects the scenic backdrop of the town and provides open space access without the need to drive a car." The District and the town hold an open space easement over another 97 acres of adjoining private land, which will remain permanently undeveloped. This parcel and land to the north is used as the headquarters of the California Province of the Society of Jesus, and as a home for retired priests.

Building the Flume Trail on the northwest side of St. Joseph's Hill was a difficult task, says District ranger Kerry Carlson. "When we decided to build the Flume Trail," he says, "we knew it was going to be a huge undertaking because it was sheer rock along that canyon that overlooks Los Gatos Creek." Carlson says that the crew consisted of District rangers, seasonal employees, and inmates of the Santa Clara County Correctional Facility. At the lead was contractor Gene Sheehan, who, over the years, built many of the District's trails. Except for Sheehan's trail-sized grader/backhoe, the only other mechanized equipment available then (the mid 80s) was a portable gas-powered jackhammer called a pionjar. "When we were out there with the pionjar breaking this rock, trying to drill into it, Gene finally said, 'We're not going to get this trail through because there's too much rock. The only way we're going to get through this is to dynamite.' And I think it was me and ranger Patrick Congdon, we said, 'Well, we know Leonard Anderson, he's the Sheriff department's bomb-squad guy. Maybe we could call him up, and maybe he'll have extra dynamite or something he wants to get rid of.' And Gene said, 'Well, pursue it. See what he says.'"

Carlson says they placed a call to Anderson, who said the bomb squad had just confiscated a case of dynamite and had it sitting in a locker. If District crews would drill holes in the rock, he would supply the explosives. Luckily, someone happened to have a video camera to record the event for posterity, says Carlson. "So there's some video of me on one of the [motorized] trail bikes, riding down the trail with this case of dynamite in the back trailer." After using the pionjar to drill holes in the rock, the crew put the dynamite in the holes and set off the blasts. "It was a good thing the Sheriff's Department was there," says Carlson, "because as things got more difficult—well, you know, those rocks get tough. 'Let's put some more dynamite in there!' So we'd start with one stick and then, well, maybe we'll put a couple of sticks in there. Pretty soon the blasts were so big in the canyon that we got a call from CHP

St. Joseph's Hill Trail Use

Bicycles: Allowed on all trails except the Flume Trail

Dogs: Leashed dogs allowed on all trails

Horses: Allowed on all trails except the Flume Trail

ST. JOSEPH'S HILL OPEN SPACE PRESERVE

Trip 33. Novitiate Loop

Length: 3.3 miles

Time: 2 to 3 hours

Rating: Moderate

Highlights: Ascending via Flume, Jones, Novitiate, and Range Trails, you climb the west flank of St. Joseph's Hill, whose grassy slopes once held vineyards used to make communion wine. Leaving the summit for another day, wander on the Serpentine Trail through an elfin forest of manzanita before joining that shrub's namesake trail as it curves west and then north to meet the Novitiate Trail. Although relatively small, this preserve is rich in plant life, as indicated by the variety of species found beside the trail. Oak and bay dominate the forest on the steep hillside above Los Gatos Creek, but higher up a wonderful assortment of chaparral shrubs vie for your attention.

Directions: From Highway 17 in Los Gatos, take the Highway 9/Los Gatos/Saratoga exit and go southeast on Saratoga Ave. After 0.4 mile turn right on Los Gatos Boulevard, which soon becomes E. Main Street. At 0.7 mile turn left onto College Avenue, go 0.4 mile and turn right on Jones Road. After 0.1 mile, park along the right side of Jones Road. There is very limited parking in this neighborhood. Just ahead is a gated entrance to Novitiate Park.

Facilities: None

Trailhead: Gate SJ01, at the south end of Jones Road

trying to figure out what the heck was going on. Traffic was slowing down on Highway 17 because of these huge explosions up in the canyon. Fortunately, the CHP was on the highway to ensure traffic flow remained steady and that no incidents occurred. This of course was the old days when permits were

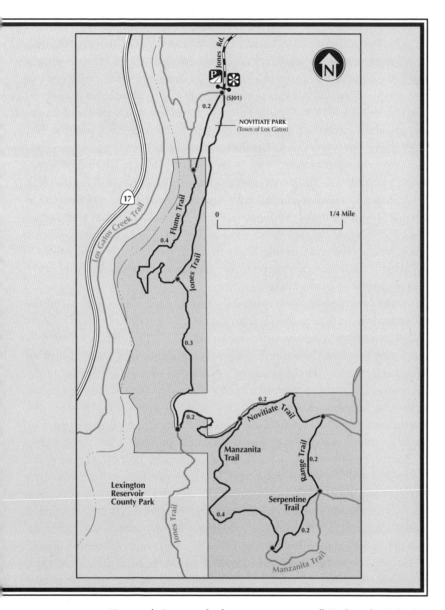

not a concern. You can't just work that way any more." Today, the District obtains all necessary permits and properly notifies all parties involved, including sister agencies and the public, for any major construction project on the preserves.

Trip 33. Novitiate Loop

A District information board and map holder are just past the trailhead, as are several Novitiate Park trails heading right. Take a dirt road straight for about fifty feet or so to a fork. The multiuse Jones Trail, which you will use on the return part of this route, is left. For now, however, veer right on the Flume Trail, for hiking only. This trail, a triumph of District trail-building ingenuity, takes its name from a waterway that once ran parallel to, but high above, Los Gatos Creek. The flume was built in 1931 as a concrete channel, and then rebuilt in the 1940s using a metal half-pipe covered with redwood planking. The District deemed it a hazard and dismantled most of it in 1985. A grassy meadow planted with trees is to your right, and a screen of French broom, an invasive nonnative, is left. The trail climbs on a moderate, then gentle, grade through stands of coast live oak, California bay, California buckeye, and olive trees. Shrubs lining the route include toyon, spiny redberry, sticky monkeyflower, and mountain mahogany. Honeysuckle vines interweave themselves in the foliage.

At the preserve boundary, marked by a wood fence with a gap, one of the Novitiate Park trails joins sharply from the right. Your trail, a single track, forges ahead on a narrow ledge through dense woodland. To the right, the hillside falls away steeply to Los Gatos Creek. (Building the Flume Trail required blasting away parts of sheer rock cliffs to create a usable trail alignment.) Now turn right and cross a bridge over a seasonal tributary of Los Gatos Creek. Coming into the open, you find yourself surrounded by chaparral—manzanita, silk tassel, and leather oak. A left-hand switchback marks the start of a moderate climb over rocky ground. A switchback to the right soon brings you to a fence with a gap.

Just beyond the fence, in the shade of tall eucalyptus trees, you meet the Jones Trail at a junction. Bearing right, take the Jones Trail, a dirt road shared by bicyclists, equestrians, joggers, and hikers. Level at first, the route now ascends on a gentle and then moderate grade. Blue elderberry and poison oak join the manzanita beside the road. Flowering in early winter and continuing through spring, manzanitas are among the Bay Area's most interesting shrubs. Their tiny urn-shaped flowers are characteristic of the heath family, and their small, tough leaves are designed to reduce moisture loss and optimize photosynthesis. Manzanitas are adapted to fire, and some species can reproduce by sprouting new shoots from an underground burl. There are about sixty species of manzanita, and most are California natives. Identification is tricky, and some species hybridize. The name refers to the plants' red berries—*manzana* means "apple" in Spanish.

When you reach the Novitiate Trail, turn left and begin a moderate climb beside a metal fence topped with barbed wire. Behind the fence, and also lining the road, is an extensive manzanita forest, one of the most beautiful in the entire Bay Area. Joining the manzanita is coast silk tassel, another early blooming member of the chaparral community, named for its dangling strings of flowers. Coast silk tassel has wavy-edged leaves, whereas Fremont's silk tassel, also found on District preserves, has smooth-edged leaves.

Rising via S-bends, the road affords dramatic glimpses of the East Bay hills and Mt. Diablo. Leather oak, indicating serpentine soil, grows nearby, as does coffeeberry. At a junction with the aptly named Manzanita Trail, you continue straight, perhaps treading on strips of eucalyptus bark and sickle-shaped eucalyptus leaves. Now on a shady, rolling course, you come to a four-way junction. Here the Novitiate Trail continues straight; the Manzanita Trail, which loops over the summit, angles right; and the Range Trail goes sharply right. Take the Range Trail, a dirt road that has a bit of pavement for the first 50 feet or so.

Soon you are treading on a dirt surface that may be covered with eucalyptus leaves and strips of bark. A rising traverse brings you to a large clearing, where habitat restoration is in progress. Once used for a shooting range, the clearing became overgrown with yellow star thistle and other invasive nonnative species. The area has since been restored by the District with native grasses, including purple needlegrass, blue wild rye, squirrel tail, meadow barley, and California brome. In addition to manzanitas, which form extensive groves nearby, the native shrubs here include silk tassel and leather oak. At a four-way junction, the Manzanita Trail goes left and straight, and the Serpentine Trail heads right.

Turn right and follow the Serpentine Trail, a single track, as it meanders gently uphill through a magical elfin forest of manzanita. A fine view to your right takes in Santa Clara, the southern edge of San Francisco Bay, the East Bay hills, and Mt. Diablo. The trail, which may be muddy during wet weather, crests a rise and begins to descend. Now you can see the Highway 17 corridor and Lexington Reservoir to the southwest. Making an almost 180° bend, your trail merges with the Manzanita Trail, a dirt road. From here follow the route description for "St. Joseph's Hill" on pages 298–99 to the Novitiate Trail. Turn left and then retrace your route to the junction of the Jones and Flume Trails. Now turn right onto the Jones Trail, a multiuse dirt road that descends along the edge of a densely wooded ravine dropping left to Los Gatos Creek.

St. Joseph's Hill Trail Use

Bicycles: Allowed on all trails except the Flume Trail

Dogs: Leashed dogs allowed on all trails

Horses: Allowed on all trails except the Flume Trail

ST. JOSEPH'S HILL OPEN SPACE PRESERVE

Trip 34. St. Joseph's Hill

Length: 3.4 miles

Time: 2 to 3 hours

Rating: Moderate

Highlights: The summit of St. Joseph's Hill offers 360° views that take in many of the communities from San Jose to San Francisco. Gazing out at all this development, you may understand and better appreciate the value of open space, whether as extensive national and state parks, or as compact urban preserves such as this one. But don't let the diminutive size fool you. The botanical diversity here is superb, and one of the most extensive manzanita forests on District lands lies along the Manzanita Trail. Elsewhere on this route, which also uses the Jones and Novitiate Trails, you encounter woodlands of oak, bay, and bigleaf maple, and open slopes that once held vineyards used to make communion wine.

Directions: From Highway17 southbound, take the Bear Creek Road exit south of Los Gatos. After 0.1 mile, you come to a stop sign at a four-way junction. Turn right, cross over Highway 17, and turn left to get on Highway 17 northbound. Go 0.4 mile to Alma Bridge Road, turn right, and go 0.7 mile to a parking area for Lexington Reservoir on the right. (There is a fee for parking in this county park parking area.)

From Highway 17 northbound, exit at Alma Bridge Road south of Los Gatos and follow the directions above.

This preserve is popular with bicyclists, and they too may be descending the Jones Trail, so stay to the right side of the road. On a windy day, the sound of rustling eucalyptus leaves almost overcomes the traffic noise from Highway 17. Tall valley oaks join the eucalyptus trees to line the rough and rocky road, which loses elevation on a moderate grade. When you reach the junction with the Flume Trail you passed earlier, simply continue straight to the roadside parking area along Jones Road.

Facilities: Picnic tables, phone, vault toilet

Trailhead: Gate SJ03, on the north side of Alma Bridge Road, across from the parking area

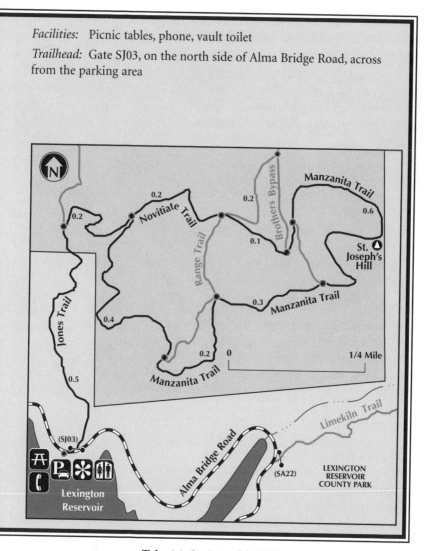

Trip 34. St. Joseph's Hill

From the trailhead, climb north on a steep dirt road that shows evidence of once having been paved. Coast live oak, valley oak, eucalyptus, and toyon grow beside the road, accompanied by California sagebrush, poison oak, and nonnative French and Spanish brooms. After several hundred yards, the grade eases to moderate, and the road curves left. During periods of wet weather, be prepared for plenty of mud! Just past two District information

*St. Joseph's Hill Open Space Preserve includes one of the most
extensive manzanita forests on District land.*

boards and a map holder, the grade relents to gentle as you enter a zone of
chaparral, including scrub oak, chamise, buckbrush, hollyleaf cherry, and
mountain mahogany. Los Gatos Creek, which parallels Highway 17, is downhill
and left. Through the foliage, you get occasional glimpses northeast toward
Santa Clara and the southern reaches of San Francisco Bay.

Hillsides draped with ferns and berry vines greet you as you enter a densely
wooded area of California bay and bigleaf maple. Descending on a gentle grade,
the road curves left near the head of a ravine and soon reaches the preserve
boundary. Climbing a bit, you arrive at a trail junction. Here the Jones Trail
continues straight, but you veer right on the Novitiate Trail, an eroded and
rocky dirt road. From here, follow the route description for "Novitiate Loop"
on pages 294–95 to the junction of the Novitiate, Manzanita, and Range

Trails. Select the Manzanita Trail and follow it uphill through dense forest that soon gives way to open slopes dotted with coyote brush. Ahead is your goal, St. Joseph's Hill, topped with a solitary cypress. As you climb, be sure to stop and admire the scenic vista that extends northward toward San Francisco and Oakland.

The (upper) Brothers Bypass Trail cuts left across a hillside that once held a vineyard. Your road curves left, giving you fine views across Highway 17 to the rugged hills of the El Sereno Preserve, described on pages 80–87. Passing the (lower) Brothers Bypass Trail on the right, you continue going left and ascending, now almost completely in the open, to the top of St. Joseph's Hill. From this spectacular vantage point, you have 360° views that take in many of the Bay Area's tallest summits, including Mt. Hamilton, Mt. Umunhum, and Mt. Tamalpais, as well as the bayside communities from San Jose to San Francisco. This makes a great spot for a picnic, and you can use the low wooden fence that borders the road as a bench. While on this aerie, be sure to scan the sky for raptors. Red-tailed hawks, American kestrels, and northern harriers are among the avian hunters you may see. The northern harrier is one of only a few raptors that shows a pronounced difference in coloration between male and female. The female northern harrier is brown, whereas the male is light gray, similar in color to a gull.

Continuing across the top of St. Joseph's Hill, you pass the solitary cypress tree you saw earlier, and then begin to wind your way downhill. Remnants of an old vineyard cling to a hillside that falls away to your right. Now the road curves sharply right and meets the (lower) Brothers Bypass Trail on the right, which you passed earlier on the other side of the hill. An almost unbroken sea of manzanita greets you just ahead. In places, you come upon the bleached skeleton of a dead manzanita, its gray bark so different from the telltale reddish hue of living specimens. At a four-way junction with the Range Trail and the Serpentine Trail, you stay on the Manzanita Trail by turning left and continuing to descend, now over rough ground. From here you have a good view of Lexington Reservoir and the parking area, far below.

At about the 2-mile point, the Serpentine Trail, which you passed at the previous junction, joins sharply from the right. Now your trail makes a sweeping curve to the left and descends on a moderate grade. After a while, it swings right and briefly enters a forest of coast live oak, bay, and toyon. Traversing an open hillside that falls steeply left, you reach the junction with the Novitiate Trail that you passed earlier. From here retrace your route to the parking area by turning left, and then left again when you reach the Jones Trail.

Salt marsh plants line the Bay's edge at
Stevens Creek Shoreline Nature Study Area.

STEVENS CREEK SHORELINE NATURE STUDY AREA

~

This tiny preserve is at the edge of San Francisco Bay adjacent to Shoreline–at–Mountain View Park. It consists of about fifty-five marshland acres bordered on the west by Stevens Creek, on the north by a salt-evaporation pond, and on the south and east by Moffett Field. Construction of the salt-evaporation ponds to the north removed the marsh from tidal action. There is no indication that the property was used for salt production, but it may have been used for hunting and grazing. It is estimated that about 80 percent of the original wetland habitats around San Francisco Bay have been destroyed by diking and filling for agriculture, industry, housing, and transportation.

This preserve is one of the District's two holdings along the Bay. Local birders know it as Crittenden Marsh, and come here to view the resident

---

Salt Marshes

Salt marshes are among the world's most productive ecosystems, and the remaining ones around San Francisco Bay attract large numbers of shore-birds, waterfowl, and waders, especially from fall through spring. The salt marsh habitat consists mainly of plants that can tolerate periodic immersion in salt water. Some of these specialized plants are found on the preserve, including cord grass and pickleweed. Other plants, such as saltbush, alkali heath, marsh gumplant, coyote brush, and fennel, grow at higher elevations bordering the marsh. Two endangered animals, the clapper rail and the salt marsh harvest mouse, are inhabitants of Bay Area salt marshes.

---

and migratory shorebirds, waterfowl, and waders that congregate on the shores of San Francisco Bay, especially during spring and fall migrations. Among the shorebird species commonly seen in this marsh are American avocets, black-necked stilts, willets, greater yellowlegs, long-billed dowitchers, dunlin, western sandpipers, and least sandpipers. Because of the relatively low salt concentration in the marsh, the preserve also attracts bird species normally associated with freshwater marshes. Other nearby birding areas include Don Edwards San Francisco Bay National Wildlife Refuge,

---

Stevens Creek Shoreline Trail Use

Bicycles: Allowed on all trails

Dogs: Not allowed

Horses: Not allowed

STEVENS CREEK SHORELINE NATURE STUDY AREA

Trip 35. Salt Marsh Stroll

Length: 1.9 miles

Time: 1 hour or less

Rating: Easy

Highlights: This tiny preserve, one of the District's two holdings along the Bay, offers visitors a chance to enjoy the salt marsh habitat once prevalent here, and to view some of the fascinating shorebirds, waterfowl, and waders who call the Bay home or pass through on their migratory flights. Birders will especially enjoy this preserve, and it is easy to combine an outing here with stops at other nearby birding hot spots, including Don Edwards San Francisco Bay National Wildlife Refuge, Palo Alto Baylands Nature Preserve, Ravenswood Preserve, and the Shoreline–at–Mountain View Park.

Directions: From Highway 101 northbound in Mountain View, take the Shoreline Boulevard exit and go north 1 mile to an entrance kiosk for Shoreline–at–Mountain View Park. Go another 0.1 mile to a parking area on the right.

From Highway 101 southbound in Mountain View, take the Rengstorff Avenue/Amphitheater Parkway exit. Stay right, and at a

Palo Alto Baylands Nature Preserve, Ravenswood Preserve, and the Shoreline–at–Mountain View Park.

The District used a matching grant to acquire this property from Peninsula Open Space Trust, which received it as a gift from Leslie Salt. The District has actively supported and participated in the creation of the Bay Trail, which one day will link parks and preserves around San Francisco and San Pablo Bays. About half of the proposed four hundred-mile trail system is in place. This preserve may play a small but important role in the completion of the Bay Trail.

traffic signal turn right and cross over the highway. At 1 mile you come to a traffic signal at N. Shoreline Boulevard, where you turn left. Go 0.3 mile to an entrance kiosk for Shoreline–at–Mountain View Park. Go another 0.1 mile to a parking area on the right.

Facilities: Vault toilet (located in Shoreline-at-Mountain View Park)

Trailhead: At the east side of the parking area

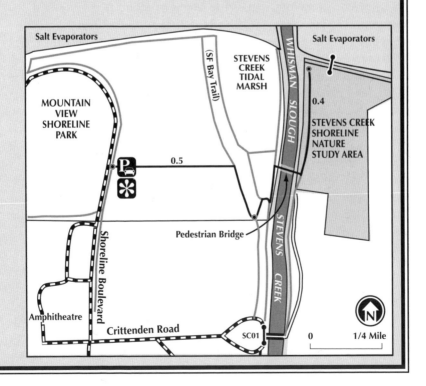

Trip 35. Salt Marsh Stroll

From the trailhead, go east across Shoreline Amphitheater's parking area E—a dirt, grass, and gravel expanse the size of several football fields. At the far end of parking area E, you get on a paved road that is curving to the right and descending to the Crittenden stormwater pump station, a low building. When you reach this building, turn sharply left onto a paved path that climbs on a gentle grade. After about 125 feet you come to a fork with a paved path. A sign indicates that the Shoreline Marshlands are left and the Stevens Creek Trail is right. Turn right, and after another 125 feet or so come to a T-junction with the Stevens Creek Trail. Here a sign reads: STEVENS CREEK TIDAL MARSH TRAIL ENTRANCE.

Just ahead is Stevens Creek, which gets its start in the Monte Bello Preserve, high above Sunnyvale and Mountain View. Following a canyon formed by the San Andreas fault, the creek flows southeast for about 7 miles before turning abruptly north when it reaches Stevens Creek County Park. A dam on the creek forms Stevens Creek Reservoir. Downstream from the dam, Stevens Creek runs parallel to Highway 85 on its way toward San Francisco Bay. The creek was named for Captain Elisha Stephens, a native of South Carolina who, in 1844, led the first wagon train over the Sierra Nevada to California.

Across the creek to the east is Moffett Field, built in the 1930s and used mostly as a naval air station and then as the NASA Ames Research Center. Rising as a backdrop behind the airfield are the East Bay hills and Mt. Hamilton. Turn left onto the Stevens Creek Trail, a paved path. After several hundred feet, cross the creek by turning right onto a metal bridge with wood planks. The bridge across Stevens Creek, connecting Shoreline to the District's Nature Study Area, was a joint project between the Coastal Conservancy, the City of Mountain View, and the District. Among the common salt marsh plants growing here are pickleweed, glasswort, alkali heath, and gumplant. Once across the bridge, you find a T-junction with a dirt road. Here turn left and enter the Stevens Creek Shoreline Nature Study Area, a District preserve.

The salt marsh to your right is a great place to look for shorebirds, waterfowl, and wading birds, especially during fall, winter, and early spring. The shorebird tribe—oystercatchers, avocets, stilts, plovers, willets, curlews, godwits, small sandpipers, dowitchers, and phalaropes—is especially interesting. Many species of shorebirds pass through the Bay Area on their way between breeding grounds in the Arctic and winter ranges in Central and South America. A few species breed locally and remain here all year. One of these, the snowy plover, is federally listed as a threatened species. Among the shorebird species commonly seen in this marsh are American avocets, black-necked stilts, willets, greater yellowlegs, long-billed dowitchers, dunlin, western sandpipers, and least sandpipers.

Where there are shorebirds and waterfowl, there may also be birds of prey, such as hawks and falcons. Common aerial hunters found above salt marshes are northern harriers, formerly called marsh hawks, and white-tailed kites. Less common and more of a threat to shorebirds and water-fowl are merlins and peregrine falcons. If you see a flock of shorebirds or ducks suddenly take flight, it may be because one of these raptors is nearby. Songbirds, such as western meadowlarks and black phoebes, may also be seen here. Flanking the Dumbarton Bridge across the Bay are the Don Edwards San Francisco Bay National Wildlife Refuge and the East Bay Regional Park District's Coyote Hills Regional Park, more good birding areas.

At the north end of the salt marsh, you come to a levee signed PRIVATE PROPERTY heading right. This marks the end of the Stevens Creek Shoreline Nature Study Area. When you have finished enjoying this small but ornithologically interesting preserve, retrace your route to the parking area.

Great egret foraging adjacent to a tidal slough

OPEN SPACE TECHNICIANS

Open space technicians perform a variety of general maintenance and construction duties, and other specialized tasks on District properties and facilities. They perform construction, cleanup, and routine maintenance on District lands, trails, roads, buildings, and other facilities. They construct District trails, and their trail maintenance duties include clearing vegetation and downed trees, and looking after drainage systems, trail bridges, culverts, retaining walls, fences, and gates. Often these tasks include carpentry, painting, plumbing, and electrical skills. Open space technicians frequently work with volunteers from the community to accomplish trail maintenance and other restoration projects on District lands. In terms of resource management, open space technicians may participate in prescribed burns of District lands, and take part in biotic or other data-collection projects. Sometimes they are called upon to fight wildland fires and help with medical emergencies and search-and-rescue operations. Open space technicians also occasionally respond to requests and inquiries from the public, and provide visitor information.

Michael Bankosh is a lead open space technician at the Foothills office. He says that resource management is a key part of an open space technician's job. "We get the whole crew together," he says, "and we choose a resource management project, which is basically managing the land we have, whether it be pulling out nonnative invasives like acacia and Scotch broom, or mowing yellow star thistle from an area, and returning it to a native ecosystem. Or going in and repairing storm damage and landslides. Or revegetating an area that was once a house pad." Other typical projects, he says, include planting oak trees and collecting native plant seeds.

Bankosh says that he is glad the District has made resource management an important goal. "It feels good when the District promotes resource management," he says, "because it's something that is now becoming a higher priority. If something's wrong with a road or a trail, you're going to go fix it for the public. But it's nice being able to spend the time on restoring ecosystems. Ultimately, I think we all care about the level of stewardship of the land we have. We all want to see that we're giving the best care we can give with the resources we have."

*Open Space Technician Ken Bolle builds the Achistaca Trail at
Long Ridge Open Space Preserve.*

Holden Neal is a lead open space technician at the Foothills office. He says that the job is rewarding, although it is frequently hot and dusty, or wet and cold. "A rewarding part of the job is when you go out in tough conditions and get the job done right. Later, somebody might come by or call and tell you, 'Hey, we really appreciate you clearing the trail, getting the poison oak off the trail, and opening it up.' At the end of the day, you feel like you've accomplished something. And it looks nice, and people are happy with it. And they really do enjoy it."

The District has two regional field offices—the Foothills office, located at Rancho San Antonio Preserve, and the Skyline office, located at Skyline Ridge Preserve. Each field office currently has two lead open space technicians, five open space technicians, an equipment mechanic operator, and up to ten seasonal open space technicians. Originally called a ranger aide, the position of open space technician was created in the late 1980s. Prior to that, District rangers performed many of the duties now handled by open space technicians.

*Views of
the San Francisco Bay
and salt marsh at
Stevens Creek Shoreline
Nature Study Area*

THORNEWOOD
OPEN SPACE PRESERVE

~

Small in size but rich in history, this 164-acre preserve is perfect for a quick stroll or a walk with your leashed dog. The name "Thornewood" honors Julian Thorne, a San Francisco land speculator, and his wife Edna. In 1908, the Thornes bought more than 600 acres along Old La Honda Road above Portola Valley, which included a large summer residence called "Montebello" by its former owner, Edgar Preston, a San Francisco attorney. The Thornes renamed the house "Portola Hall," and proceeded to subdivide their land into small parcels for summer homes in what they called Portola Hills. August Schilling, whose San Francisco business sold tea, coffee, and spices, bought many of the parcels, including the one where Portola Hall was located. Schilling changed the name of the house again, this time to "Broad Oak." He also converted an old winery into a thirty-two-room guest house called "Sunny Run," where people came for seminars and retreats.

Schilling's estate was extensive and included a redwood-ringed reservoir that dated from the area's logging days in the 1850s. Called "Lake in the Woods," the reservoir was in the midst of old logging roads that the Schilling family and their guests used for hiking and horseback riding. The landscape was "improved" by the addition of artificial lakes, waterfalls, rock formations, viewpoints, and such. The 0.7-mile trail through Thornewood Preserve passes some of this terrain on its way to Lake in the Woods, now called Schilling Lake. In addition to coast redwoods, you stroll by stately oaks, California bays, and Douglas-firs. Spring is a fine time to view the early blooming chaparral shrubs and forest wildflowers that line the route. Broad Oak, Schilling's mansion, was demolished in 1953, but not before it had been sprayed with chlordane dust, cyanide gas, and DDT, and then burned, to rid it of thousands of bees that kept attacking the wrecking crew.

Oak woodland at Thornewood Open Space Preserve

After selling all the other parcels in the Portola Hills subdivision, the Thornes kept nearly ninety acres for their use, and in 1928 they built a summer home designed by noted architect Gardner Dailey. Some of Dailey's other projects included the American Embassy in Manila, a hotel in Honolulu, the Varian Physics Lab at Stanford, and the farm buildings at Filoli. Julian Thorne died in 1930 at age 55. Edna, a member of the Woodside Garden Club, continued to supervise her garden and estate for many years. She left the property at her death to the Sierra Club Foundation, but did not provide

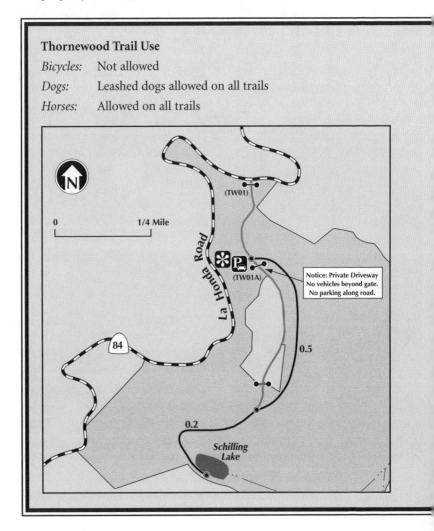

Thornewood Trail Use

Bicycles: Not allowed

Dogs: Leashed dogs allowed on all trails

Horses: Allowed on all trails

money for upkeep or repairs. The foundation created a committee to oversee the property and plan appropriate uses for it. Fundraising through "Walk-A-Thornes" and volunteer efforts succeeded in raising money and completing some of the needed repairs, but paying taxes and meeting the requirements of the Woodside Planning Commission proved too burdensome. After holding the property for seven years, the Foundation donated it to the District in 1978. Today, a private party who has leased the property is restoring the house and grounds.

THORNEWOOD OPEN SPACE PRESERVE

36. Schilling Lake

Length: 1.5 miles

Time: 1 hour or less

Rating: Easy

Highlights: This easy out-and-back ramble follows a single-track trail through a forest of oak, bay, and Douglas-fir, and then descends a dirt road past stately coast redwoods to secluded Schilling Lake. Flowering chaparral shrubs and early blooming wildflowers make this route an ideal choice for an early spring outing.

Directions: From I-280 in Woodside, take the Highway 84/Woodside Road exit. Follow Highway 84/Woodside Road southwest through Woodside and then southeast to a junction with Portola Road at 3.3 miles. Bear right to stay on Highway 84, now La Honda Road. At 4.9 miles from I-280, turn left at a brick wall marked 895–897. Go 0.1 mile on a single-lane road to a parking area on the right.

From the junction of Skyline Boulevard and Highway 84 in Sky Londa, take Highway 84/La Honda Road north 1.9 miles and turn right at a brick wall marked 895–897. Go 0.1 mile on a single-lane road to a parking area on the right.

Facilities: None

Trailhead: Just left of gate TW01A, about 60 feet southeast of the parking area on the paved entrance road

Trip 36. Schilling Lake

At the trailhead are two District information boards and a map holder. The trail to Schilling Lake, a single track, is just to the right of the information boards. (The paved road continues past gate TW01A to a closed area, where the Thornewood house is under restoration by a private party who is leasing the property from the District.) You follow the trail through a forest of coast live oak, black oak, California bay, Douglas-fir, and madrone. Tangles of berry vines mingle with coffeeberry, gooseberry, toyon, and nonnative French broom. In late winter or early spring, look for the large triangular flowers and cheerful blue-and-white flowers of hound's tongue, an early bloomer. This is also a good time to look for birds—they may be easier to spot while the foliage on many trees and shrubs is sparse.

During the rainy season, the trail may be wet and muddy. Two switchbacks help you lose a bit of elevation, and now the trail finds a level course across a hillside that drops to your left. Ferns abound, and several burbling streams flow under the trail through culverts. The rain forest feel is briefly interrupted by a stand of chaparral, including manzanita, chamise, and sticky monkeyflower. Also nearby are chaparral currant, another early bloomer, and blue elderberry. Returning to a forest of bay trees and moss-covered oaks, you soon reach a narrow ravine spanned by a bridge. A seasonal creek flows through the ravine in winter, creating delightful miniature cascades as the water splashes from one pool to the next. On a sunny day, the light filters through the foliage, creating sparkling highlights on the water's surface.

At about the 0.5-mile point, you merge with a dirt road joining sharply from the right. Descending on a gentle grade, you begin to pass stands of majestic coast redwoods and a few tall pines. The road reaches a low point just west of Schilling Lake, which is nestled in a cool, shady forest. Here a creek flows under the road through a culvert. Just beyond the creek is a junction, left, with another dirt road. Turn left, cross a second culvert, and then bear left at a fork. The lake is now on your left, and on a sunny day it is marked with the long, narrow shadows of the redwoods, Douglas-firs, and pines that tower above its southern shore. A sign on your right alerts you that the preserve boundary and the start of private property, marked by a fence, are just ahead. From here retrace your route to the parking area.

Seasonal stream flowing among the ferns at
Thornewood Open Space Preserve

The Anniversary Trail climbs Windy Hill and offers superb views along the way.

WINDY HILL
OPEN SPACE PRESERVE

~

Windy Hill is aptly named. Coastal breezes from the Pacific, often bearing loads of thick fog, rush over the ridge top and whistle across the grassy slopes below. The shape of the terrain, combined with periodic fires and grazing, have kept the upper hillsides here mostly free of trees and shrubs since Spanish missionaries passed by in 1769. Forests of Douglas-fir, oak, madrone, and California buckeye line the steep gulches that radiate eastward and downhill from Windy Hill's twin summits. These woodlands block the wind and also provide welcome shade on warm days. Views of the Bay Area and the San Mateo coast from atop Windy Hill are unrivaled, and the summits are easily accessible from parking areas on Skyline Boulevard. Hawks and falcons soar overhead in plain view, but you may need binoculars or a trained ear to identify elusive forest and grassland songsters. A fine variety of shrubs and wildflowers will delight native-plant enthusiasts. Approximately nineteen miles of trails await your exploration. Leashed dogs are welcome on several trails, and mountain bicyclists will enjoy the Spring Ridge Trail, which connects Skyline Boulevard with Portola Valley. Windy Hill is an ideal spot for kite flying. Hang gliding, paragliding, and remote-control gliding are allowed by special permit. Call the District office: (650) 691-1200.

Joyce Nicholas was the District's docent coordinator from 1981 to 1990, and she has been guiding visitors to District preserves as a docent since 1977. A bird lover, she was on a quest for a tiny warbler-like bird named for a hard-to-see red patch on its head. "Oh, for years I've kept looking for a ruby-crowned kinglet and hoping that it will flash," she says. "I've seen a ruby-crowned kinglet flash its color twice in twenty years, and one evening late in the day we saw a ruby-crowned at Sausal Pond that flashed over and over." Nicholas remembers other wildlife she has seen at Sausal Pond, which is near the Portola Road entrance to Windy Hill

Preserve. "There used to be a green heron there—we haven't seen it recently. But we did see hooded mergansers there for a short time this winter. The bullfrogs there are amazing, and turtles haul out on some of those logs. We've seen three at once. One year that I know of, there were at least a dozen wood ducks there—a dozen wood ducks hiding under the willows at the northern end of the pond."

The 1,300 acres of this preserve, which forms the scenic backdrop for Portola Valley, were once part of a 13,300-acre Mexican land grant owned by Maximo Martinez. After his death in 1863, the rancho was divided and sold to ranchers and farmers who tried to eke out a living on the often inhospitable hillsides. The key to success was access to water, either from the springs that give Spring Ridge its name, or from Corte Madera Creek, which collects water from several tributaries on its way through Portola Valley. Some of the land's features echo the names of its early settlers. William Jones was an early logger and farmer, hence Jones Gulch. Hamms Gulch is named for the Hamm family, who owned about 550 acres on the upper slopes of Windy Hill and across what is now Skyline Boulevard. Other landowners in the area included the Orton family, who probably planted the cypress trees you can still see today on the upper part of the Spring Ridge Trail, and John Francis Neylan, attorney for William Randolph Hearst. Herbert Law, a well-to-do San Francisco entrepreneur, at one time owned much of the land that became Windy Hill Preserve. Law bought the land to ensure a steady supply of water for Willowbrook Farm, which grew medicinal plants.

The twin summits of Windy Hill Open Space Preserve

*Limbs of a massive Douglas-fir radiate outward
from the trunk like spokes from a hub.*

In the 1960s, some of Windy Hill was owned by developers, but geological constraints and local building regulations made their plans for residential housing difficult. In 1981, Corte Madera Associates donated about 500 acres of land, valued at more than $3 million, to Peninsula Open Space Trust (POST), which had been founded in 1977. One year later, POST sold the property to the District for half its value, bestowing a fabulous gift on the public and providing the nonprofit land trust with seed money to fund more acquisitions. In 1987, the District purchased Spring Ridge and the upper part of Windy Hill. Beginning in 1982, POST began raising money to improve the preserve's trails. The Portola Valley Trust contributed $16,000, and donations from more than three hundred people helped raise a total of $67,000 for trail construction. District staff, California Conservation Corps members, and local volunteers worked with ax and shovel to improve existing ranch roads and hack out new alignments. Trail builder Gene Sheehan, a District contractor, provided the motorized grading. You can enjoy the fruits of their labor as you traverse the trails of Windy Hill Preserve.

John Escobar, the District's former assistant general manager, remembers supervising volunteers from Portola Valley during the trail-building project. "Being in my late 20s," he says, "my assessment was, here are folks who don't do much physical labor. I thought it would take about a year and a half. They said,

Windy Hill Trail Use

Bicycles: Allowed only on the Spring Ridge Trail, and on the multi-use trail south from gate WH01 to the main parking area off Skyline Boulevard

Dogs: Leashed dogs allowed on all trails except the Eagle and Razorback Ridge Trails, and the Lost Trail south of its junction with the Hamms Gulch Trail

Horses: Allowed on all trails except the Anniversary Trail

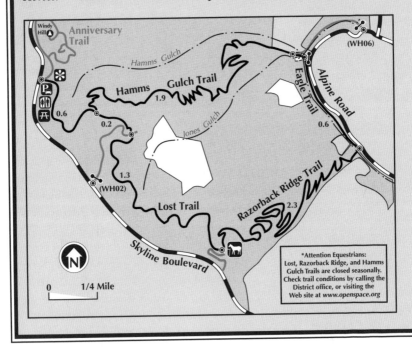

*Attention Equestrians:
Lost, Razorback Ridge, and Hamms Gulch Trails are closed seasonally. Check trail conditions by calling the District office, or visiting the Web site at www.openspace.org

'No, it will be open by spring, six to seven months.' They were amazing—perseverance and commitment! Got the trail done in six months. Everything but one bridge near Portola Road." Escobar says that he and others poured concrete for the bridge footings on a Monday, and then, with a crew of eight, built the bridge in a single day. They were working against the clock, because the dedication ceremony was set for the following Saturday. When the volunteers began their trek up the Hamms Gulch Trail to attend the festivities, they were delighted to find the newly built bridge waiting for them as a tribute to their hard work and devotion.

WINDY HILL OPEN SPACE PRESERVE

Trip 37. Hamms Gulch

Length: 8 miles

Time: 4 to 5 hours

Rating: Difficult

Highlights: This adventurous semi-loop uses the Hamms Gulch, Eagle, Razorback Ridge, and Lost Trails to explore one of the District's best-loved preserves. Dropping about 1,000 feet in 3 miles, you follow cool and shady Hamms Gulch downhill through a lush forest of Douglas-fir, California buckeye, and bigleaf maple to the banks of lovely Corte Madera Creek. Aided by many switchbacks, you gradually win back lost elevation, and then contour on a course roughly parallel to Skyline Boulevard for an easy return to the parking area. Bring binoculars to catch glimpses of forest birds flitting through the trees, and scan the skies for raptors such as hawks and falcons. Native plant enthusiasts will be delighted by the variety of trees and shrubs found along this route.

Directions: From the junction of Skyline Boulevard and Highway 84 in Sky Londa, take Skyline Boulevard southeast 2.3 miles to a parking area on the left.

Facilities: Picnic tables, vault toilet

Trailhead: At the northeast corner of the parking area

Trip 37. Hamms Gulch

Once past the picnic area, which has three District information boards and a map holder, you come to a split-rail fence with a gap. Beyond the fence are two trails: the Anniversary Trail to Windy Hill, left, and the Lost Trail, right, part of the Bay Area Ridge Trail. As its name implies, there is often wind at the upper reaches of this preserve, and also, in summer, fog. Turn right and after about 100 feet reach another fence, this one with a gate that controls equestrian use. During wet weather horses are prohibited and the

Equestrians love Windy Hill Open Space Preserve for the long-distance riding and scenic vistas.

gate is closed. (When the gate is closed, hikers can pass through a narrow gap in the fence.)

Now the single-track trail climbs on a gentle grade through a corridor of coyote brush and berry vines. Douglas-fir, California bay, and tanbark oak tower beside the trail. At left, an expansive view stretches from the Stanford campus and Palo Alto to the East Bay hills and Mt. Diablo. An inviting rest bench beckons, but so does the trail, which winds amid stands of coast live oak and madrone. A fine diversity of native shrubs are found nearby, including toyon, coffeeberry, snowberry, sticky monkeyflower, thimbleberry, and blue elderberry. Dark-eyed juncos may be flitting about, and you may be rudely accosted by a Steller's jay, watchbird of the forest.

At a junction with the Hamms Gulch Trail, a single track, turn sharply left and begin descending via switchbacks. Massive Douglas-firs, with limbs the size of ordinary tree trunks, stand sentinel next to the trail. This is a beautiful forest, providing shade and shelter from the wind. You pass through a lovely fern garden presided over by California buckeyes, among those trees to lose their leaves earliest each season, and bigleaf maples, colorful in fall. Evergreen huckleberry and hazelnut thrive here as well. Curving right, you pass an unofficial trail leading left to a promontory.

In a dense forest, you continue to descend a ridge by following the twists and turns of its gullies and ravines, some of which hold seasonal creeks. Approaching a grassy slope crossed by power lines, the trail angles left and returns to the forest.

Take a moment to scan the sky and the power lines for raptors—aerial hunters such as hawks and falcons. North America's smallest falcon, the American kestrel, is often seen hovering above open fields, searching with its keen eyes for prey such as insects, reptiles, small mammals, and sometimes birds. Also at home here is the northern harrier, told by its long tail, white rump, and low, wobbly flight.

Around the 2-mile point, you reach a rest bench on the left, with a fine view of Windy Hill. This is a great place to take a break. Beyond, the trail continues to lose elevation on a grade that alternates between gentle and moderate, with Hamms Gulch steeply downhill and left. Soon you reach a fence and another equestrian gate. Just beyond the fence, the Hamms Gulch Trail veers right and is joined on the left by a connector to the Spring Ridge Trail. You stay on the Hamms Gulch Trail, and after several hundred yards reach a bridge over the creek flowing through Jones Gulch.

Crossing the bridge, you come to a paved road in about 100 feet. To the right is the preserve boundary, so turn left and then cross Corte Madera Creek on a stone bridge that has a paved surface. Once across the creek, look right to find the start of the Eagle Trail, maintained by the town of Portola Valley and closed to bikes. This single-track trail parallels the rocky bed of Corte Madera Creek, which is to your right. Before too long, the trail deposits you on Alpine Road. Walk along the road shoulder for about 100 yards, and then regain the trail, which descends to the right.

Soon returning to Alpine Road, follow it for several hundred feet to a paved driveway on the right. Crossing Corte Madera Creek on a bridge, the driveway turns right, but you continue straight and begin to climb a dirt-and-gravel road. After a short, moderate climb, leave the road on a single-track trail, the Razorback Ridge Trail, marked with a trail post and an arrow. After about fifty

---

How to Tell Madrone and Manzanita Apart

Drawing close to a stand of madrone, you may notice the tree's resemblance to manzanita, a common California shrub. Both are members of the heath family and share certain characteristics: peeling bark, urn-shaped flowers, and red berries. How to tell them apart? Madrone is generally tree-sized, has orange bark, and large, oval leaves, whereas manzanita is usually a compact shrub with reddish bark and stiff, spade-shaped leaves. Manzanita and madrone are particularly lovely when draped with lace lichen, which resembles the Spanish moss found in the Southern United States.

feet, the trail curves right and comes to an equestrian gate. The moderate but relentless climb continues—thankfully, via switchbacks in the shade. Gooseberry and wood rose join other shrubs typical of a Douglas-fir forest.

The deep canyon holding Damiani Creek is to your left, and around the 4-mile point you begin a long, rising traverse that ascends to a vantage point with a view of Windy Hill. Other views along the trail—aided by good visibility and binoculars—sweep northward to San Francisco Bay, three of its bridges, and the cities of Oakland and San Francisco. Now switchbacks take you back and forth across the crest of a ridge, which has an overgrown dirt road running down its spine. The road is fenced to prevent hikers and equestrians from using it as a terrain-damaging shortcut. Someday, its traces will disappear completely.

A huge Douglas-fir just left of the trail may provide an ideal roost for a flock of band-tailed pigeons. These country cousins of urban pigeons are larger and

Windy Hill Trail Use

Bicycles: Allowed only on the Spring Ridge Trail, and on the multiuse trail south from gate WH01 to the main parking area off Skyline Boulevard

Dogs: Leashed dogs allowed on all trails except the Eagle and Razorback Ridge Trails, and the Lost Trail south of its junction with the Hamms Gulch Trail

Horses: Allowed on all trails except the Anniversary Trail

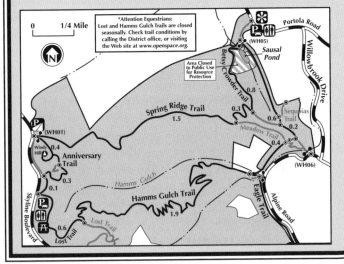

more finely decorated. Roosting in large flocks in the forest, they often take flight with a startling commotion when approached. At a junction with the Lost Trail, angle right, pass a watering trough for horses, and then follow a mostly level grade. Now following a ridge downhill, you give up several hundred feet of hard-won elevation near the head of Jones Gulch before leveling again.

A trail sign, left, confirms that you are following the Lost Trail toward Hamms Gulch. In a weedy area to the right of the trail, look for western creek dogwood, a water-loving shrub with red twigs, large green leaves in opposite pairs, and white flowers that open from late spring through midsummer. You cross a scrub-covered hillside before reaching a four-way junction with a dirt-and-gravel road. Continuing straight across the junction, climb on a gentle grade to meet the Hamms Gulch Trail on the right. From here retrace your route to the parking area by going straight.

WINDY HILL OPEN SPACE PRESERVE

Trip 38. Spring Ridge

Length: 7.6 miles

Time: 4 to 5 hours

Rating: Difficult

Highlights: Using the Betsy Crowder, Spring Ridge, Anniversary, Lost, and Hamms Gulch Trails, this leg-stretching semi-loop climbs more than 1,000 feet from Portola Valley to the flower-studded slopes of Windy Hill. Along the way, you pass through groves of oak, madrone, and California buckeye, which lead to rolling grasslands sweeping steeply uphill. Windy Hill's twin summits offer unrivaled views of the San Francisco Bay Area and the San Mateo coast. The descent is through densely forested Hamms Gulch, where Douglas-firs and bigleaf maples provide welcome shade on a warm day

Directions: From I-280 southwest of Palo Alto, take the Alpine Road/ Portola Valley exit. Take Alpine Road south 3 miles to a stop sign at the intersection of Alpine and Portola Roads. Turn right and go 0.9 mile to a parking area on the left.

Facilities: Vault toilet

Trailhead: At the southwest end of the parking area

Trip 38. Spring Ridge

Before leaving the parking area, look carefully at the power pole that stands just south of the vault toilet. Acorn woodpeckers use it to store their namesake food, and it is riddled with their holes. Now you follow a single-track trail uphill from the parking area and, in about seventy-five feet, reach a junction. There are two District information boards and a map holder here. A trail used by equestrians joins sharply from the left. Bearing right, travel through a brushy area shaded by California bay trees and a large valley oak. Northern flickers, another member of the woodpecker family, are often seen and heard here.

Several hundred yards from the trailhead is a T-junction with a dirt road. The Spring Ridge Trail, a multiuse path, is left, but instead turn right and almost immediately find the Betsy Crowder Trail on your left. This hiking and equestrian path honors Betsy Crowder, who was a District board member from 1989 until her death in 2000. She was also active in the District's volunteer program, and was one of the authors of *Peninsula Trails*, published by Wilderness Press. As you start off on this trail, you pass a fence with a seasonal gate that prevents access by horses during wet weather. (When the gate is closed, hikers can pass through a narrow gap in the fence.)

The earthen dam that forms Sausal Pond is on your left, partially hidden behind a screen of trees and shrubs. Coast live oak, black oak, madrone, and eucalyptus are some of the species found beside the trail. Level at first, the trail now climbs gently past stands of California buckeye and toyon, crossing several culverts along the way. In late winter and early spring, look for the buckeye's large, round seeds, sometimes called horse chestnuts, on the ground. When these seeds sprout, they split open and send out a thick, green taproot that penetrates the soil. This anchors the seed and helps provide the newborn tree with water and nutrients.

Traversing a grassy hillside dotted with coyote brush, you soon reach a fence with a seasonal gate. About 100 feet ahead is a T-junction with the Spring Ridge Trail, a dirt road. Here you turn right and begin a curvy ascent through a good birding area—open fields alternating with groves of venerable coast live oaks. Steller's jays, California towhees, wrens, and golden-crowned sparrows are among the more common species found nearby. Spring Ridge is named for the many springs in the area, which made the surrounding land valuable to early settlers and ranchers. Passing the Meadow Trail, left, at about the 1-mile point, you emerge from a wooded area and have a magnificent view uphill across rolling slopes to the twin summits of Windy Hill. This is one of a few District preserves offering such vast open terrain for your viewing enjoyment.

The road, which may be muddy during wet weather, climbs steadily on grades that run the gamut from gentle to steep. A few level sections allow you to stop, rest, and enjoy the views. You may be lucky enough to spot one or more of this preserve's common raptors—red-tailed hawk, American kestrel, northern harrier, white-tailed kite—patrolling the skies or roosting in a tall Monterey cypress. Be sure to turn around and admire the scenic vista that extends across San Francisco Bay to the East Bay hills.

As you near Skyline Ridge, you may begin to feel the effects of the Peninsula's coastal climate. The wind may increase, and great billows of fog may pour over the ridge. This preserve is aptly named! When you reach gate WH01 and two District information boards and a map holder, both just east of Skyline Boulevard, turn left. Just ahead is a fork. Here a multiuse path veers right, but your route, the hiking-only Anniversary Trail, angles left. The Anniversary Trail, built in 1987, commemorates the District's fifteenth anniversary and also the tenth anniversary of Peninsula Open Space Trust, a local nonprofit land trust that provided major support for the acquisition of this preserve.

Just shy of the three-mile point, you come to a rest bench and an unsigned trail departing to the right. To visit the preserve's highest point, turn right and follow this short trail to Windy Hill's north summit. From this impressive vantage point, you have 360° views of the San Francisco Bay Area and the San Mateo coast. When you have finished enjoying this beautiful spot, return to the Anniversary Trail and bear right. Now you follow the trail as it curves around the base of the north summit. At a saddle where two more rest benches await, you pass a trail to Windy Hill's south summit, which is about twenty-five feet lower than its rival. These high vantage points and the hillsides just below them provide great birding opportunities. Spring sightings here of lesser goldfinch and lazuli bunting may encourage you to bring binoculars.

The Anniversary Trail continues from the saddle by clinging to a narrow ledge cut in a hillside that slopes left. In spring, the wildflower display along this trail may be stunning. Look for such grassland favorites as California poppy, checker mallow, lupine, yarrow, bellardia, and fiddleneck. Descending on a gentle grade, the trail makes a sharp bend to the left and brings you to a wood fence with a gap. Just beyond, the multiuse path joins sharply from the right. Now on level ground, you soon reach the end of the Anniversary Trail at its junction with the Lost Trail, which is left. A District parking area, a picnic area, and a vault toilet are just ahead. Here you turn left onto the Lost Trail and follow a portion of the route description for "Hamms Gulch" on page 324 (beginning with paragraph 1 and ending with the second-to-the-last sentence in the first full paragraph on page 325). When you reach the junction of the Hamms Gulch Trail and a connector to the Spring Ridge Trail, bear left.

Hamms Gulch, which holds a seasonal tributary of Corte Madera Creek, is downhill and left. This is a lush and lovely area, where Douglas-fir, bay, bigleaf maple, and madrone are joined by snowberry, honeysuckle, berry vines, and ferns. Now the trail swings left and runs parallel to Corte Madera Creek itself, which is on your right. Soon the trail curves left again and meets the creek in Hamms Gulch, which you cross on rocks. About 100 feet ahead, the trail switchbacks right and climbs gently alongside Corte Madera Creek. A dense, riparian corridor is beside the creek, but uphill and left is a savanna of mostly valley oaks, giving this part of the route a park-like ambiance. Many of the oaks are draped with strands of lace lichen, and some hold large clumps of mistletoe.

At a junction, the Meadow Trail departs left, and a trail and a dirt road, both going to gate WH06, go right. Here you continue straight, now on a dirt road. At the next junction, the Spring Ridge Trail departs left, and again you go straight. Just ahead, you pass the Sequoias Trail, which angles right. Continuing straight, you pass through a possibly wet and muddy area. Willows and coyote brush line the road. A low-lying, marshy area holding the upper reaches of Sausal Creek is to your left. Sausal Pond, designated a "critical wildlife habitat," is just ahead. The pond is home to wood ducks, and large wooden boxes have

The Anniversary Trail climbs Windy Hill and offers superb views along the way.

The evening mist descends on coastal hills west of Skyline Boulevard.

been placed on nearby trees to provide them with safe nesting sites. Green herons also live here, and sometimes great blue herons, their much larger cousins, drop by for a visit.

Sausal Creek, which is just left of the road, flows out of the pond via a concrete spillway. Just ahead is the junction where you began this loop. When you reach it, simply turn right and retrace your route to the parking area.

PENINSULA OPEN SPACE TRUST
A Key Preservation Partner Organization

Peninsula Open Space Trust (or POST, as it is affectionately known) was founded in 1977. At that time, the District was a five-year-old public agency in the early stages of its land acquisition program. Herb Grench, then District general manager, was looking for a way to expand the District's capacity to raise funds for land acquisition. "The supporters of the District were mostly environmentalists," he says. "But the people I knew who helped to create the District didn't represent a lot of wealth in the community, just a lot of people-power. It was my feeling that there were a lot of people of means who would be very supportive of open space preservation. I didn't know how to reach these people, especially as a public agency." Grench says he looked to organizations like Sempervirens Fund and Save-the-Redwoods League as models for a private, nonprofit land trust.

"So I talked to a few people that I knew," Grench says, "and somehow we generated enough interest to get the ball rolling. Of course, once that group of successful business people got going they were bound to be successful." Thus was POST born. Grench counts the creation of POST among the high points of his career at the District. One of the people Grench contacted was Ward Paine, an early venture capitalist. Paine then recruited a board of trustees that included former Stanford University Vice-President Bob Augsburger, who became POST's first executive director, and *Sunset* magazine publisher Mel Lane. "MROSD is a government agency," says Paine. "It has taxing powers, and all the institutional stuff that goes with a government entity. Many of the pieces of property that the District is interested in the availability of around the Peninsula are owned by individuals or families. And these individuals and families, generally speaking, might not have considered keeping the property as open space, and might be more interested in working with a nonprofit entity rather than a government agency, if they so decided to pursue keeping the property as open space."

There were several reasons for this reluctance, says Paine. "The most typical problem you have is that the property was acquired by an individual, and upon his death, it is spread amongst a large group of new owners, usually the children of the initial buyer. Some of these children are well off, but don't live in the area anymore. Some of them are very comfortable and have high conservation values, and others have no [conservation] values. So you have to weave through this to satisfy each and every owner. And that is a very tricky business. You have to be able to develop confidential relationships with the principals and their legal representatives who you are working with to solve these problems." Paine says that POST has used a variety of techniques, including donated gifts, bargain sales, open space easements, and selling to conservation buyers, to acquire and protect property. Land acquired by POST is then most often sold or transferred to a public agency, such as the District, or to a private party who agrees to certain conservation restrictions.

Started on a shoestring budget, POST scored its first big success in 1981, when it received about 537 acres of land on Windy Hill as a donation from Corte Madera Associates, a land-investment group. POST then sold the property to the District for half of the fair market value, receiving about $1.5 million. This money was used to create POST's revolving land acquisition fund. "POST had a flexibility that MROSD didn't," Paine says. "Our Executive Director, Bob Augsburger, knew one of the property owners of

Windy Hill. At that time, the zoning was for 400 houses or so. People envisioned Windy Hill just covered with housing. And it became very obvious, because of earthquake problems initially, and then pressure from the conservation movement, that that probably wasn't going to happen. Bob was able to approach this group of individuals, and we negotiated a deal, which MROSD couldn't do." The District is one of the largest acquirers of property from POST—however, POST has also transferred property to other entities, including California State Parks, the Golden Gate National Recreation Area, the counties of San Mateo and Santa Clara, and Don Edwards San Francisco Bay National Wildlife Refuge.

Organizationally independent of the District, POST is not confined to set geographical boundaries. Its area of interest reaches from San Francisco Bay to the San Mateo coast and extends down the Peninsula to San Jose. POST's early goals seem incredibly modest, given the organization's success: raise $1 million for open space, and protect ten important properties on the Peninsula. Today, POST is more than three-quarters through a $200 million fund-raising drive—aided by $50 million each from the David and Lucile Packard Foundation and the Gordon and Betty Moore Foundation—to save more than 20,000 acres on the San Mateo coast. POST has secured nine of the original ten Peninsula properties it targeted for protection, for a total of nearly two hundred properties protected. Among the organization's milestones: the 1987 purchase, through state bond and government funds, of the 1,270-acre Cowell Ranch on the San Mateo coast; the 1990 purchase of the Phleger Estate, which expanded the Golden Gate National Recreation Area; the 1997 purchase of Bair Island in San Francisco Bay; and the 2002 acquisition of Driscoll Ranch, which protected about 3,600 acres of open space in the coastal hills northwest of La Honda.

Audrey Rust, who has been POST's president since 1986, says the current $200 million "Saving the Endangered Coast" campaign "targets unprotected properties from Pacifica to Pescadero, west of Skyline Boulevard, that are threatened by development and expected to change hands in the next few years." According to the organization's Web site, *www.openspacetrust.org,* the properties in which POST is interested occupy strategic locations, contain critical wildlife and plant habitat, offer scenic views and recreation opportunities, or contain productive farmland. In addition to the major foundation grants, the campaign is being helped by POST's approximately 9,000 individual donors. POST is governed by a thirteen-member board of directors and has a staff of about twenty people at its Menlo Park office.

Picnickers enjoying the view to the west at Skyline Ridge Open Space Preserve

PUBLIC PROGRAMS & ACTIVITIES

Take a hike! Ride a bike! Get on a horse! The District offers docent-led activities for all user groups and every level of fitness. Visitors can learn about earthquake geology on the San Andreas Fault Trail at Los Trancos Preserve, or revel in colorful displays of spring wildflowers atop Russian Ridge Preserve with a knowledgeable guide. Tour a historic home, a working farm, or one of California's early wineries. Take the children along for Family Outdoor Discovery Programs or seasonal events hosted on District preserves. The District provides many ways for the public to become involved with open space. In addition to the beautiful preserves and wonderful trails, there are a number of historic buildings the District has restored and preserved for visitors to enjoy. There is also a nature center on the shore of Alpine Pond at Skyline Ridge Preserve. Except as noted, information about the nature center, docent-led programs, and the various historic buildings listed below is available from the District office: (650) 691-1200, or on the Web site at *www.openspace.org.*

David C. Daniels Nature Center

The David C. Daniels Nature Center features habitat exhibits, touchable displays, and an interactive pond mural. The center is open to the public 12:00 to 5:00 P.M. (hours are subject to change) on weekends from April through mid-November. Knowledgeable docent hosts welcome visitors of all ages and cultures, and share information on local natural history.

Deer Hollow Farm

Deer Hollow Farm at Rancho San Antonio Preserve is a working homestead with sheep, goats, pigs, rabbits, chickens, ducks, geese, a cow, an organic garden, and orchard. The primary purpose of the farm is to serve as an educational center where school classes, community groups, and families can observe, explore, and participate in a family farm. Classes are offered during the school year for children in grades K–12; subjects covered include the farm, wilderness, and Native Americans. During the summer, students in grades 1 through 9 participate in weeklong camp sessions. A few staff members and many volunteers keep the farm operating. The farm, located on District land, is funded through a cooperative agreement between the City of Mountain View, Santa Clara County, and the District, with support from the Friends of Deer Hollow Farm. The farm is open to the public Tuesday, and Thursday through Sunday, 8:00 A.M. to 4:00 P.M.; and Wednesday 8:00 A.M. to 1:00 P.M. For more information, call Deer Hollow Farm: (650) 903-6430.

Fremont Older House

This historic home once belonged to Fremont Older, a crusading newspaper editor, and his wife Cora. The home and grounds have been restored by a private party, Mort and Elaine Levine—also former local newsfolk—who have a long-term lease on the property from the District. Visitation to the house and beautiful gardens is available on an annual docent-led Fremont Older house tour in the spring.

Grant Cabin

This is the oldest remaining building at Deer Hollow Farm, built in the 1850s. It was on the property when Theodore and George Grant, two brothers from Boston, arrived in 1860 to homestead. The cabin has been reframed, restored, and furnished with artifacts by the District.

Picchetti Winery

This was the home of the Picchetti brothers, Italian immigrants who came to the Santa Clara Valley in the 1870s and started a winery on the slopes of Monte Bello Ridge. The Picchetti Ranch is historically significant because it represents Santa Clara Valley's rich agricultural heritage and the families who operated vineyards and wineries here. Picchetti Winery is listed on the National Register of Historic Places and the Santa Clara County Heritage Resource Inventory. The District has restored historic buildings on the property, including the winery building, blacksmith shop, homestead house, and fermenta-

Deer Hollow Farm is one of the attractions at Rancho San Antonio Open Space Preserve.

Historic Red Barn in La Honda Creek Open Space Preserve

tion barn, among others, commemorating the winery's heritage. Today, the winery is leased by the District to a private party, which produces wine under the Picchetti label. The winery is open daily from 11:00 A.M. to 5:00 P.M. On Sundays, visitors may enjoy live music from 1:00 to 4:00 P.M. The winery offers tasting (for a small fee) and picnicking on the winery grounds, adjacent to the preserve trails, and is available for events, parties, and corporate meetings. For more information, call (408) 741-1310 or visit the winery's Web site *www.picchetti.com.*

Thornewood Estate

Once the summer home of Julian Thorne (a San Francisco land speculator) and his wife Edna, the Thornewood Estate is now leased by the District to a private party who is restoring the house and grounds. The estate is currently not open to the public.

Red Barn

The District recently completed restoring the historic Red Barn, located in La Honda Creek Preserve. The barn once served as a social center for the local ranchers and their families, and is a visual reminder for travelers on Highway 84 of the area's important agricultural heritage. The barn is currently not open to the public.

VOLUNTEER AND DOCENT PROGRAMS

The District relies strongly on the help of volunteers to effectively accomplish its mission: protecting and restoring natural communities, and educating the public about open space. "Our volunteers are such a valuable part of the Open Space District," says board member Jed Cyr. "There is no way District staff would be able to provide all the services the volunteers generate for the public. Our volunteers assist the District by providing many additional sets of eyes and ears, allowing for much better management of District lands." In 2003, approximately five hundred volunteers contributed more than fourteen thousand hours of service to the eight distinct volunteer programs listed below. These dedicated volunteers have a strong commitment to the District's mission, and the District strives to provide involvement opportunities, thorough training, and quality programs.

Preserve Partners, established in 1989. Each year, between three and four hundred volunteers participate in trail maintenance and construction, tree planting, cleanup projects, invasive nonnative plant removal, fence construction, and other resource management projects. Two to three Preserve Partners projects are scheduled each month, and each project accommodates ten to twenty-five volunteers. In addition, other projects are organized when requested by groups outside of the District's Preserve Partners program, such as local business, school, Scout, user groups, and other community groups. The resource management

*Preserve Partners volunteers and Skyline Ranger Chris Barresi
repair a damaged trail pad and install a culvert on the Peters Creek Trail
at Long Ridge Open Space Preserve.*

specialist, rangers, open space technicians, and specially trained volunteer crew leaders provide leadership and training at the project site.

Marc Auerbach is a former longtime member of the Preserve Partners program. "I moved here from Southern California, and I wondered why I hadn't moved here sooner," he says. "One of the things that really attracted me was the green hillsides, not knowing anything about the Open Space District or its land management or preservation role."

"The projects are quite varied, and it's more about finesse and technique than it is about brute strength," Auerbach says. "The District provides the tools and the training. Preserve Partners may do anything from collecting native plant seeds to repairing trails and building retaining walls. Nearly every District preserve has benefited from volunteer efforts."

Auerbach says that the staff are often surprised by how much the volunteers can accomplish. "I've never been in any day's program where the volunteers haven't risen to whatever challenge was given to them, and accomplished more than the rangers or District staff ever thought was possible."

At Pulgas Ridge Preserve, Auerbach was enlisted to help remove invasive nonnative plants such as acacia and eucalyptus. This is an ongoing project, and over the years, Auerbach says, he has seen results. "I go back a year later and I see the oaks starting to grow. We continue to remove the nonnative vegetation, and started spreading some native seed to help with the grassland restoration. It's interesting to see the whole ecosystem at work, and trying to bring it back into balance."

Crew Leaders, established in 1998. Volunteer crew leaders assist in leading various outdoor volunteer projects. Under the supervision of a District staff member, the crew leader directs a small group of volunteers in the construction of trails, and the routine maintenance of District lands, trails, roads, and other facilities. Members are required to complete an extensive training program, including two evening-training and five field-training sessions, and assist with at least four volunteer projects per year.

Jane Huber tells how she got involved with the District's volunteer program, and what the job of crew leader entails. "I was hiking in one of the preserves and noticed an upcoming volunteer project," she says. "It sounded interesting. This must have been about seven years ago. So I went on my first project, which was building a fence. I did some more projects, and then that's when the District started up with the volunteer crew leaders, and so I went through that training."

Huber says that crew leaders have training that other volunteers do not. They show up early, stay late, and generally assist District staff. Each project is different.

Crew leaders Jerry Wroblewski and Kat Rudd repair a section of the Lost Trail at Windy Hill Open Space Preserve.

"Well, there is no typical day," says Huber. "That's part of the whole fun process. Whoever the staff person is, whether it's a ranger or an open space technician, they're on site first. And they've got all the tools with them. If we're using special equipment, or gravel, or lumber, or whatever, it's there as well." District staff brief the crew leaders about the project before the volunteers start arriving, Huber says.

Once the volunteers arrive and sign in, the entire group, which may be ten to fifteen people, travels to the work site, either in District vehicles or on foot. Everything needed for the day, including tools and supplies, goes too. Following a safety lecture and a short talk about the history of the District, work begins. Depending on the nature of the project and the size of the group, volunteers may form smaller teams to tackle various tasks. "If it's something more complicated like fence building," says Huber, "we have to show people unless they've done it before. If it's broom pulling, then you have to make sure that they know which vegetation is actually broom. We explain to them what poison oak is as well. We then split up into groups and get to work. The rangers, open space technicians, or resource management specialist supervises the work." At the end of the day, there's the satisfaction in knowing that you've done something to help improve a small piece of open space.

Trail Patrol, established in 1993. This group of volunteers, which includes equestrians, bicyclists, hikers, runners, and companion dog patrollers, talk with preserve visitors about trail safety and etiquette, provide information, report trail conditions to staff, and monitor conservation easements. There are approximately eighty trail patrol volunteers, who are required to attend an initial training program, patrol a minimum of four hours per month, and attend quarterly membership meetings and enrichment training sessions. These volunteers spent more than four thousand hours patrolling District trails in 2003.

Rodger and Lorraine Alleman got involved with the District's volunteer trail patrol in 1997. "We both have had a lifelong interest in mountains and the outdoors," says Rodger, "and after we retired this seemed to be a way to get out and go hiking, which is good for us physically. We've both been through the cancer routine twice, and we think that exercise is a good thing to do, and so this presented itself as an opportunity." Rodger says that they learned about the trail patrol when he encountered volunteer members while visiting a preserve. "We want to do it every day if we can," he says. "It's been a godsend to us because we don't have to breathe a lot of the exhaust, and you get out in the wilderness and we're working with people and helping people." Rodger says they also feel good about helping the District monitor its preserves. "It's been a joy because we think we're doing ourselves a lot of good as well as the District, and I know people that stop us or that we stop appreciate our being there."

The Allemans regularly patrol the trails at Rancho San Antonio, which is near where they live. "We go one direction one day," says Rodger, "and if we want to take the same trail, we go in the opposite direction the next day. We try to do a different trail every day—we're talking about an average of, say, five times a week." The Allemans say they keep an eye on trail conditions, looking for downed trees and other hazards. If any problems exist, the Allemans note them in their daily report to the District via e-mail or through the District's Web site. They also collect items for the District's lost and found, which over the years have included cameras, cellular phones, and car keys. Rodger says trail patrollers are taught to carry a length of rope, which can be given to dog owners who failed to bring a leash.

Patrollers field questions about the local flora and fauna, and especially about the difference between bobcats and mountain lions, Lorraine says. "We have seen the results of deer kills by mountain lions, or we assume they're mountain lions. And we have had people reporting carcasses to us."

Lorraine says most of their contacts involve people who want to know where a particular trail goes or how to get to a certain destination. "We hand out a lot of maps," she says. "Rancho San Antonio is great because there are lots of loop trails and you don't have to backtrack. One of the main things people want to know is how long a trail is and is it steep. My favorite question was, 'Does this trail go anywhere?' I liked that."

Outdoor Activity Docents, established in 1977. The District's sixty-five volunteer docents create and lead activities for the public on open space preserves. These activities include hikes, mountain bicycle excursions, and horseback rides, all with interpretive elements. Docents complete a comprehensive eight- to nine-week training program, conducted by staff and others with expertise in local natural and cultural history. Training includes classroom and field sessions. Outdoor Activity Docents agree to lead at least eight activities per year. The activities are advertised in the "Outdoor Activities" section of the District's quarterly public newsletter *Open Space Views.*

Joyce Nicholas is a longtime District docent, and at one time coordinator of its docent program. "I saw a little ad in the newspaper in 1977," she says. "This was the second docent class that the District had held. They had acquired some properties, and at Monte Bello Preserve, they had established Waterwheel Creek Trail. So they decided that it would be good to have a program using volunteers to get the public on the land, and introduce the public to this particular preserve and the idea of open space and what the Open Space District is all about. So that's how it started." In addition to the Waterwheel Creek Trail at Monte Bello Preserve, Nicholas says that docents soon were leading walks on the popular San Andreas Fault Trail at Los Trancos Preserve. This is still one of the District's best-attended walks.

The early years of docent training consisted of walking District preserves, walking the trails, and learning about the human and natural history of the Santa Cruz Mountains. "I knew about the birds," says Nicholas. "I learned about the plants. Had we learned any geology? Yes, we certainly did. Tim Hall, a former teacher from Foothill College, he is the most gifted teacher you can imagine. He makes the subjects so exciting that I was just overwhelmed. This whole idea of plate tectonics was fairly new at that time. It seemed like everything I was learning was so incredibly exciting, and to this day that's where my interests lie in natural history." Nicholas says there was always a great fear among docents that one of them would get "a real, honest-to-gosh geologist" on a guided walk along the San Andreas Fault Trail.

The original docents, says Nicholas, would lead groups of anywhere from twelve to twenty people. Larger groups would require more than one docent. Most of the trips were by request. "There had been a lot of interest generated by the whole business of getting this District formed," she says. "Groups like the Sierra Club really wanted to get out there, and the native-plant people really wanted to get out there. And here was their chance finally to be on this piece of

Students on a Spaces and Species environmental education field trip
led by Outdoor Education Leader Simone Smith marvel at
Alpine Pond at Skyline Ridge Open Space Preserve.

land, so they're the ones who signed up in the very beginning." The Boy Scouts and the Girl Scouts also took advantage of guided walks, especially at Los Trancos Preserve. In addition to the by-request trips, Nicholas says there were drop-in walks every Sunday.

In 1981, Nicholas was hired by the District to be its docent coordinator, a position she held until 1990. Her job included overseeing not just the docent program, but all of the District's volunteer activities, including volunteer trail maintenance and volunteer trail patrol. Training for docents by this time included a presentation by the District general manager, a talk about trail safety and handling emergencies, and a lecture on Native American history. "During those years we added so many new trails, it was very exciting," she says. "One of the main ones was the Stevens Creek Nature Trail at Monte Bello Preserve. We did weekly wildflower walks in the spring, and we really worked on outreach. We developed the Fremont Older house tour. I wrote a monthly docent news-letter and I listed a calendar and showed where docents were needed. And it was about that time that we started doing the evening hikes and those were incredibly popular, because otherwise people couldn't be on the preserves legally after they closed."

In recent years, Nicholas has spent most of her volunteer time for the District at the nature center on Alpine Pond, seasonal home of Snickers, the District's gopher snake. "I've been up there when Snickers has performed, eating her mice with an appreciative audience," Nicholas says. "The little kids flock in there and some of them have to be dragged out, they don't want to leave." For Nicholas, children are "future voters" and future supporters of the District. It is fine, she says, to "preach to the choir" by leading hikes for Sierra Club members or native-plant enthusiasts. But reaching others is what outdoor education and the docent program is all about. "I think outreach is very important," she says.

Outdoor Education Leaders, established in 1995. The District's school field trip program, "Spaces & Species: Exploring Natural Communities," is led by Outdoor Education Leaders in teams of four to a class. After completing a six-week, hands-on training program, Outdoor Education Leaders dedicate two days each month during fall and spring to taking students in grades three through six on this innovative environmental education outing at Skyline Ridge Preserve and the David C. Daniels Nature Center. The field trip program focuses on the local environment, fosters stewardship of the land, and correlates to the state of California's guidelines in science and history/social science. "The program's design fits well into the curriculum needs of elementary and early middle school students," says Renée Fitzsimons, current docent programs coordinator. "Children in this age range are still outwardly excited about learning, and they share their enthusiasm and joy for discovery of the natural world with ease." The District is able to offer about forty field trips per year, with the involvement of fifteen to twenty active docents.

Nature Center Host, established in 1996. The District's fifteen or so friendly Nature Center Hosts rotate the staffing of the David C. Daniels Nature Center at Alpine Pond. The center is open 12:00 to 5:00 P.M. (hours are subject to change) on weekends from April to mid-November, providing the public a chance to visit on a drop-in basis. Knowledgeable hosts greet visitors of all ages and from all cultures, and share information about the District and the natural and cultural history of the Skyline Ridge area. Training for this program consists of an orientation session and an onsite (nature center) session taught by District staff.

Special Project Volunteers. The number of volunteers in this program fluctuates; there are currently about a dozen. These volunteers assist with administrative projects, including researching preserve history, updating maps, answering phones, helping with mailings, assisting staff with data entry, maintaining historic buildings, counting visitors at open space preserves, and staffing community outreach events.

Community Outreach Volunteers. These volunteers staff the District display at various outreach events. They have the opportunity to educate Bay Area constituents at local art and wine festivals and other outreach venues.

VOLUNTEER AND DOCENT PROGRAMS STAFF

The District has two full-time coordinators and a community affairs representative to administer these programs.

The volunteer programs coordinator is responsible for recruiting preserve partners, crew leader, trail patrol, special project and community outreach volunteers, and coordinating projects with staff and volunteers. The volunteer programs coordinator handles inquiries from groups and individuals who are interested in volunteering and, if possible, matches them up with appropriate projects. Other duties include organizing meetings, training sessions, and recognition events, keeping track of volunteer hours and projects completed, and writing a quarterly newsletter for volunteers.

The docent programs coordinator focuses on the District's interpretive and education programs. The docent programs coordinator recruits docents, and

Outdoor Activity Docent Katherine Greene leads a wildflower hike on the Ridge Trail at Russian Ridge Open Space Preserve.

conducts and trains for the Outdoor Activity Docent, Outdoor Education Leader, and Nature Center Host programs. The coordinator also produces a newsletter for the docents and the "Outdoor Activities" section of the District's quarterly newsletter for the public, coordinates the scheduling of docent-led activities and nature center hosts, and works closely with schools to offer environmental education field trips.

One of the roles of the community affairs representative is building communities. This is achieved by supervising the volunteer programs coordinator (who puts together volunteer projects helping to protect and restore natural communities) and the docent programs coordinator (who oversees the District's interpretive and education programs that foster community understanding of the importance of open space). Building communities requires bringing together various District staff, volunteers, community groups, and individuals to achieve the District's mission: protecting and restoring natural communities, and educating the public about open space.

Each volunteer helps to spread the District's message. Besides allowing the District to complete projects that might otherwise not be accomplished, the volunteer programs have contributed to good public relations for the District. The District's volunteer programs provide an opportunity for people to learn more about the District and the environment, and to become actively involved in the District's mission. If you would like to volunteer or obtain more information, call the District office: (650) 691-1200.

Nature Center Host Steve Salveter assists visitors with the interactive pond community display at the David C. Daniels Nature Center.

District field staff member sawing a downed tree

MANAGING
OPEN
SPACE

District staff in 2004

PEOPLE

District staff currently consists of approximately seventy-five employees in five departments: operations, planning, public affairs, real property, and administration. It takes many people in a number of different positions to provide the opportunities and services visitors enjoy in the open space preserves. Each of these positions is important to the District's operation, and each of them has a direct impact on how the District serves the public.

Operations is divided into four subgroups: *Operations administration* develops operations policies and handles resource management. For the operations program, this subgroup administers labor negotiations, purchasing, and field staff training. This group makes sure that field staff has the equipment needed to take care of District properties, and that the lands are protected and safe to visit. It includes an operations manager, a management analyst, a resource management specialist, a support services supervisor, and an administrative assistant.

Field supervision oversees the field operation of the Foothills and Skyline areas and provides direction and guidance to the staff in the field. Each of the two areas has an area superintendent, two supervising patrol rangers, a maintenance and construction supervisor, and a maintenance, construction and resource supervisor.

Patrol staff provides visitor information, resource protection, public safety, and routine maintenance. Rangers interact directly with open space preserve visitors, answering questions, providing directions, interpreting nature, enforcing regulations, responding to emergencies or unusual situations, and making sure that signs, trail maps, and other forms of information are available to the public at the preserves. There are seven rangers in each of the two areas, Skyline and Foothills.

Brendan Downing is a supervising ranger at the Skyline office: "On Memorial Day weekend, District rangers were shorthanded due to unfilled positions and staff injuries. I noticed that on Memorial Day there was one ranger on until 2:00 P.M. I didn't feel good about this, so on impulse I decided to come in one hour early. No sooner did I go in service than I heard the one ranger on, Chris Barresi, responding to a bicyclist accident on Page Mill Road. I responded Code 3 and was in the area about ten minutes later, when the request came to set up a helicopter landing zone. I communicated with Stanford Life Flight and they landed shortly thereafter. The patient had a very painful angulated arm due to the fall.

After the helicopter left for the hospital, I stopped in at a full parking lot in Russian Ridge Preserve to be flagged down by a woman whose vehicle was stuck in a ditch. While pulling her vehicle out with a chain, I received a call from dispatch that visitors had reported bats in the Los Trancos Preserve information board. After finishing with the stuck vehicle, I left for Los Trancos Preserve and upon arrival found two little brown bats that had taken a liking to the warmth inside the information board. The access slot was missing a cover and the information board made an enticing bat box. After slowly removing the display board and tapping on the glass, the critters exited for another roost. The rest of the day went typically—dog-prohibited redirects to other preserves, lots of visitor contacts with questions. Just shows how a day can be on Skyline."

Maintenance and construction staff build and maintain District trails, parking lots, fire roads, bridges, vault toilets, fences, and other projects. Among other duties, maintenance and construction staff make sure that trails drain properly during winter rains, that poison oak does not overly encroach a trail, and that vault toilets are clean and well stocked for public use. Each area has staff comprising an equipment mechanic operator, two lead open space technicians, five open space technicians, and up to ten seasonal open

District staff carefully monitor a prescribed burn conducted as part of the Grassland Management Program at Russian Ridge Open Space Preserve.

space technicians. In addition, the Foothills area has a farm maintenance worker who works at Deer Hollow Farm at Rancho San Antonio Preserve.

Planning. The District's planning department is responsible for formulating plans, policies, and procedures for the management and development of open space preserves; conducting resource inventories and other scientific study of the District's lands; preparing environmental restoration, habitat enhancement, and resource management plans; developing and maintaining the District's Geographic Information System (GIS); emphasizing preservation and enhancement of resources in Use and Management Plans and in the design of capital improvement projects and public access facilities; and ensuring continued compliance with environmental regulations. The planning department staff includes a GIS intern, two planning technicians, two open space planner I positions, two open space planner II positions, a senior planner, a resource planner, an administrative assistant, and a planning manager.

Public Affairs staff gets the word about the District out to the public and the media, to other organizations, and to elected officials. They accomplish this by preparing and distributing news releases, responding to information requests, and providing a District booth at local events. The public affairs staff coordinates the publishing of all the District's trail maps, newsletters, and other written materials, and also implements special events and works on legislation for the District. The department offers community volunteer and environmental education programs that provide volunteers with opportunities to participate in the protection of, restoration of, and education about open space. The department includes a public affairs manager, a public affairs specialist, a public affairs administrative assistant, a community affairs representative, a volunteer programs coordinator, a docent programs coordinator, an interpretive aide, and several hundred volunteers.

Ana Ruiz is a planner II in the District's planning department; she describes her work day as follows: "With a calculator and ruler in one hand and a calendar or a Palm Pilot in the other, a phone sitting on one shoulder and a camera dangling from the other, a map on our lap and a computer monitor staring in front, planner IIs are responsible for managing public improvement projects at the various preserves. They hire, coordinate, and monitor the work of consultants who help design these projects, and contractors who build them. Meanwhile, planner IIs also ensure that permits are obtained and environmental review is performed in a timely fashion."

Real Property. This program is responsible for purchasing land, as well as managing property that the District rents or leases for special uses (such as agriculture and housing). In addition, this department works cooperatively with preserve neighbors, encouraging open communication and an exchange of ideas, to protect the public lands through programs such as easement monitoring. The acquisition/property management/land protection staff is constantly evaluating land, and negotiating for the next addition to the District's preserve system. Real property, along with other District departments, also continually explores opportunities to supplement its funds through existing grand programs. This department consists of a real property manager, a real property specialist, an administrative assistant, a senior acquisition planner, and a land protection specialist.

Administration supports all of the other District departments and the District's elected board of directors. The administration staff prepares board meeting agenda packets, pays employees and accounts, and handles legal issues, liability protection, and human resources. The department includes the general manager, the assistant general manager, an administration/human resources manager, general counsel, an attorney, a human resources management analyst, an administration management analyst, a human resources administrative assistant, a controller, a senior accounting specialist, an accounting clerk, a senior administrative assistant/office manager, a receptionist/administrative clerk, and a network specialist.

RESOURCE MANAGEMENT

Planning

In 1994, the District adopted a set of resource management policies that defined the way District staff would manage resources on District lands—including plants, animals, water, soil, terrain, geological formations, and historic, scenic, and cultural features. These policies were designed "to ensure the long-term protection of natural and cultural resources on District preserves." Because of the rapid growth in the amount of land acquired by the District since 1994, and the complexity of managing and restoring native ecosystems, a new five-year strategic plan was announced in 2002. This strategic plan identifies key goals for future resource management efforts. Among these goals are:

• To develop a resource management planning process
• To inventory and map natural and cultural resources

- To prepare resource management plans for key open space preserves and other high priority sites
- To protect and enhance the natural biodiversity of the District's preserves
- To protect and enhance habitat for special-status plant and animal species
- To restore seriously degraded sites to natural conditions
- To remove populations of invasive nonnative plant and animal species

Craig Britton is the District's general manager. "In the early years," he says, "when we'd buy a piece of land, we would announce in the paper that it was open to the public. And part of our program was, if you're hiking, you can go anywhere on District land. Equestrians or bicyclists really have to stick to designated trails. But as a hiker, if you're walking along and you see something, and you want to go picnic and sit underneath the trees somewhere, there's no problem with that. What we learned is that uses were getting out ahead of our planning." Britton says that as a result, well-meaning visitors were often cutting trails through inappropriate places. "So we don't really do that anymore," he says. "When we buy a piece of property we set it aside for comprehensive planning first."

Specifically, the District intends to identify and map valuable wildlife habitats, such as wildlife movement corridors, water sources, and sensitive nesting areas. Unique plant communities—such as wetlands, serpentine grasslands, and riparian corridors—will also receive special attention. District staff will monitor certain wildlife species—such as mountain lions, deer, bats, bluebirds, and amphibians—to check on the health of the ecosystem. Designated areas will be earmarked for limited or no public access to protect valuable wildlife habitat and unique plant communities. Throughout the process, monitoring programs will help District staff evaluate the success of their efforts. Data collected will help planners avoid locating new trails on erosive slopes or through sensitive habitats. "Once we have that information," Britton says, "then we'll develop a master plan, which will be a public process where we'll get public input to our planning process. We'll look at existing trails and some of the problems that we've encountered, or the areas of special concern. We can design a trail system and an access plan that will enhance the environment."

Using the recently completed Sierra Azul resource inventory as a model, the District will inventory special-status plants and animals—those that are rare, threatened, or endangered—and their habitats in each District preserve. District staff will prepare maps of the locations of these special-status species and their habitats, and then use the maps and other information collected in the field to protect and restore them. The District has a number of degraded areas on certain preserves, primarily left over from previous property owners, which also need to be restored. These include former use sites such as abandoned roads, off-road vehicle areas, illegal trails, former dump sites, quarries, and gun ranges. Among the preserves targeted for restoration efforts are Sierra Azul, Bear Creek Redwoods, La Honda Creek, and El Corte de Madera Creek. Some of the District's restoration projects involve volunteers from the community, who contribute thousands of volunteer hours annually.

District board member Larry Hassett would like to see more emphasis placed on planning. "Right now we have a resource specialist, and that resource person has to do an awful lot of projects," he says, "and without a lot of money or funding. I could easily see where our resource management staff would grow so we can do a better job of managing the lands. Do the eucalyptus trees belong there or should they be removed? How do we get rid of star thistle on the preserves? How do we keep, or is it appropriate to keep, Windy Hill free from chaparral? The open grasslands are disappearing—is that a resource management issue that we should be addressing now? So that's an area where I see the District needing to focus more attention and probably dollars as well."

PROGRAMS

The District has several resource management programs on specific preserves that have been very successful. Among these are grassland restoration at Russian Ridge Preserve, the removal of invasive nonnative plants at Pulgas Ridge Preserve, and the trapping of feral pigs at Long Ridge and Skyline Ridge Preserves.

Russian Ridge Grasslands

Russian Ridge Preserve hosts a wide variety of native grasses, such as purple needlegrass, California brome, blue wild rye, California fescue, meadow barley, and June grass. Wildflowers in these grasslands include California poppy, red maids, Johnny jump-up, purple owl's-clover, checker mallow, and mule ears. In 1996, the District began studying ways to remove star thistle and other invasive nonnative plants (including Harding grass) from the grasslands at Russian Ridge Preserve. The aim was to restore the grasslands to a more natural state and to encourage the growth of wildflowers and other native plants. From 1997 to 2000, the District tested a number of methods to find an effective solution. These methods included hand control using weed-eaters, tractor mowing, careful application of herbicide, grazing by goats and sheep, prescribed burning, and planting native seeds.

All the methods used in the Russian Ridge Preserve study resulted in an initial decrease in the amount of area covered by nonnative plants. With grazing and prescribed burning, the area of nonnative plants increased in the second year, although these same methods also resulted in an increase in the area and types of native species over both years. Based on this and other studies, a combination of methods is usually most effective at restoring native grasslands—as long as they are specifically adjusted to the site conditions. For example, prescribed burns followed by selective herbicide treatment can be a cost-effective way to control large stands of yellow star thistle. Mowing also controls yellow star thistle, but only if it is conducted several times a year at critical periods in the early summer, and is followed with selective herbicide spraying or spot weeding. At highly disturbed sites, it may be necessary to subsequently seed in native plants with special equipment, although this can be expensive. Goat grazing is a good way to control weeds on steep slopes where access is difficult. Prescribed burning requires approval from the California Department of Forestry, which is sometimes difficult to obtain.

The District intends to continue to restore native grasses and other native plants at Russian Ridge Preserve using feasible and effective methods. Some of these methods—including fire, seeding, and weed control—may have been used by Native Americans in the Santa Cruz Mountains, according to longtime area resident Janet Schwind. "They actually practiced a form of agriculture," she says. "They managed the wildlands not only through fire but maybe even some planting. They encouraged things. They weeded. They may have brought some seeds and planted them closer to their villages. Fire was definitely a form of agriculture. In fact, the Spanish report a lot of fires going on." Schwind says the Native Americans here may have wanted to keep meadow areas free of brush to make hunting easier and to stimulate the growth of edible plants.

Deane Little is a member of the District board of directors. "Sometimes we try to restrict activities that are highly visible," he says, "like off-trail cycling, and it's important that we do that. But I believe that the intrusion by non-native invasive species, which do not have natural pests here in North America, poses a much greater ecological threat. Perhaps the worst is star thistle, which is common on so many of our preserves. It out-competes native species, wildflowers, and really reduces the diversity of species. If you go to Russian Ridge Preserve where we've done some prescribed burns and have beaten back the star thistle on top of Borel Hill, you just see an amazing diversity of wildflowers and native plants." District general manager Britton says grassland management is a top priority. "If you don't have grazing and you don't have burns of any kind, you're eventually going to get chaparral and, I guess ultimately, forest. You know, we don't have that much time to wait. So that's one of the things that the [District] board is wrestling with—how are we going to deal with and retain our open grassland?"

Pulgas Ridge Restoration

Pulgas Ridge Preserve is the site of the former Hassler Health Home, a large treatment center for tuberculosis patients operated from 1926 until 1972 by the City and County of San Francisco. The District acquired the property in 1983 and the buildings were demolished in 1985. In June 1999, District staff prepared a poster explaining the ongoing habitat restoration project at Pulgas Ridge Preserve, which involves removing eucalyptus, acacia, broom, and other invasive nonnative plants.

"The resource management mission of the Midpeninsula Regional Open Space District is to protect and restore the diversity and integrity of its resources for their value to the environment and to people, and to provide for the use of the preserves consistent with resource protection. The Pulgas Ridge Habitat Restoration Project aims to restore this site to a more natural environment that will have higher habitat values for wildlife and recreational use. This will be done through vegetation management. The primary project has two goals. The first is to enhance the natural values of the land by replacing invasive nonnative vegetation with plants native to the area. The second is to create self-sustaining native vegetation that will require little or no maintenance in the long term."

Although some people think that eucalyptus trees are native to California, they were actually introduced from Australia in the 1850s as a prospective get-rich-quick lumber scheme. This venture failed because the trees take up to two years to dry and season properly. Eucalyptus thrived, however, and now covers many acres in our state. Blue gum *(Eucalyptus globulus)* is the most common eucalyptus in California and is found in a variety of ecosystems. While some birds and other mobile species, such as monarch butterflies, can make use of its structure, the blue gum inhibits the coexistence of most other plant species and the life forms that depend on them, making this stately tree a significant threat to biological diversity.

There are several species of acacia present at Pulgas Ridge Preserve, and all of them can be invasive. The one most commonly seen here is silver wattle acacia *(Acacia dealbata).* These trees have finely divided feathery leaves, and in late winter are covered with pale yellow flowers, which are followed by brown pea-shaped pods.

French broom, Scotch broom, and Spanish broom are familiar yellow-flowering shrubs often seen along roadways. They are perhaps the most widespread invasive nonnative shrubs in the Bay Area. Broom often forms

---

What Is a Nonnative Plant?

A nonnative plant is a species that has been introduced into an environment different from that in which it evolved. Because invasive nonnative plants have the ability to grow quickly, they have dominated disturbed areas, and are crowding out native plants by forming impenetrable thickets, shading out native plant seedlings, competing for nutrients and water, and even fundamentally changing the soil to favor their kind. Invasive nonnative plants provide little habitat value for native fauna. Most insects, birds, and other animals have adapted to use relatively few plant species for food, shelter, or nest sites. A loss of their preferred species can result in their decline or even extinction. If a sufficient number of plant species, or even a few "keystone" species, are eliminated, the whole ecosystem may collapse. (This text has been adapted from the poster of the habitat restoration project at Pulgas Ridge Preserve.)

---

impenetrable thickets and is found in nearly all types of habitats. Mature plants can reach fifteen feet or more in height and produce thousands of seeds each year.

Many invasive nonnative plants can be pulled by hand or dug out, as long as the plants are small and the soil is moist. The use of a tool called a weed wrench can make the job easier with mid-sized plants. If the plant is deep-rooted, the root can be cut 4 to 5 inches below ground, and this will usually kill the root. Tree-sized plants are best removed with a hand saw or chainsaw, followed by an application of herbicide on the stump. (Most invasive nonnative species resprout from the cut stump and must be treated with an herbicide to kill the root system; the herbicide is applied with a paintbrush to avoid contacting other plants.)

Because many invasive nonnative species have seeds that remain dormant but viable for decades, follow-up in the form of patient, persistent removal of seedlings is essential to prevent new seeding while the existing seed bank is gradually exhausted. Only a small percentage of the seed bank will germinate each year, so although there may be fewer plants to pull each year, eliminating these plants is a long-term effort. Annual visits to the site to remove any new growth of invasive nonnative species will need to occur for at least the next ten years. Volunteers from the community have been involved with this project, usually in the form of pulling acacia and eucalyptus seedlings, and also broom.

Habitat restoration is a long-term commitment. Control of invasive nonnative species, revegetation, maintenance, and monitoring are proposed to continue at Pulgas Ridge Preserve until the year 2016. Various factors will determine the rate and success of this restoration project—most notably staff time, availability of funds, and public support. A focused effort on the preserve over the past several years has resulted in considerable progress in restoring the area to a more natural state. Continued focus and momentum will assure that the District's goals are met and that Pulgas Ridge Preserve is returned to a healthy, self-maintaining ecosystem with high biological diversity.

Feral Pigs

Feral pigs on District lands may be descendants of European pigs released in Monterey County in the 1920s, or they may have come from escaped domestic stock. Whatever their heritage, these destructive animals pose a unique management challenge. Feral pigs *(Sus scrofa)* compete with native species for food, namely acorns, bulbs, and tubers. They also eat worms, insects, mushrooms, fruits, small mammals, birds, and carrion. Rooting with their flat-tipped snouts in search of food, pigs can do extensive damage to soil and leave it subject to erosion. Marc Auerbach is a former member of the District's Preserve Partners program. "We were trying to fence off a streambed area where the pigs had been rutting around," he says. "Boy, they do a lot of damage. Unbelievable! They just churn up the ground, and it looks like a tractor's run back and forth after they've rutted around. It's just amazing. They burrow into the ground to get the roots and just churn everything up in their path."

Feral pigs cause crop and structure damage, and may spread foot and mouth disease and trichinosis. Feral pigs can be very dangerous to humans when threatened or cornered. They are prodigious breeders. A female pig can reproduce at around six months old, and can produce two litters of six to eight piglets annually. Under favorable conditions, such as a large acorn crop, more piglets will be born and more will survive.

District board member Larry Hassett, who lives in the South Skyline area, says that by the late 1990s, feral pigs were showing up near Highway 9. "They have slowly been migrating to the north," he says. "About three years ago, our driveway was the farthest northern sighting that the feral pigs had come. So now they are way beyond our driveway. Neighborhood groups got together and

Feral pig; photo taken at Rancho San Antonio Open Space Preserve

started to trap them, and convinced the Open Space District to participate with a trapping program. Now they're the lead agency in catching the most feral pigs up there." The District's trapping program uses large box traps baited with fermented corn as the most efficient and humane way to trap these destructive animals. A professional trapper then shoots the trapped pigs and takes their carcasses to a tallow shop. The trapping program started in September 2000. By spring 2004, more than 280 pigs had been removed from District lands. The District is currently in the maintenance phase of this program to keep the pig population under control.

SENSITIVE SPECIES

District lands, which stretch from the shore of San Francisco Bay to the crest of the Santa Cruz Mountains, are rich with a remarkable diversity of plants and animals. Some of these are rare, threatened, or endangered. Others are being closely monitored because their populations are in decline or their habitats are disappearing. District staff conduct regular surveys of selected animals, including mountain lions, deer, bats, bluebirds, and amphibians. The District also maintains a rare-plant inventory describing each plant's location and status. Among the most interesting rare plants on District lands, according to Cindy Roessler, the District's resource management specialist, are western leatherwood, Mount Hamilton thistle, and Metcalf Canyon jewel-flower—herbaceous plants that occur on serpentine soil. Kings Mountain manzanita is another District specialty, she says. Some of the animals found on District lands and waterways are federally listed as either endangered or threatened. These include clapper rail, marbled murrelet, snowy plover, steel-head trout, salt marsh harvest mouse, San Francisco garter snake, and California red-legged frog. Among the District's rare, threatened, or endangered plants are Santa Cruz manzanita, Santa Clara red ribbons clarkia, fragrant fritillary, smooth lessingia, scrub oak, white-rayed pentachaeta, Santa Cruz wallflower, Marin flax, and fountain thistle.

SUDDEN OAK DEATH

First reported in Marin in 1995, sudden oak death is causing great concern among land managers and forestry experts in California. This highly con-tagious fungal disease is caused by the pathogen *Phytophthora ramorum*, and has already killed tens of thousands of oaks and tanbark oaks in northern

Leaf infected with sudden oak death

California. A total of sixteen plant species in California are known to host the disease, including commercially and ecologically important coast redwood and Douglas-fir. Other hosts include black oak, coast live oak, Shreve oak (a variety of island scrub oak), tanbark oak, rhododendron, California bay, bigleaf maple, madrone, various manzanitas, huckleberry, California honeysuckle, toyon, California buckeye, and coffeeberry. Not all infected hosts succumb to the disease. So far at least, no mature coast redwoods or Douglas-firs have developed symptoms or died from it. Sudden oak death has been found in twelve California counties. These include all nine Bay Area counties, plus Humboldt, Mendocino, and Monterey counties. On District lands, the disease has affected coast live oak, black oak, and tanbark oak in Long Ridge Preserve, and coast live oak and tanbark oak in Skyline Ridge Preserve.

Symptoms of the disease in true oaks—black oak, coast live oak, and Shreve oak—include the appearance of what one Web site devoted to sudden oak death calls "a bleeding canker, burgundy-red to tar-black thick sap oozes on the bark surface." As the disease progresses, the tree may become infested with bark beetles and fungus. Finally, the tree's leaves may turn brown or begin to disappear altogether. Infected tanbark oaks may develop similar symptoms but may also be entirely free of bark bleeding. The other hosts of sudden oak death show symptoms primarily on their leaves and occasionally on their stems. Sometimes these symptoms are severe enough to kill the host plant, especially with heath family members such as huckleberry, madrone, and rhododendron. There are sixty other species of the pathogen *Phytophthora* world-wide, but the one killing California's oaks is puzzling as to its origin. No one knows whether it has newly invaded from elsewhere or was here for many years, waiting to strike. For more information on sudden oak death, visit the California Oak Mortality Task Force Web site, *www.suddenoakdeath.org*.

EPILOGUE:
THE OTHER SIDE OF THE MOUNTAIN

~

A JOURNEY TO PROTECT THE FUTURE

Perhaps the brightest star on the District's immediate horizon is the great promise of the San Mateo County Coastside Protection Program. The San Mateo Coast, with its verdant rolling hills, rural agricultural lands, and spectacular views of the Pacific, is unparalleled in its pristine beauty, abundant resources, and rural way of life—all of which are in grave danger of being lost to the pressures of urban expansion and development. This is why the District, in 1997, at the request of three coastal elected bodies, and with the subsequent encouragement of a majority of the area's voters, began to explore the possibility of expanding its boundaries to the coast—an area as vast as it is beautiful, encompassing the 140,000 acres of coastal landscape in San Mateo County, from the southern boundary of Pacifica to the Santa Cruz County line, and west of Skyline Boulevard.

Spanning more than seven years, the process for this program has included more than forty public meetings designed to encourage the coastside residents to share information, ideas, and concerns with the District's board and staff. These meetings have been vital in shaping the Coastside Protection Program. Responding to residents' concerns about eminent domain, the District's board unanimously agreed to eliminate its use in the coastal region and to purchase property from willing sellers only. The Board formalized this commitment by adopting a Willing Sellers Only Ordinance, thus ensuring that the District would never exercise its power of eminent domain on the Coast. The Board also entered into a Memorandum of Understanding with the San Mateo County Farm Bureau to make this promise even more secure and permanent by jointly

Father with children walking into the sunset at
Windy Hill Open Space Preserve

sponsoring legislation to remove the power of eminent domain in the Coastside Protection Area. The Farm Bureau is giving its full and unqualified support to the District's program, and the District's Coastside Protection Program received a significant boost when Governor Arnold Schwarzenegger signed the legislation into law. "The District is strongly committed to sharing this important responsibility of protecting and preserving the San Mateo Coastside with local residents," says Craig Britton, the District's general manager. "We have the farmers and ranchers on the coast to thank for preserving the agricultural and rural heritage of this unspoiled coastline. The District's program will back up that longtime landowner commitment as the District prepares to bring its resources to specific coastside projects and preservation efforts."

In October 2003, the District submitted its formal application for the Coastside Protection Program to the San Mateo County Local Agency Formation Commission, or LAFCo, which conducted public hearings on the Program before deciding whether to grant its approval.

The District awaited LAFCo's decision with bated breath. So much is at stake: Fields rich with peas, beans, artichokes, Brussels sprouts, and flowers. Hillsides dotted with horses, cattle, sheep, and goats. Wetlands. Creeks. Redwoods. And great, sweeping, unimpeded views of the Pacific. In April 2004, in a historic victory for supporters of open space preservation along the San

The District is working to protect the pristine beauty, abundant resources, and rural way of life of the San Mateo coast through its Coastside Protection Program.

Mateo coast, the San Mateo County LAFCo voted to approve the District's Coastside Protection Program.

This action clears the way for the District to buy land from willing sellers for the purpose of protecting the region's coastside from inappropriate urban sprawl and manage land on the coast for the benefit of the public. There are still steps to take to complete this ambitious program, but the District continues to work with its friends on the coast to make this vision a reality. In September 2004, the program cleared its final hurdle when a San Mateo County Superior Court judge rejected a request from opponents to stop the program, confirming that there were not a sufficient number of protests to force the program into an election on the November 2004 ballot.

Land, once developed, is difficult and most times impossible to restore. Land gone is gone forever, preserved, if we are lucky, only in a photograph. In 1950, Ansel Adams photographed one of the thousands of orchards that filled Santa Clara Valley, the "Valley of Heart's Delight." It makes a nice picture. But wouldn't it be nicer still to have the picture *and* the orchard?

Meanwhile, the District will continue its stewardship of land within its current boundaries, and look forward to continuing its long and fruitful history of working with other government agencies, private organizations, nonprofit groups, and individuals to preserve land and create regional trails and low-

impact recreational opportunities throughout the Peninsula. In October 2003, the Bay Area Ridge Trail Council, Santa Clara County Parks and Recreation Department, the District, and community members and leaders celebrated the opening of a new staging area at the Hicks Road entrance to Sierra Azul Preserve, and the dedication of an important segment of the Bay Area Ridge Trail that begins near Almaden Quicksilver County Park and connects through the Sierra Azul Preserve to Lexington Reservoir County Park—some 11.8 miles away. When complete, the Bay Area Ridge Trail will be a continuous, multiuse trail spanning five hun-dred miles around San Francisco Bay's ridgelines. The District is honored to have so many of its trails dedicated as part of the Bay Area Ridge Trail, and is looking forward to completing the segment of this important regional trail system that lies within the District's boundaries.

In its Regional Open Space Study, the District has explored the possibility of numerous other regional trails. One of these is the City-to-the-Sea Trail, which would begin at the District's Ravenswood Preserve in East Palo Alto and then wind its way through Menlo Park, Redwood City, and Edgewood Park and Preserve before continuing across San Francisco watershed land, ascending through Golden Gate National Recreation Area's Phleger Estate to Skyline Boulevard, and then descending through Purisima Creek Redwoods Preserve to Purisima Creek Road and on to Cowell Ranch State Beach, where Peninsula Open Space Trust has recently purchased land in this trail corridor.

Another, the Bay-to-the-Bay Area Ridge Trail, would connect the District's Stevens Creek Shoreline Nature Study Area in Mountain View to the in-process Stevens Creek Trail, which will meander alongside Stevens Creek through Mountain View, Sunnyvale, Los Altos, and Cupertino until it reaches Lower

Stevens Creek County Park. The trail will then continue through District lands (and what are now private lands) until it reaches the Bay Area Ridge Trail in Upper Stevens Creek County Park.

A regional trail the District has long wanted to provide is now built—the Achistaca Trail in Long Ridge Preserve. Named after an Ohlone subtribe that lived in what is now Castle Rock State Park, the Achistaca Trail offers a direct connection from the Ridge Trail to the Skyline-to-the-Sea Trail, which begins in Castle Rock State Park near Saratoga Gap Preserve and continues on to Big Basin Redwoods State Park and the Pacific. Now visitors have direct access to the Skyline-to-the-Sea Trail and the coast from any of the five or so preserves and parks near or next to Long Ridge Preserve.

There are a number of possibilities for other regional trails, including one connecting Palo Alto to the Skyline area through Stanford lands and Foothills Park, and another connecting Los Gatos Creek Trail to the northern end of Sierra Azul Preserve. Another would connect the southern end of Sierra Azul Preserve to the District's Loma Prieta Ranch property in Santa Cruz County, and then continue from there to the Soquel Demonstration Forest, and the Forest of Niscene Marks State Park. And in Santa Cruz County, people are working hard to connect the Forest of Niscene Marks to the California Coastal Trail.

And then there is the restoration of what some say is Old Page Mill Road—the road originally built by William Page in 1868 to haul lumber from his mill in what is now Portola Redwoods State Park to the Embarcadero in Palo Alto. The District-owned section of this road lies in Skyline Ridge Preserve and currently provides a short two- to three-mile out-and-back hike to Lambert Creek. When restored in its entirety, with a new bridge crossing and substantial trail repair, this road will provide a direct connection to Portola Redwoods State Park. Whether it actually was Page's original road, although intriguing, hardly matters. The fact remains it was *someone's* original road, and preserving it, besides providing a vital regional trail connection, would be preserving yet another piece of Peninsula history.

Along with making regional trail connections, the District also looks forward to opening new preserves (such as the currently named Mills Creek) and new areas of preserves now only partially open (such as Teague Hill, La Honda Creek, Sierra Azul, and Bear Creek Redwoods). Teague Hill is open to the public, but access is very limited, with only a small part of the Bay Area Ridge Trail crossing its northwest corner and connecting it to San Mateo County's Huddart Park. However, once the planning process for its trail system is complete, Teague Hill, which is adjacent to Huddart Park, Wunderlich

Park, and the El Corte de Madera Creek and Purisima Creek Redwoods Preserves, will provide a central hub of trails that will join these neighboring parks and preserves.

Mills Creek (an interim name designation) lies on the coast side of Skyline Boulevard, 2.3 miles south of Highway 92, and is one of the District's newer preserves. Not yet open to the public, Mills Creek is the northern gateway into District lands, and is an integral part of a larger greenbelt that includes Burleigh Murray Ranch State Park, the San Francisco Crystal Springs Watershed land, and lands currently owned by Peninsula Open Space Trust (POST). Mills Creek, because of this strategic location, serves as home to sixteen species of special concern (including Townsend's western big-eared bat, golden eagle, and Monterey pine), and provides an important migration corridor for deer and mountain lion. For its human visitors, it will provide the first connection into Burleigh Murray Ranch State Park from Skyline Boulevard, and panoramic views of the coast and the Pacific as spectacular as any to be found on the Peninsula.

So what is it that determines when a preserve can be opened to the public? Occasionally, if preexisting ranch roads and fire roads are in good condition and there is an area large enough to accommodate parking, those areas can be opened to the public almost immediately upon purchase. Otherwise, the District waits until the preserve's resources have been assessed, the community consulted, and a comprehensive, long-range master plan has been prepared. Master Plans serve as a guiding vision to protect resources, and to direct development of low-impact recreational uses such as trails, staging areas, and other rustic facilities.

The master planning process begins with a resource inventory and an assessment of the opportunities and constraints presented by the land. Based on these findings and extensive public involvement, a conceptual plan that sets priorities for future resource management, low-intensity trail development, and regional trail connections is then developed. Once completed, this plan is presented to the District's board and the public for consideration and approval. And always—at the beginning of the master planning process and after its implementation—there are the resources to consider, manage, and protect, no matter how many trails, interpretive facilities, and staging areas are built. A program to remove nonnative invasive plants must be developed to enhance and encourage native plants; water must be kept pure; unique geological formations must be protected; wild creatures, endangered and otherwise, must have a viable habitat; archaeological and cultural sites must be considered for preservation; past and

Issues such as use of the landmark Red Barn and opportunities to utilize grazing as a tool for restoring and maintaining grassland biodiversity will be addressed in the master planning process for La Honda Creek Open Space Preserve.

current agricultural uses must be evaluated. Even the trails themselves become part of resource management—many must be closed during the wet season to prevent erosion, repaired if damaged, and occasionally even permanently closed in order to give the land a chance to rest and restore itself. At El Corte de Madera Creek Preserve, the district is embarking on a comprehensive program to protect and restore the watershed while maintaining opportunities for year-round, multiple-use recreational activities and environmental education.

La Honda Creek Preserve has a number of interesting issues that will be addressed in its master planning process, including use of the landmark Red Barn, and opportunities to utilize grazing as a tool for restoring and maintaining grassland biodiversity. This preserve also has a number of remarkable natural features, such as a rare albino redwood, and habitat for the endangered California red-legged frog and federally threatened steelhead trout, which will be protected through a comprehensive resource management plan.

Sierra Azul and Bear Creek Redwoods Preserves, because of their close proximity to each other and their similar roles as conservation areas, are being included in one master plan. The development of an inventory of the preserves' resources is already underway, and includes botany and wildlife, geology and soils, hydrology and water quality, historic and archaeological resources, and the existing road and trail system. At more than 17,000 acres and growing, Sierra Azul Preserve is by far the District's largest preserve, and is remarkable for the diversity of its resources, which include steep chaparral-covered hillsides, open grasslands, lush canyon streams that flow year-round, and stands of coastal redwoods. This incredibly rugged landscape is also home to some of the Bay Area's most elusive wildlife—golden eagle, mountain lion, and federally threatened species such as steelhead trout (in Guadalupe Creek) and the California red-legged frog. This master planning provides an unparalleled process to protect these species while also providing more opportunities for increased public access, including access to Mt. Umunhum.

Mt. Umunhum, fondly referred to by its admirers as "Mt. Um," is the centerpiece of Sierra Azul Preserve. Unfortunately, public access to the summit has not been possible because of the abandoned Almaden Air Force Base. Built at a time when no one worried about asbestos, lead paint, or chemical pollution, the abandoned base that sits atop Mt. Um is a toxic quagmire. When the District bought the property at fair market value in 1986, the Department of Defense agreed to have the Army Corps of Engineers remove underground fuel tanks and old transformers, but declined to do more at Mt. Umunhum. The planned soil sampling for future cleanup is now being scheduled; additional cleanup that the Army Corps is studying includes the former dump site, cesspool and evaporator ponds, and soil contamination around the underground tanks. So the lead paint, asbestos, chemicals, and fifty-some-odd buildings remain, and cleaning them up will cost many millions of dollars. Currently, local politicians are working hard to encourage the federal government to help finance the cleanup, as it did at Marin County's Mt. Tamalpais, which once had a toxic-laden, abandoned missile silo facility of its own. There is also a group of concerned citizens, the Friends of Mt. Umunhum, eager to help the District get their local mountain cleaned up. It will require the cooperative efforts of everyone involved, and it will be a tremendous challenge, but the cleanup of Mt. Um *will* happen. And when it does, Mt. Um, with its panoramic views of the Santa Clara Valley and Monterey Bay, will more than rival its Marin cousin.

Just across Highway 17 from Sierra Azul Preserve, offering more modest, but nonetheless spectacular, views from its grassy hilltops, lies Bear Creek Redwoods Preserve. With its oak and redwood forests, open grasslands, old vineyards, a working stable, the remaining buildings of Alma College, and an adjacent, privately owned retreat/conference center, everything about Bear Creek Redwoods Preserve is extraordinary. Even its acquisition was extraordinary in that it was accomplished in one astonishing $25 million, 1,065-acre deal that immediately saved 260 acres from becoming fifty homes and a golf course, and forever preserved 805 additional acres of grassland and redwood forest as open space. The District had had its eye on this land for more than

*Bear Creek Redwoods Open Space Preserve; master planning for this preserve,
as well as for Sierra Azul Open Space Preserve,
is a part of the District's journey to protect the future.*

twenty years, but it was always out of financial reach. And the purchase still would not have been possible had it not been for a generous fund-raising effort by POST, and two outstanding grants from the Wildlife Conservation Board and the San Francisco Bay Area Conservancy Program of the California Coastal Conservancy. These partners provided $10 million towards the purchase of the preserve.

Another recent grant from the Coastal Conservancy has enabled the District to acquire an additional 198 acres of redwood forest from Presentation Center, an interfaith retreat and conference center adjacent to Bear Creek Redwoods Preserve, owned and operated by the Sisters of the Presentation (a Catholic religious congregation deeply committed to the environment and environmental education). In return, the Sisters of the Presentation have an easement across District land for a parking lot for their new, "green" welcoming center and dining facility, which will have passive solar orientation, straw-bale walls, integrated photovoltaic panels, and a living roof. Needless to say, the District is overjoyed to be able to share the stewardship of this remarkable preserve with such an exceptional neighbor. Again, the word "extraordinary" comes to mind.

It is also extraordinary to find mature redwood and Douglas-fir forests on the bay side of the Santa Cruz Mountains, which only increases the environmental value of this already astonishing preserve. That it should also be in such close proximity to urbanized Santa Clara County (downtown San Jose is only twenty minutes away), and virtually next door to Sierra Azul, St. Joseph's Hill, and El Sereno Preserves (as well as Lexington Reservoir and Sanborn Skyline County Parks) makes its value to present and future generations inestimable.

The San Francisco Bay Area has one of the largest, most productive systems of public open space to be found in any urban area in the United States. We owe so much to those who first realized the enormity of what could be lost—and who made sure that it wasn't. We owe even more to those who are yet to come.

We simply need that wild country available to us, even if we never do more than drive to its edge and look in. For it can be a means of reassuring ourselves of our sanity as creatures, a part of the geography of hope.

—Wallace Stegner,
The Wilderness Letter

—ANNE KOLETZKE

Appendix A
SUGGESTED READING

History

Lavender, David, *California*. Lincoln: University of Nebraska Press, 1972.

Richards, Rand, *Historic San Francisco*. San Francisco: Heritage House Publishers, 1999.

Midpeninsula Area and Santa Cruz Mountains

Payne, Stephen M., *Santa Clara County: Harvest of Change*. Northridge, CA: Windsor Publications, 1987.

Rusmore, Jean, *The Bay Area Ridge Trail*. 2nd ed. Berkeley: Wilderness Press, 2002.

Rusmore, Jean, et al., *Peninsula Trails*. 3rd ed. Berkeley: Wilderness Press, 1997.

Stanger, Frank M., *Sawmills in the Redwoods*. San Mateo: San Mateo County Historical Association, 1967.

Stanger, Frank M., *South from San Francisco*. San Mateo: San Mateo County Historical Association, 1963.

Young, John V., *Ghost Towns of the Santa Cruz Mountains*. Santa Cruz: Paper Vision Press, 1979.

Natural History

Alt, David, and Donald W. Hyndman, *Roadside Geology of Northern and Central California*. Missoula, MT: Mountain Press Publishing, 2000.

Barbour, Michael, et al., *Coast Redwood*. Los Olivos, CA: Cachuma Press, 2001.

Burt, William H., and Richard P. Grossenheider, *A Field Guide to the Mammals, North America, North of Mexico*. 3rd ed. Boston: Houghton Mifflin, 1980.

Clark, Jeanne L., *California Wildlife Viewing Guide*. Helena, MT: Falcon Press, 1992.

Coffeen, Mary, *Central Coast Wildflowers*. San Luis Obispo, CA: EZ Nature Books, 1996.

Faber, Phyllis M., *Common Wetland Plants of Coastal California*. 2nd ed. Mill Valley, CA: Pickleweed Press, 1996.

Faber, Phyllis M., and Robert F. Holland, *Common Riparian Plants of California*. Mill Valley, CA: Pickleweed Press, 1988.

Kozloff, Eugene N., and Linda H. Beidleman, *Plants of the San Francisco Bay Region*. Berkeley: University of California Press, 2003.

Lanner, Ronald M., *Conifers of California*. Los Olivos, CA: Cachuma Press, 1999.

Little, Elbert L., *National Audubon Society Field Guide to North American Trees, Western Region*. New York: Alfred A. Knopf, 1994.

Lyons, Kathleen, and Mary Beth Cooney-Lazaneo, *Plants of the Coast Redwood Region.*
    Boulder Creek, CA: Looking Press, 1988.

National Geographic Society, *Field Guide to the Birds of North America.*
    4th ed. Washington: National Geographic Society, 2002.

Niehaus, Theodore F., and Charles L. Ripper, *A Field Guide to Pacific States
    Wildflowers.* Boston: Houghton Mifflin Company, 1976.

Pavlik, Bruce M., et al., *Oaks of California.* Los Olivos, CA: Cachuma Press, 1991.

Peterson, Roger T., *A Field Guide to Western Birds.* 3rd ed. Boston: Houghton Mifflin
    Company, 1990.

Schoenherr, Allan A., *A Natural History of California.* Berkeley: University of
    California Press, 1992.

Sibley, David Allen, *The Sibley Guide to Birds.* New York: Alfred A. Knopf, Inc., 2000.

Stebbins, Robert C., *A Field Guide to Western Reptiles and Amphibians.*
    2nd ed. Boston: Houghton Mifflin Company, 1985.

Place Names

Durham, David L., *Place-Names of the San Francisco Bay Area.* Clovis, CA: Word
    Dancer Press, 2000.

Gudde, Erwin G., *California Place Names.* 4th ed. Berkeley: University of California
    Press, 1998.

Marinacci, Barbara and Rudy Marinacci, *California's Spanish Place-Names.* 2nd ed.
    Houston: Gulf Publishing Company, 1997.

Appendix B
INFORMATION SOURCES

Government Agencies
California State Parks — *www.parks.ca.gov*
San Francisco District — (415) 330-6300
Santa Cruz District — (831) 429-2851

Don Edwards San Francisco
Bay National Wildlife Refuge (USFWS) — *www.desfbay.fws.gov* (510) 792-0222

Golden Gate National Recreation Area (GGNRA) — *www.nps.gov/goga* (415) 561-4700

Midpeninsula Regional Open Space District — *www.openspace.org* (650) 691-1200

San Mateo County Parks and Recreation — *www.eparks.net* (650) 363-4020

Santa Clara County Parks and Recreation — *www.parkhere.org* (408) 355-2200

Other Organizations
Bay Area Hiker — *www.bahiker.com*

Bay Area Open Space Council — *www.openspacecouncil.org* (510) 654-6591

Bay Area Ridge Trail Council — *www.ridgetrail.org* (415) 561-2595

Bay Trail—Association of Bay Area Governments (ABAG) — *www.abag.ca.gov* (510) 464-7900

California Native Plant Society — *www.cnps.org* (916) 447-2677

California Oak Mortality Task Force — *www.suddenoakdeath.org*

Committee for Green Foothills — *www.greenfoothills.org* (650) 968-7243

Greenbelt Alliance — *www.greenbelt.org* (415) 398-3730

Natural Resources DataBase — *www.nrdb.org*

Peninsula Access for Dogs (PADS)   *www.prusik.com/pads*

Peninsula Open Space Trust (POST)   *www.openspacetrust.org*
(650) 854-7696

Responsible Organized Mountain Pedalers (ROMP)   *www.romp.org*
(408) 380-2271

San Mateo County Horsemen's Association (SMCHA)   *www.smcha.org*

Save-the-Redwoods League   *www.savetheredwoods.org*
(415) 362-2352

Sempervirens Fund   *www.sempervirens.org*
(650) 968-4509

Sierra Club (Loma Prieta Chapter)   *www.lomaprieta.sierraclub.org*
(650) 390-8411

The Nature Conservancy   *www.nature.org*
   California Field Office   (415) 777-0487

Whole Access   *www.wholeaccess.org*
   (Trails are referred to as "Easy Access"   (650) 363-2647
   by the District.)

Appendix C
NEARBY PARKS

District Preserve	Nearby Park
El Corte de Madera Creek	Wunderlich Park (San Mateo County)
Foothills	Foothills Park (City of Palo Alto) Hidden Villa (Nonprofit Organization)
Fremont Older	Stevens Creek County Park (Santa Clara County)
Long Ridge	Portola Redwoods State Park (California State Parks)
Los Trancos	Foothills Park (City of Palo Alto)
Monte Bello	(1) Hidden Villa (Nonprofit Organization) (2) Upper Stevens Creek County Park (Santa Clara County)
Picchetti Ranch	Stevens Creek County Park (Santa Clara County)
Pulgas Ridge	(1) Edgewood Park and Preserve (San Mateo County) (2) San Francisco Watershed Lands (City of San Francisco)
Purisima Creek Redwoods	(1) Phleger Estate (Golden Gate National Recreation Area) (2) Huddart Park (San Mateo County)
Rancho San Antonio	(1) Hidden Villa (Nonprofit Organization) (2) Rancho San Antonio County Park (Santa Clara County, Managed by Midpeninsula Regional Open Space District)

Ravenswood	(1) Palo Alto Baylands Nature Preserve (City of Palo Alto) (2) Don Edwards San Francisco Bay National Wildlife Refuge (U. S. Fish & Wildlife)
Saratoga Gap	(1) Castle Rock State Park (California State Parks) (2) Sanborn Skyline County Park (Santa Clara County) (3) Upper Stevens Creek County Park (Santa Clara County)
Sierra Azul	Almaden Quicksilver and Lexington Reservoir county parks (Santa Clara County)
St. Joseph's Hill	Novitiate Park (Town of Los Gatos) Lexington Reservoir County Park (Santa Clara County)
Stevens Creek Shoreline Nature Study Area	Shoreline–at–Mountain View Park (City of Mountain View)
Teague Hill	Huddart Park (San Mateo County)
Thornewood	Wunderlich Park (San Mateo County)

PHOTO CREDITS

The following people hold copyright to the photographs (and painting) as listed:

Chris Braley: p. 28;
Carolyn Caddes: pp. 218–19;
California Historical Center Foundation, De Anza College, Cupertino, Calif.
(courtesy of): p. 177;
Katie Cooney: pp. 24, 350;
Frank Crossman: pp. 73, 88, 110–11, 112, 142, 149, 178, 186, 200, 208–9, 239, 273, 307,
310–11, 317, 320;
Craig Cummings: p. 98;
Kenneth L. Fisher (from the collection of): pp. 76, 77, 190, 288, 289;
Karl Gohl: pp. 9, 25, 29, 62, 68, 91, 154 (bottom), 174 (top), 191, 204, 253;
Dianne Hunt: p. 338;
Paul Jossi: back cover painting;
Peter LaTourrette: pp. 58–59, 69, 176;
Tom Lausten (from the collection of): pp. 132–33;
MROSD: pp. 21, 24, 33, 34–35, 36, 38, 48–49, 55, 65, 80, 84–85, 105, 126, 140–141, 154
(top), 155, 162, 164, 180, 184, 185, 196, 205, 214–15, 225, 226–27, 250, 256, 257,
261, 265, 285, 290, 292, 300–1, 302, 309, 313, 334–35, 341, 348–49, 351, 359, 361,
363, 364–65, 368, 370;
Palo Alto Weekly (courtesy of): p. 14;
Curt Riffle: p. 347;
David Weintraub: front cover, pp. 50, 92, 94, 95, 99, 102, 106, 114, 122, 123, 130, 137,
158–59, 165, 168, 172, 174 (bottom), 175, 197, 199, 220, 228, 230, 231, 234, 242,
244–45, 260, 281, 284, 318, 321, 324, 330, 331, 337, 339, 344, 346.

The District has made an effort to properly credit the photographer's work; however, the District is not liable for any errors in attribution other than to make reasonable effort to correct any errors or omissions. Please contact the District should you find an error with any attribution.

ABOUT THE AUTHOR

David Weintraub is a professional writer, editor, and photographer based in South Carolina and Cape Cod. Prior to 2003, David lived in San Francisco for sixteen years. His photographs and articles have appeared in many newspapers, books, and magazines, including *Audubon, Bay Nature, Backpacker, Sierra, Smithsonian,* and *Sunset.* He has published six books with Wilderness Press: *East Bay Trails; North Bay Trails; Monterey Bay Trails; Adventure Kayaking; Cape Cod and Martha's Vineyard; Top Trails: San Francisco Bay Area; Afoot and Afield;* and *San Francisco Bay Area.* You can visit David on the Web at *www.weintraubphoto.com.*